S0-ADN-617

My Life of Turmoil

My Life of Turmoil

A Jewish Immigrant's Story and Warning

~LARRY WENIG~

EPIGRAPH
RHINEBECK, NEW YORK

Contact the publisher for information:
Epigraph
27 Lamoree Road
Rhinebeck, N.Y. 12572

Printed in The United States of America.

Library of Congress Control Number: 2007933947

ISBN 978-0-9789427-9-3

Bulk purchase discounts for educational or promotional purposes are available.

First Edition

10 9 8 7 6 5 4 3 2 1

Epigraph
A Division of Monkfish Book Publishing Company
27 Lamoree Road
Rhinebeck, N.Y. 12572
www.epigraphps.com

Contents

Preface

My first book, *From Nazi Inferno To Soviet Hell,* told the story of my Holocaust experiences, escaping the Nazi atrocities in Poland only to suffer at the hands of Soviet Communists, who forced my family to live in a gulag outside Siberia. But quite a number of people have approached me after lectures based on that book suggesting that I should write another, this one about my accomplishments in my new blessed country, the United States of America, which I came to at the age of 22.

When I give lectures about the history of the Muslim religion and the Koran, these audiences also urge me to write such a book, and they plead with me to explain and educate my fellow Americans about the danger we are facing from the evil Muslim fundamentalists, jihadists, Hezbbolah, Hamas, and the Yasser Arafat's Fatah terrorists.

9/11 was a wake up call for all of us, namely that we are no longer safe, despite the natural protection afforded us by our Atlantic and Pacific Ocean boundaries. I had learned a long time ago in Uzbekistan the hatred Muslims have for us "Infidels." I lived in Uzbekistan for 3½ years in a mud room next to a cow, and for one year attended a school with a predominantly Muslim student body.

Despite my great accomplishments in my beloved America, becoming a successful attorney, and being married to a beautiful and wonderful wife, and my good, wonderful children and grandchildren, I can't forget the Holocaust. Memories of the Holocaust cause me sleepless nights, and are with me throughout the day. As a Holocaust survivor, I am always concerned about the safety, security, and survival of Israel as a Jewish State.

My other concerns are the safety and security of my fellow Americans. During my lectures on the history of the Muslim religion and the Koran, I noticed the ignorance of my fellow Americans about radical Islam, and Islamofascism. I feel that it is my duty and obligation to explain to my fellow Americans and the other "Infidels" on our planet the dangers we are facing from the Islamofascists and Jihadists.

Yet, with all the problems we are faced with, I want to state my gratefulness to my adopted country, America, for in no other country could I have found such happiness and been so successful.

God bless America.

Chapter 1

COMING TO AMERICA

To the best of my recollection, it was a dreary day toward the end of March in 1946 when we received a letter from the American consulate in Munich, Germany. At that time we were in a displaced-persons camp in the city of Badgastein, in the American-occupied zone of Austria.

My father opened the letter, which was typewritten in English, a language that neither he, my mother, my sister Hella, nor I could read. I told him that I knew a woman in the camp who had some knowledge of English. He told me to go ask her if she could read the letter.

Mrs. Shelupski was a very nice person, an attractive young married woman with dark blonde hair, beautiful blue eyes, a tiny nose, and tiny lips. Her husband had been a partisan in the Bielski Brigade, a Jewish unit fighting the Nazis in the forests of eastern Poland during the war.

She opened the envelope and started to read the letter. Her mouth opened wide. "Lusiek," she screamed, "your family has been approved by the American government to go to America! How lucky you are! You're the first family in our DP camp to get an approval." My eyes lit up and my body trembled in disbelief. "You have to be in Bremerhaven by the beginning of June, where an American boat, the *Marine Flasher,* will take you to New York," she continued.

I thanked Mrs. Shelupski and kissed her right in front of her husband. I explained that it must have been my rich uncle Irving in New York, my father's brother, who had made the arrangements. I pleaded with them not to tell anyone in the camp. I was worried that people might be jealous. And I did not want to disappoint the friends with whom my sister and I had agreed to go to Palestine. Mrs. Shelupski promised to keep our news a secret.

I ran as fast as I could to tell my parents. I raced into our room waving the letter and shouting, "We've been accepted by the American government to go to New York in June! We have to go to Bremerhaven and from there we will go to New York."

My mother turned to me with tears in her eyes. "Lusiek, is it true that we will no longer be wanderers, sneaking across borders, hiding from KGB agents, living in camps? Will we once again be normal human beings?"

"Yes," I replied.

My father, his eyes misty, said in a low sad voice, "If only Mundek and Shmulek were alive today." My father was actually my stepfather, and Mundek and Shmulek, his sons from a prior marriage, had been my stepbrothers. Mundek had not been with us on June 28, 1941, when the KGB sent us from the Soviet-occupied Polish city of Lwów to Gulag 149, on the edge of Siberia. Six days earlier, on June 22, when Germany invaded the Soviet Union, Mundek had gone to hide with a Polish Christian family he knew. Instead of hiding him, they turned him over to the Nazis. He escaped and ran toward the San River, but was shot and killed as he tried to get across.

My other stepbrother, Shmulek, was killed on September 12, 1945, during our escape from Communist-controlled Poland. Assisted by Bricha, the Zionist underground organization, we were traveling by train from Poland, via Czechoslovakia, to the American-occupied zone of Vienna. Just before we got there, KGB agents on the train apparently recognized Shmulek, or perhaps Shmulek only thought did. Perhaps they threw him off the moving train, or maybe he jumped off. Either way, he died 12 miles from the safe haven of Vienna.

Despite these sad memories, we rejoiced in our good news. But good as the news was for the family, I just didn't feel right. My friends in the DP camp had decided to go to Palestine, with the assistance of the Zionist underground, to help build a Jewish state there. The new friends, both younger and older than I, were survivors of the Nazi death camps. Some of them, with tattooed numbers on their arms, were from Auschwitz, others had been in Treblinka, Theresienstadt, or Mauthausen, and some had fought against the Nazis as partisans in the forests of eastern Poland. They told me about the torture and unspeakable crimes perpetrated by the Nazis against Jews. One particularly bestial act favored by the Nazi brutes was to pick up a Jewish baby and smash it against a wall, killing it in front its parents.

These new young friends of mine had decided that it was the solemn obligation of Holocaust survivors to go to Palestine by any means and help build a Jewish state. Hella and I had planned to go to Palestine with them, but our father practically went down on his knees, weeping and pleading with us not to break up the family. I just couldn't tell these dedicated Zionists that I would soon be leaving for America to please my parents.

We didn't share the secret of our departure with anyone in the camp until the day before we left. When we told our friends that we would be leaving for America the next day, they couldn't believe it; they couldn't believe that I, such an ardent Zionist, would desert them and our cause. Some of them refused to shake hands with me or to say goodbye.

We packed our few belongings in a battered suitcase and took a taxi to Salzburg. From there we went by train to Munich, and from Munich by train to the port of Bremerhaven, where the American troop transport *Marine Flasher* was waiting to take us to New York.

We embarked in the morning. The *Marine Flasher* was certainly no cruise ship, and it had virtually no amenities, just stacks of bunks and a mess hall. The passengers were almost all displaced persons, both Christians and Jews. Most of the passengers were single young people; there were very few families.

Embarking, checking documents, and loading supplies took almost an entire day. My father and I were housed in the men's section of the ship, my mother and sister in the women's section.

We didn't know a single soul on the ship, and the numerous passengers spoke a Babel of many different languages. We knew Yiddish and Polish, and were also familiar with Russian, but we made no contact with any of our fellow passengers on that first day, and our only conversations were among ourselves.

That evening aboard ship, we were served our first, delicious American meal, and unbelievably, it included a good-sized portion of meat. As darkness fell, we went to our bunks. My father was in the lower bunk, and I was in a bunk above him. I went to bed in my underwear, as we had no pajamas. I was very tired and tried to sleep, but I couldn't even close my eyes. My mind was working feverishly, brimming with questions that called for answers. The first question that tortured me was how I would fulfill the silent oath I had taken on August 11, 1945, in the Polish city of Kraków.

We had arrived in Kraków in July 1945, after escaping from the Soviet Union. We were met at the railroad station by representatives of a local Jewish committee who assigned us temporary housing in a residence it maintained. There we met concentration camp survivors and other refugees who had just come out of hiding. They told us some harrowing tales about the crimes the German had perpetrated on the Jews of Europe.

The next day we went to Auschwitz, which is not far from Kraków, to see it for ourselves. The sights that I saw there will be imprinted on my brain forever. Huge stacks of thick ropes made out of human hair. A mountain-high stack of soap made from human fat. Gold and silver crowns pulled from human teeth. Thousands upon thousands of leather shoes. There was no escaping the knowledge that this was a death factory where human beings had been gassed and cremated.

Who were the accursed monsters who had committed such unspeakable crimes? What kind of creature orders or commits such heinous acts? Human beings could not have done that to one another. My eyes, glazed and unforgiving, seemed drawn from their sockets to the exhibits. My legs felt drained of blood and buckled under me.

Back in our residence the veil of travail followed me. I could not eat. I dropped down onto a cot and covered my eyes with my hands. I thought about us. If we had not fled from Poland in 1939, we too might have fed the flames in Auschwitz. We had suffered frostbite, we had suffered deeply in the Soviet Union, but the sufferings of those death-camp victims had been so much greater. They were dead and I was still alive. How many other nations had contributed to that evil? Why had no one done anything to stop it?

The next morning I went to get a haircut, since my hair was wild and bushy. The barber shop was owned by a Polish Christian, and there were several other customers. I had a long wait, but eventually one of the barbers called me to take a seat in his chair. While he cut my hair, I listened to the conversations around me. Mostly they were about the war, how terrible it had been, and what tremendous destruction Poland had suffered. As clippings from my hair fell to the floor, so did my heart when I heard someone say, "We must forever be grateful to Hitler. He got rid of the Jews."

They all nodded in agreement, yet I could say nothing. If I dared to utter even one word in defense of the Jews, or had announced that I was a Jew, I was afraid my throat would have been slit. I was afraid to speak, to cry out in protest. I just sat silently, absorbing the pervasive anti-Semitism.

On August 11, while out for a walk, I suddenly heard shouts and screams. Like a stampede, people were running through the street, shouting that the Jews had killed a Christian boy and used his blood to bake matzos for the Passover holidays. I saw the mob severely beating a man. I had to assume he was Jewish. I turned around and, although barely more than a skeleton, I ran as fast as I could, faster than I had ever run in my life. I managed to elude the mob and ran into the building where we were living, shutting the door against the wild, uncontrolled throngs in the street.

After these two events--the incident in the barbershop and the pogrom against Jews in Kraków only a few weeks after the end of World War II--I told myself that for Jews to survive as a people, there must be a Jewish homeland, a Jewish state. That very day, August 11, 1945, I took a silent oath that I would dedicate all my time and all my strength to the establishment of a Jewish state in the territory of the ancient kingdom of Judea, which the Romans had renamed Palestine after they crushed the Judean revolt.

Now, brooding on the silent oath I had taken that August day, I asked myself, "What am I doing on this boat?" It was not that I did not want to go to America, but I had broken my oath.

The next thing that crossed my mind was my fear of Stalin's Soviet Union. In the schools I had attended there, I had been taught that the Soviets hoped to make the entire world Communist through a world-wide Communist revolution. I thought about the Institute for Eastern Studies and its students in the city of Fergana in Uzbekistan. Revolutionaries from all over the world were trained there. Many of the students were Asians. No one dared to approach or speak to them. They were frightening, and, like them, Stalin always frightened me.

My mind was roiling that first night on the ship, bombarded with unanswerable questions. I was almost 22 years old, I had no trade or profession, I could not speak English. How would I earn a living in America? My experiences with the "justice" system in the Soviet Union had given me an interest in law. I also had a great interest in history, and most of all, I was a student at heart. But how would I support myself if I went to school? Then another question popped up: now that I was 22 years old, an age at which some fellows married, how could I support a wife? The last question that popped into my mind was how I would be treated by my father's family in America, because I was, after all, a stepson, and not a blood relative.

All these questions cut into my mind like laser beams, and they demanded answers. I tossed from side to side, but couldn't find any. I could not sleep; my life was in turmoil.

In the morning, my father called from his bunk below and asked how I had slept. I did not want to make him feel bad, so I responded that I had slept well.

We dressed and climbed to the upper deck, where we found mother and Hella, along with many other passengers. We went to the dining hall for breakfast. I noticed that the sky was very cloudy, and we could feel ship swaying from side to side as a slight wind began to churn up the water.

The dining hall was almost full, and noisy with the din of numerous languages. Whenever I heard Polish, Russian, Yiddish, Ukrainian, or Czech, I pricked up my ears in comprehension. We conversed a little in Polish with the people at our table. Our breakfast on that second day consisted of scrambled eggs, bread and rolls, and excellent coffee with milk, quite a contrast to the dismal fare we had been used to.

Late that afternoon we entered the English Channel. Buffeted by heavy winds, the ship rocked up and down, and we began to feel a bit unsteady. We went below to lie down in our bunks. The wind turned into a huge storm, with waves that tossed our ship up and down. Our bunks shook violently, but even so, my father and I decided go to the dining hall for supper. We simply could not resist the good food, a luxury we had not had for more than six years.

We met very few passengers on our way to the dining hall. Many of our fellow DPs were afraid to chance the shaky stairs as the storm became stronger and stronger. Our ship was like a child's toy being hurled about by the storm. My father and I had to hold each other's hands in order not to fall. We reached the dining hall and met mother and Hella. We had a good dinner, but after dinner we were afraid to walk on the top deck. Huge waves were crashing across it, and the crew warned us not to go up there as we might be blown overboard by the furious wind.

We went below for the night, hoping that the storm would end soon. But we hoped in vain, for the storm became stronger and stronger, and it felt as though our bunks were being levitated. Some of our neighbors begin to vomit. I too was nauseous and felt that I was on the verge of vomiting. I called down to my father, and receiving no answer, I climbed down to see how he was faring. He was very pale and unable to talk. He said in a whisper that he felt that he was going to be ill. As I looked around, I noticed other passengers standing against the wall vomiting. Very soon I began to do so, as well. Everyone in sight was vomiting.

I decided to go up on deck to get some fresh air. There were a number of passengers on the deck, obviously for the same reason. Then I saw something I had never seen before. An elderly man with a long white beard came up on deck. He took out a large tallit, a Jewish prayer shawl, and placed it, as required by Jewish law, on his shoulders. He stretched his hands upward and cried out to God in Yiddish, "God, you saved me from concentration camps, please help me again, and let me not die now on this boat." It was an indescribable scene. He then bent over, and began to vomit right in front of us. We could not keep our footing, the ship was rocking so violently, and every few seconds another person would vomit.

All of a sudden there was a scream from the front of the deck. The passengers there began shouting that a man had jumped overboard. The captain had the ship circle the area several times, hoping to rescue the passenger, but to no avail. He was just swallowed by the huge waves. A depression settled over all of us, and we thought that we were all going to die there on the boat.

I went back to my bunk. My father was still deathly white and could not even try to talk. I made an effort to sleep but again could not. Many thoughts flashed through my mind. I remembered my hometown in Poland: Dynów, where I had been born. I remembered my two older stepbrothers, who had perished in the Holocaust. I also recalled what the peasants in Gulag 149 had told me when we complained about the harsh conditions and the brutally cold winter: "Pryvikniesh, yesli niet, ty zdechniesz: You'll get used to it, and if not, you'll just drop dead." It was actually very encouraging at the time. I must have finally fallen asleep, because when I woke up in the morning, the ship was no longer rocking. I tried to speak to my father, but he was still unable to talk.

I went up on deck. Some passengers were there already, and I could see smiles on their faces. The sea was calm and our ship was forging ahead. The captain informed us that we were now out of the English Channel and entering the Atlantic Ocean, and from now on the weather would be good. He also said us that we had just come through one of the worst storms he had ever experienced.

The rest of the crossing was smooth, and finally, after a long voyage, we approached New York harbor. Everyone was on deck, gazing at the skyline of New York City. Suddenly a woman pointed her finger and shouted in Polish, "Statuta Wolnosci!"--the Statue of Liberty. It is difficult to describe our excitement when we saw that magnificent statue. Many passengers, myself included, had tears in their eyes.

We disembarked at Ellis Island. The customs inspection did not take very long, because our possessions consisted of one battered old suitcase. I did not even have a jacket. We were met at the dock by my father's brother, Uncle

Irving, his wife Ruthie, and their two sons, Norman and Jerry. We all began to weep. Uncle Irving told my father, "Don't cry, you're in America now."

Uncle Irving had come with two cars. We were driven to my uncle's brick house on Fish Avenue, in the Bronx. I do not recall the address, but it was a detached private house in a good area. We looked around the house, which appeared magnificent to us. Once seated in the living room, we gave our new family a brief account of our sojourns over the past eight years.

After a few minutes of small talk, Uncle Irving took father and me to the basement, which was nicely paneled and had a fine wood floor. He directed us to a separate room in the basement, which was a bar. It had four upholstered leather bar stools, a wood counter, shelves containing many bottles of liquor and wine, and overhead recessed lights.

My father asked Uncle Irving what time the bar opened, and when the customers would arrive. My uncle replied that it was his private bar, and that many homes in America had similar bars. Our mouths gaped in astonishment; we had never in our lives seen such luxury.

We were speaking in Yiddish. My father commented "Amerika ganef," which translates literally as "America is a thief," but here conveys the sense "Only in America could you become so rich without stealing." In Europe, especially in Poland, people looked at America with great envy because it was so rich and Americans had such a high standard of living.

Uncle Irving offered my father a drink, but I refused any liquor. Aunt Ruthie called us to dinner. We went upstairs and were directed to the dining room. Mother and Hella were already there.

It was a large room with a large table covered with a white tablecloth. Around the table were eight upholstered chairs. In front of each chair was a large white porcelain plate on top of which was a small porcelain plate. To the left of the plates was a large white paper napkin on which rested two silver forks, and to the right of the plates was a silver knife, a soup spoon, and a teaspoon. I looked at the table setting in disbelief. In the Soviet Union my only eating utensil had been a wooden spoon. No wonder my father used the term "America ganef."

Aunt Ruthie asked us to take seats at the table. The first thing I did when I sat down in that comfortable chair was to pick up the napkin and tear it in half. My uncle asked, "Why are you tearing the napkin?" I responded, "We have to save paper." My uncle laughed, "In America we have plenty of paper; there is absolutely no reason to tear the napkin in half." Obviously, my uncle didn't know that in the Soviet Union there were no paper napkins. In the Soviet Union there was no toilet paper. In Stalin's workers' paradise, newspaper was our toilet paper. Smokers used newspaper to roll cigarettes from their machorka tobacco.

Dinner consisted of green salad, tomatoes, vegetable soup, and a large serving of American steak. We ended the dinner with excellent apple pie and coffee. Never before had I eaten such a delicious meal, not even in Poland before the war, when we had been quite wealthy.

After that delicious dinner, we sat down in the living room, and Uncle Irving asked us about our war experiences. Each of us spoke in turn. Our conversation was in Yiddish, a language in which both Uncle Irving and Aunt Ruthie were fluent. My two cousins, Norman and Jerry, listened and then my aunt interpreted for them, because they did not know Yiddish. My cousins were handsome boys, very warm and affectionate. They were shocked by the details of our sufferings during the war.

I was sitting in a chair next to Uncle Irving, which gave me an opportunity to watch his face as he listened to our experiences. Uncle Irving was very handsome, stocky and not too tall, with black hair and dark eyes. There wasn't a wrinkle on his face. He was very opinionated, very sure of himself. Although saddened by our sufferings during the war, he told us to leave our past behind and to think positively, because we were now in free and blessed America.

I said in response that, as a Jew, I could not and would never forget what had happened to European Jewry during the war. Because of the Holocaust, I continued, we had to devote ourselves to bringing about the establishment of a Jewish state in the ancient kingdom of Judea, which was now called Palestine.

Uncle Irving said that I should concentrate on getting a good job or think about going into some business. America was the greatest country in the world, full of opportunities if one applied oneself: work hard and you can achieve success--the sky's the limit in America. He told us how he had become very wealthy and successful in the metal manufacturing business.

I told my uncle that I was by nature a student, and I would like very much to continue my education and become a lawyer or a diplomat. He replied that I must be dreaming, that I was living in a fantasy world.

At this point Aunt Ruthie interrupted. "Irving, we should speak about this another time." Aunt Ruthie, with her smooth, pale face, green eyes, and light red hair, was a very warm, kind person. You could see the grief in her face when we described our horrendous experiences during the Holocaust.

She suggested that we now go to the apartment Uncle Irving had prepared for us in the building he owned at 50 East 191 Street in the Bronx. We were surprised to learn that our good Uncle Irving had provided an apartment for us. He told us that this apartment building was the last one built in the Bronx prior to the beginning of World War II.

We left my uncle's house in the two cars and arrived at the building in about half an hour. It was located across from beautiful St. James Park. As we entered the building we noticed a concierge in a splendid uniform. The building consisted of two sections, each with its own elevator. Our apartment was on the fifth floor, 5D.

When we opened the door, we could not believe our eyes. The apartment was magnificent. It had a large sunken living room, a foyer, a large kitchen, and a large bedroom. It was furnished with beautiful new furniture, and the kitchen was fully equipped with brand-new appliances, including a refrigerator. Moreover, the refrigerator was full of food, and the kitchen cabinets were full of new dishes and cooking utensils. The kitchen had a fine new table with six chairs. The living room was furnished with a new sofa bed and armchairs, and there were pictures on the walls. The large bedroom was furnished with a complete new bedroom set.

The white-tiled bathroom had a large cabinet with a built-in sink, and over it a large mirrored cabinet with shaving material, powder, and other bathroom necessities. There was a bathtub and shower. After our gulag in Siberia, the mud house in Uzbekistan, and the DP camp in Austria, the apartment seemed like the Taj Mahal.

Unimaginably, it had a telephone. We could not believe that we had our own telephone. The last time we had used a phone was in 1939 in our house in Dynów.

As Uncle Irving and his family left, he urged us to get a good night's sleep after this arduous and exciting day. We kissed one another goodbye, and we thanked him over and over for all the wonderful things he had done for us.

We were dead tired, but we didn't want to go to sleep. We couldn't believe this wonderful turn of events. We felt as if we had been resurrected and granted a new lease on life. However, we were so tired and exhausted that we had to sleep.

Hella was assigned the bed in the foyer, I was given the pullout sofa bed, and my parents went to sleep in the bedroom. I wanted so much to sleep, yet again I couldn't fall asleep. My mind was bombarded with the same questions that had plagued me that first night on the *Marine Flasher*. What was I doing in this beautifully furnished apartment when so many of my people, who had suffered so much during the Holocaust, were still bedded in bunks in DP camps in Germany and Austria?

Why was I lying in a comfortable bed when so many other Holocaust survivors were braving the dangerous passes across the Alps to reach ports in Italy and France and be smuggled into Palestine on dilapidated hulks that were barely seaworthy? Why wasn't I with them, on the way to Palestine to build a Jewish state? Was I a traitor? What should I do? Would I be able to continue my education in America? I just couldn't answer all the questions that were flooding my mind. I was so tired and exhausted that I finally fell asleep. I must have slept very well, because my mother had quite a bit of trouble waking me up in the morning. I was the last one in the family to get up on our second day in New York.

Chapter 2

LEARNING ABOUT MY NEW COUNTRY

My mother prepared breakfast, which consisted of scrambled eggs, rye bread, which we buttered, and coffee with milk and sugar. These were some of the things with which Aunt Ruthie had filled our refrigerator.

As I got up from that wonderful breakfast, I looked out the kitchen window and noticed a short woman waving to me. Her window, in the other section of our building, was also on the fifth floor and faced our kitchen window. I waved back, although I had no idea who she was.

After our delicious American breakfast, we sat and talked. We were very happy with the new turn in our lives, yet we were very tense. The bright sun shone through our windows, but we didn't feel safe enough to walk down the street. We didn't know any English, and we didn't know where to go. We turned on our radio and listened to some music and some people talking. We liked the songs and the melodies, but of course we couldn't understand the words or what the people were saying.

Uncle Irving and Ruthie came over later that day without the boys, who were attending a military school outside New York City. Aunt Ruthie brought a large supply of food, some of which was in brightly colored boxes. For the first time in my life I saw corn flakes. Aunt Ruthie explained that many Americans had this cold cereal for breakfast with milk. She also brought numerous packages of kosher meat. My mother had told Ruthie that we kept a kosher home.

Aunt Ruthie helped my mother prepare dinner. It consisted of chicken noodle soup, chicken, and potato pancakes. Then we finished off our excellent meal with delicious chocolate cake and tea.

After dinner we went into the living room for a long talk. Uncle Irving told us that we had other relatives in New York, an uncle and a niece. The uncle, Samuel Eiss, was married, and his wife's name was Ettie. The Eiss family lived in the East Bronx. They had five children, four daughters and a son. The son had been in the American Army and was killed on the beach at Anzio during the invasion of Italy.

The niece, Peppi, was married to Bernard Turner. They had two sons, and lived in Brooklyn. Samuel Eiss and Bernard Turner, upon arriving in New York, had gone to work in Uncle Irving's factory. Now Samuel Eiss was in the diamond business, and Bernard Turner owned a grocery store in Brooklyn. They were both eager to visit us as soon as possible.

Uncle Irving told us that he owned a large factory in the Bronx that manufactured metal kitchen sink cabinets and radiator covers. During the war the factory had manufactured various items for the military. Now that home construction had resumed after the long hiatus during the war, his factory was very busy and he could not keep up with all the orders for his products.

Uncle Irving also told us that in the New York area there were several hundred families from our hometown, Dynów. Some of them had come to New York before World War I. People from European cities and villages generally formed organizations based on their place of origin. Jews called these societies landsmanshaften. The Dynower Krenken Untershtitsung Fareyn ("Dynów Sick People's Support Organization") gave financial support to immigrants from Dynów in the event of sickness or financial destitution. It had its own cemetery in Woodbridge, New Jersey, where members of the society were buried. From time to time it sent money to Jews still living in Dynów.

We learned from Uncle Irving that newcomers to America were called Greeners, greenhorns. He told us not to be offended by the word. When he came to America in 1924, he too had been called a Greener.

I asked my uncle about the woman who had waved to me that morning. He said that her last name was Flender and her husband was a fur manufacturer. She had come to America many years before from Kraków and she spoke both Polish and Yiddish. He had told Mrs. Flender about us and had asked her to help us, and in particular to show us around the neighborhood.

Uncle Irving got up and made a telephone call, speaking to someone in English. When he finished, he told us that he had asked a couple who lived in the building to come up to our apartment. Mr. and Mrs. Berman soon arrived, and he introduced them. They had come to America from Poland many years before; they were fluent in Yiddish and could still speak some Polish. They said that they were ready to help in any way they could. They told us that they were manufacturers of ladies' girdles. When they saw that we had a radio, they told us about WEVD, a Yiddish radio station that was on the air most of the day, and they showed us its number on the dial. They recommended the comedian Zvi Scooler and the political commentary of Shlomo Ben Israel, who reported the international news.

I told the Bermans that I wanted to continue my education and that history was my favorite subject. After our experiences during the Holocaust, I said, I fervently believed that we must have a Jewish state in Palestine. They said that they too were Zionists and shared the same goal. Mrs. Berman had spoken to Mrs. Flender, and together the two of them would take us around the neighborhood and to the local stores. They promised to call for us the following Saturday.

"It's getting late," my uncle said, "and we have to go home soon, as tomorrow is a working day. Now let's talk." He used the Yiddish word tachlis, which means "talk business."

"You will not have to pay rent for this apartment, because I am letting you have it rent-free. You, Yoshu [Joseph], you will work in my factory. You, Meciu [Miriam], you will just stay home and be a housewife, and you, Hella, will go to school." Finally, "Now Lusiek, you will have to look for a job, and earn money, and contribute some of your earnings to your parents."

"But I want to go school," I said.

Uncle Irving snorted loudly, "You're 22 years old, and you want to go to school? What for?"

"I want to be a lawyer," I said.

"Let me give it to you straight," he replied. "You're 22 years old, you don't speak English, and you want to be a lawyer! I don't know whether you know it, but law is not a very good profession. In the depression lawyers were jumping off the rooftops because they couldn't make a living. Listen, Lusiek, when you meet a girl and want to marry her, she isn't going to ask you how much you know, she'll ask if you earn enough to provide her with a nice living. You'd better wake up to the realities of life in America. Your head is in the clouds. We have to go home now, but think, Lusiek, think hard about what I've said to you tonight."

We thanked Uncle Irving and Aunt Ruthie for everything and kissed them good night. I was very grateful for all their kindnesses, but I was devastated to learn that I would not be able to go to school and continue my education.

I said good night to my parents and fell into bed. My head was spinning again, and my life seemed to be collapsing in front of me. I wondered whether my uncle's attitude could be explained by the fact that we were not blood relatives. I needed to continue my education and achieve my goal, but how? Who should I speak to, where would I find someone to advise me, how I should proceed? At the same time, I understood that I was 22 years old and didn't speak English. I did speak other languages, but what good would they do me in America? My mind was searching for answers, and that night I didn't find any. I was ready to grasp at straws to achieve my dream, but lying in bed that night, I couldn't find a single one. I tossed from side to side, ready to scream. But even if I did, who would listen or pay attention?

My mother came over after she cleaned up the kitchen and kissed me on the forehead. I think that she understood my feelings. My life was in turmoil.

The next morning we received phone calls from Uncle Samuel Eiss and Cousin Peppi Turner, who wanted to come visit that night with their children. I already knew them both because they had visited us in Dynów in the 1930s before leaving Germany for America.

Ten people arrived shortly after seven o'clock that evening: the Eiss family--Uncle Samuel, his wife Ettie, and their daughters Elsie, Lisa, Rose, and Ruthie--and Cousin Peppi with her husband, Bernard, and their sons, Norbert and Nathan. Both families brought boxes of cake. After the usual hugging and kissing, they asked about some of their friends from our hometown who had perished during the Holocaust. I was appointed by my parents to give an account of our war experiences. I noticed again that they were warmer to my parents and my sister than to me. I sensed that they considered me an outsider. The only one who somehow seemed friendly to me was Lisa Eiss. I felt an inner hurt, and I felt that hurt for many years at our family gatherings.

We all spoke Yiddish except Norbert and Nathan Turner, who didn't speak the language well. I sensed some jealousy on their part that we, the greenhorns, who had just arrived only two days before, had such a beautiful apartment in a beautiful new building

The two Turner cousins were attending high school in Brooklyn, and Cousin Ruthie, the youngest and prettiest of the Eiss daughters, attended high school in the Bronx. They knew that my father was going to work in his brother's factory. They asked about my plans. As always, I replied that I wanted to be a lawyer. They too warned that at age 22, and with no knowledge of English, I should be realistic and look for a good job or learn a trade.

Naturally I had expected my relatives to encourage me. Instead, on all sides, I found myself surrounded by land mines ready to explode. Virtually everyone advised against the plan that meant to much to me. I was devastated, on the verge of tears. The only encouragement came from Lisa, the smartest and best educated of the Eiss daughters. All three Eiss girls had office jobs. Rose Eiss, another attractive girl, told me that one Saturday she would take me to Manhattan and show me the skyscrapers and other interesting sights.

As it was getting late, my mother made coffee, and we enjoyed the delicious cakes they had brought. They told us that as soon as we were settled, they would invite us to their homes. I was sad, perhaps even depressed, after their departure, but I felt that I mustn't give up, I had to pursue my goal, no matter how difficult that might be.

On our first Saturday morning in New York, we heard the doorbell ring. I glanced through the peephole and recognized our neighbor, Mrs. Berman. I opened the door. She told us that she and Mrs. Flender, the other Polish-Yiddish-speaking tenant, were ready to take me for a walk

It felt good to communicate with these new American neighbors, to speak with them in Polish and Yiddish. As we walked out of our magnificent lobby, they explained that we would begin by looking around Fordham Road, the commercial center of the Bronx, which was within walking distance of our building.

When we reached Fordham Road, they pointed out Alexander's Department Store, on the corner of Fordham Road and the Grand Concourse. They explained that the Grand Concourse was the main street of the borough. As we strolled along Fordham Road, I was aghast to see so many large stores, as well as so many pedestrians on both sides of the street. Suddenly I noticed two policemen walking in our direction, and I took off like a shot. My companions ran after me and asked what was wrong. They were both amused and moved when I told them that in the Soviet Union you avoided the police, because they could haul you off to prison for any reason or for no reason at all. My companions assured me that I had nothing to fear from American policemen and that in the United States the function of the police was to protect the people, not to persecute them. I accepted their assurances with some skepticism. It was very difficult to ignore the terror implanted in my mind and body by the KGB during the Stalin regime.

After our long stroll along Fordham Road, we turned onto the Grand Concourse. The two ladies pointed out the many high-rise apartment buildings. They took me into the lobby of the Paradise Theater, the largest and the most popular movie house in the Bronx. They described the ornamental ceiling of the theater proper, painted to look like a blue sky. It was a wonderful stroll, and a wonderful introduction to my new world.

By now I thought of the two women as my friends. Mrs. Berman told me that she had one child, a daughter, who was looking for a husband. Mrs. Flender told me that she had two unmarried sons. The oldest, Murray, worked with his father in their fur business. The younger son, Harold, was attending City College and hoped to become a novelist, and in fact, in later years he did become a prominent writer.

I told my companions that I wanted to be a lawyer. They too questioned my plan: You're 22 years old, you haven't finished high school, you don't know English! Think about it, they said. I told them about my great love of history and foreign affairs. Mrs. Flender said that her son Harold was also interested in history. She promised to introduce me to him, and perhaps he would have some ideas about how I could continue my education.

Along the way they pointed out the many stores, including the bakery where they bought their bread and cakes, and they tried to teach me some English. Among other places, they showed me Krum's, which they described as the largest ice cream and candy store in the Bronx.

When we returned to our building, I thanked them both for their kindness in giving up their time and introducing me to my new neighborhood. They said that they felt a moral obligation to help people like us who had suffered so much during the Holocaust. They said that they would try to help us adjust to our new surroundings.

When I returned home I told the family about my experiences that morning. My mother had been very concerned about my long absence. Her state of mind was still the same as when we were in the Soviet Union. There, if you were absent for longer than expected, the presumption was that you had been picked up by the KGB and put in jail. It took quite a long way before we were free of this paranoiac conditioned reflex.

Sunday morning I turned on the radio and listened to WEVD. It was such a pleasure to hear Yiddish on the radio. I listened to the quasi-comedian Zvi Scooler, who called himself Der Grammeister ("Rhyme Master") because he rhymed his statements, and I was very impressed by the commentator who so perceptively analyzed the national and world news, specifically the news from Palestine.

While I was listening to the radio, we got a phone call from Munia Waining, an officer of the Dynower Krenken Untershtitsung Fareyn. He told my father that he and his family would like visit us that afternoon, together with some of the society's other officers. My father looked forward to the visit, because he had known most of them in the old country. They had come to America in the 1920s.

Early in the afternoon of our first Sunday in New York, the doorbell rang. My father looked through the peephole, opened the door, and exuberantly greeted Munia Waining, whom he had known in our hometown. Munia came with his wife and his daughter, Basia. Father and Mother kissed them. I noticed that they brought a white box, which they gave to my mother. They said that it was a box of cookies from a very good bakery.

After introducing themselves, they told us that they lived in an apartment house on Davidson Avenue, not very far from our building. We all sat down in the living room. They said that Uncle Irving had notified the Dynower society in New York of our arrival. Munia told us that he worked in a grocery store, and I was surprised to learn that Basia, who was born in New York, was fluent in Yiddish. She was about 16 years old, tall and very attractive. She told me that she was attending high school. My parents and Munia reminisced about the old days in the Dynów that was no more.

In a few minutes the doorbell rang again. My father opened the door to three men, exclaiming "Yankel! Pinchu!" but the third one he did not know. My father introduced to us Yankel (Jacob) Ores, the president of the Dynower society, and Pinchu (Pinchas) Kessler, the vice-president. They introduced the third man, Max Fishman, the treasurer. Max had not been born in Dynów but had joined the society after marrying a Dynower girl in New York. All three had brought cakes and cookies. I brought in some chairs from the kitchen and we sat down in the living room.

Yankel Ores worked in a grocery store, Pinchu Kessler worked in a metal factory, and Max Fishman worked in a kosher butcher shop. They asked us to tell them everything that had happened in Dynów from the beginning of the war, and especially about their relatives and friends. We were the first survivors from Dynów to arrive in America after the war.

My father, as usual, designated me to give an account of that era of pain and suffering. I began by describing Dynów as it was in 1939. The town had a vibrant Jewish community and three Orthodox synagogues. Most of the Jews were manufacturers, merchants, and craftsmen, such as tailors and cobblers. The medical doctors were Jewish. We had two Jewish schools, one religious and the other secular.

The German army occupied Dynów in the early days of September 1939. They rounded up about 300 Jews and machine-gunned them in a nearby forest on the first night of Rosh Hashanah. They also burned down our three synagogues, killing the Jewish refugees who were sleeping in them that night.

After these horrible events, the rest of the town's Jewish populace fled across the River San. In the villages on the other side the river we were surprised to come across units of the Red Army. We asked them what they were doing there. Their officers responded that they had come at the invitation of the Polish peasants and workers. Of course that was a lie. The Red Army was there because of the treacherous agreement Stalin had entered into with Hitler in the last week of August. Pursuant to this agreement, the Soviet Union invaded and occupied the eastern part of Poland.

The surviving Dynów Jews settled here and there in the Soviet-occupied part of Poland. We eventually made our way to the city of Lwów. There, because my father had been a wealthy merchant, we were classified by the KGB as "capitalists and enemies of the people," and in consequence we were sent to a gulag on the outskirts of Siberia. We remained in the gulag for a year and a half. From there we ended up in the Soviet Muslim Republic of Uzbekistan, close to the border of Afghanistan. In Uzbekistan we lived for 3½ years in a mud room next to a cow. We escaped from the Soviet Union after the war, in June 1945, by bribing the KGB. The great majority of the Jews of Dynów, so far as we knew, had perished in the Holocaust; many of them were exterminated in Auschwitz.

Our visitors were deeply saddened by my account, especially when they realized that I had no information about their relatives and friends.

I asked, "What did you American Jews do, when you learned about what was happening to European Jewry during the war, what did you do about the Holocaust?" They said they hadn't known about it.

"Didn't you read your newspapers, or listen to the radio?"

They said there had been nothing in the papers or on the radio. I asked if President Roosevelt was a friend of the Jews. In one voice they unanimously declared that Roosevelt was the best friend the Jews ever had.

Now the topic of conversation changed, and they told us about our Jewish landsmen from Dynów in America and about the activities of the Dynower society in New York City, which had several hundred members. They met on Sunday evenings once a month in a room they rented in a building on the Lower East Side of Manhattan. The members of the society worked at all kind of jobs, and three members had become quite rich. These rich men were the Feldman brothers, who owned one of the largest liquor distributorships in New Jersey, located in Hoboken; Harry Stelzer, one of the biggest ladies' belt manufacturers in New York, whose factory was located in the garment district, and who lived in an exclusive building on Fifth Avenue; and the third was Uncle Irving, who was a very successful metal manufacturer. All of these wealthy men were active members and supporters of the Dynower society.

"You are very fortunate to have such a good and wealthy brother who will help you financially," said Pinchu Kessler. "We have been in New York since the 1920s, and we are still living in dilapidated old walk-up apartments; you just came over a few days ago, and you live in a palace."

President Yankel Ores told us that the full membership had been notified of our survival and our arrival in New York. The society was going to hold a special meeting on a Sunday in August, and he asked me to give a full report on Dynów and its Jewish people during the war. I willingly agreed and looked forward to addressing the whole membership of the society.

The conversation now turned to their life in Dynów before they left for America. They talked about relatives, friends, and neighbors, many long gone. They reminisced about the old days. Yankel Ores, Munia Waining, and Max Fishman were serious-minded men. In contrast, Pinchu Kessler was a kibbitzer. He turned to my father: "Greener, what will you do now, in America?" He knew that my father had been a wealthy merchant in Dynów. I butted in. "Why do you call my father Greener?" I asked. He answered, "When you guys come to America, you talk stupid sometimes and you act silly."

I asked if he could give me an example. "Okay," Pinchu said, "Here is an example for you. A Polish Jew whose name was Mechel--in English it would be Michael--came to visit his brother in New York in July of 1939. Relatives and landsmen came to visit him in his brother's house. When his brother and his family and the landsmen asked him about their hometown in Poland, he sounded very sad. He never looked people in the eye: when you spoke to him, he looked at the walls and the ceilings. His brother's two sons discussed their uncle's behavior, and the fact that he never had a smile on his face. The nephews wanted to do something to make their uncle Mechel happy, so they took him to see a baseball game. They bought good seats and took him to Yankee Stadium.

"The stadium was packed to full capacity, because it was an important game. In a short time, the Yankees hit a home run with the bases loaded. The crowd in the stadium, including the nephews, went wild. They stood up, they were screaming, cheering the Yankees. Mechel sat quietly and didn't say a thing. The nephews got angry and said to him, 'Uncle Mechel, how can you just sit so quietly and not cheer and applaud? Uncle Mechel, can't you see that the Yankees just hit a home run with the bases loaded?'

"Uncle Mechel felt embarrassed. He had never seen a baseball game, and he had probably never heard of baseball, but he knew that something big had happened, because the crowd was standing up, cheering and applauding. He turned to his nephews and asked, 'Tell me, dear nephews, is this home run with the bases loaded good for the Jewish people?'

"How can you Europeans be that stupid? How does a home run with bases loaded affect Jewish people? Now," Pinchu continued, "you understand why we call you Greener."

I couldn't let this pass. "You see, Pinchu Kessler," I responded, "Uncle Mechel is a smart fellow, and you are the Greener. You obviously don't read the papers or listen to the radio. Anti-Semitism in Europe, especially in Poland in the late thirties, was so virulent and so violent that any Jew in Poland in July 1939 would be right to ask whether a home run with bases loaded was good for the Jews."

The three other officers of the Dynower society began to laugh, saying in Yiddish, "Git gezugt" ("You told him!"). Even the young girl Basia said, "You're absolutely right, Lusiek." Pinchu said nothing.

We now began to discuss our plans for our new life in America. They all knew that my father had been a merchant in Poland. Munia Waining asked, "Yoshu, what are you going to do? Have you discussed it with your brother Itchu (Irving)?"

My mother joined in and said that Uncle Irving wanted Father to work in his factory. She would be staying home as a housewife. Then Pinchu Kessler asked me, "Lusiek, you look so pale and emaciated, are you sick or something?" Mother responded that I was not sick, but that my wan appearance was the result not only of our sufferings but also of my constant worrying and sleepless nights. "He worries about almost everything," she said. "He feels guilty that he didn't go with the illegal boats to Palestine. He feels that Jews will never be safe unless there is a Jewish state in Palestine. He is afraid of the Soviet Union. He believes that Stalin cannot be trusted and that one day America will have trouble with the Soviet Union. All the problems of the world are on his mind." She was caressing my head as she spoke about me. "He is upset that he does not speak English. However, his biggest concern is that he wants to continue his education and become a lawyer. He also has a great interest in history, and he is talking about going into the diplomatic service."

"How old are you, Lusiek?" asked Pinchu Kessler.

"I am 22 years old," I said.

"Lusiek, you're dreaming, your head is the clouds!" said Pinchu. The other members of the Dynower society nodded in agreement. "You're 22 years old, you don't speak English, and you want to go school?" asked Pinchu. "Who is going to support you, who is going to pay for your education? Stop dreaming, be realistic and get yourself a good job. You know what? I've got an even better idea. Find yourself a rich girl, that will solve all your problems."

Once again I was devastated. It felt as if everyone was conspiring against me, throwing obstacles in my path. I made no reply to Pinchu. Basia took my hand and said, "Don't worry, you'll be alright!"

The hour was late, and my mother served coffee and cake. Our guests had meant well, and before they left they reminded me about the meeting in August when I would give a detailed account of the last days of the Jewish community of Dynów. After their departure I remained sullen and depressed. I helped Mother with the dishes and went to bed.

The next morning, Uncle Irving dropped Aunt Ruthie off at our apartment. He said he would return in the evening to have supper with us. Aunt Ruthie took me and Hella to a small department store called Robert Hall, located on Jerome Avenue, a short walk from our apartment. There she purchased two pair of slacks, two shirts, and a jacket for me. She bought Hella some dresses and some nightgowns.

On the way back to our apartment from our shopping spree, I picked up the *Yiddish Morning Journal*. Aunt Ruthie commented that it was good to read the Yiddish paper to keep up with the news of the day, but it was more important to begin to learn English. I told her the few English words I had picked up here and there. My aunt sat down in our living room, and began to give me and Hella some lessons in English. I wrote down what she told us in a notebook. And I began to listen to English radio stations, such as NBC and CBS.

Uncle Irving arrived toward the end of the day to pick up Aunt Ruthie. He told us that he had arranged for father and me to be driven down to his factory by one of his employees. We went the next morning.

The factory was located at 230 Manida Street. I was amazed at its size. It was a large building, a huge noisy place filled with all kinds of heavy machinery. There were at least 60 workers. Some of the machines were cutting large metal sheets. The welding machines emitted gigantic sparks. In one area, metal cabinets were spray-painted white. In another, the cabinets were heat-dried. I was very impressed. My father was proud of what his brother had achieved in America. His face lit up, and he smiled broadly.

After our tour of the factory we went into my uncle's office. He was on the telephone, and his office manager, Sam Rund, introduced himself. He spoke a little Yiddish and told us that he, too, had an apartment in our building. He told us that my uncle was speaking to his stockbroker. I had never heard the word "stockbroker" before and asked what it meant. Sam told us all about corporations, stock issues, and trading of shares on the stock exchange. You could make a lot of money or be completely wiped out, he said. He told us that many people had lost all their money in the Wall Street crash and killed themselves. He ended by saying that you had to be a gambler to get involved in the stock market. I wasn't the least bit interested--all I had in my pocket were the two dollar bills my uncle had given me after our arrival in New York.

When he got off the phone, Uncle Irving said to me, "Greener, become a manufacturer, and don't waste your time with school." I didn't say anything. He introduced his office staff. Father was so impressed with the factory that I thought he was going to roll up his sleeves and go to work then and there.

We had sandwiches for lunch in my uncle's office. Father said that he was ready to go to work right now, but Irving advised him to rest for at least another couple of weeks. However, he told me to start looking for a job right away. He told father that Sam Rund lived in our building, and would drive him to and from work.

Later on, when we discussed the visit, father was excited about the factory. I too was impressed, but I was disheartened because my uncle was trying to discourage me from going to school. My problem was finding someone to support me and pay for my education.

When we entered the lobby of our building, we found Mrs. Flender waiting for the front elevator with her younger son, Harold. They invited me to come up to their apartment to get some ideas from him.

It was a beautifully furnished, two-bedroom apartment. Mrs. Flender had told Harold about me. Although I was beginning to have some inkling of English, I could speak fluently only in Yiddish or Polish, so she interpreted for me. Harold was a young man in his early twenties--quite tall with nice blue eyes, a clean-shaven face, and thick, light brown hair. He had graduated from CCNY with a bachelor's degree in English literature. His dream was to write novels, and he also had a great love of history and international events. He had no interest in his father's fur business. I felt that I had finally met someone who shared my interests.

Harold very much wanted to hear about my experiences in the Soviet Union. I told him what we had been through, and also my views on Stalin's plan for world domination. Then I told him about my personal problems, specifically that I wanted to continue my education and become a lawyer, but so far everyone had been discouraging me. Harold's response was comforting: the people I had spoken to were not well enough educated to understand those who have a thirst for knowledge. He urged me not to be discouraged.

Harold had a friend in our building who would be graduating from law school in a few days, and he promised to introduce me to him, offering to help me in any way he could. I thanked Harold very much, for he had lifted my sprits enormously, and went home.

When I returned to our apartment, I found my family in an upbeat mood. Obviously, my father had told mother and Hella about the factory where he would soon be working.

The phone rang, and I answered it. It was Peppi Mildwurf, a friend of my mother's from Dynów who had come to America in the late 1920s. When I told mother, she cried, "Peppi Mildwurf, my dear friend," and grabbed the phone. After the telephone conversation she announced, "The Mildwurfs and the Feldmans will be coming to see us tonight."

The concierge called us on the house phone around six, informing us that several people were on the way up. The doorbell rang and mother opened the door, crying, "Peppi, Peppi, my dear friend Peppi!" They hugged and kissed, and they had tears in their eyes. Peppi introduced her husband, Max, and the three Feldman brothers. My father had known the Feldmans in Dynów. They had been poor there, but since coming to America in the early 1920s, they had become successful businessmen and were very wealthy. They owned one of the largest liquor distributorships in New Jersey. The two older brothers were married and had children. The youngest brother, Izzy, was single.

Everyone sat down and began reminiscing about the old days in Dynów. Once again, at my father's request, I gave an account of the war years. Our guests were saddened. Izzy had tears in his eyes. He looked at Mother and said, "Miriam, I am glad that you survived, and from now on you will be a newborn person. You will have nothing to worry about."

All three Feldman brothers were short and stocky. The oldest brother had gray hair, but Izzy had black hair and dark eyes, and emanated warmth.

He was deeply affected by my tale, and by the deaths of so many people he had known; you could see tears in his eyes. Meanwhile, my mother was in a corner of the room with her childhood friend Peppi. I am sure that they discussed my mother's divorce from my natural father and her subsequent marriage to my stepfather.

Peppi's husband, Max, was the most educated of the men. All of them were ardent Zionists and they agreed on the necessity for a Jewish state in Palestine. I told them that I planned to dedicate myself to the realization of the dream of establishing the Jewish state.

Mother and Peppi joined our conversation just as I was explaining that I wanted to continue my education as a full-time student. Max Mildwurf asked about my educational interests, and whether I was interested in any particular profession. I responded that I had a great interest in history and international affairs, especially problems related to the Soviet Union, and that I wanted to become a lawyer.

And now the same old litany: "So you want to be a lawyer. Larry, Larry, you must be dreaming. You are 22 years old, you don't know English, you still haven't finished high school, and you want to be a lawyer in America. I sympathize with you, but be realistic. You are banging your head against a wall."

I felt as if someone had stuck a knife through my heart. Somehow I had imagined that Max Mildwurf, a well-educated man, would understand me and encourage me.

Noting my dejection, Peppi entered the conversation. "I have a cousin, Sol Fine, whose parents also came to America from Dynów. Perhaps he can give you some advice." Sol Fine had become an engineer and lived with his mother and sister Goldie in the Bronx. Peppi said that she would call him and ask him to come to see me.

Peppi and her husband had a jewelry store in Hoboken, New Jersey, but sent all their customers' repairs to a jewelry manufacturer in Manhattan. She told me she would speak to the manufacturer about giving me a job. "The jewelry business is very good now, and perhaps you could go into it," she said. "You know what else I want to tell you? Sol's sister Goldie is looking to get married. Perhaps we will make a shidduch." That's Yiddish for arranging a marriage.

Now I was being told not only to forget about school and go into the jewelry business, but to meet Goldie, who was looking to get married. Marriage at this juncture was the last thing on my mind.

Peppi asked to use our phone. She made a call and had a lengthy conversation in English. I heard the names Sol and Goldie. When she finished, Peppi announced that she had made arrangements for Sol and Goldie Fine to visit us the next day.

The hour was getting late, and mother served cake and coffee to our guests. Izzy took my mother aside and told her that he would keep in touch and visit us again. Our guests bade us good night; we hugged and kissed each other, and they left our apartment.

I was so dispirited that I told my parents I had a headache and wanted to go to sleep. I fell into my bed like a brick. I pounded my pillow with my fist. I kept asking myself why everyone was against me. Why was everyone trying to discourage me? Why couldn't they understand that all I wanted was to get an education? I tried to sleep but could not; I kept tossing from one side of my bed to the other. I was heartbroken, but after a few hours of tossing and turning, I finally fell asleep.

The next morning, Mother came over as I sat with my feet dangling off the bed and kissed my forehead. She knew that I was suffering a great deal; she was the only one in the family who understood me. My stepfather and my stepsister had absolutely no understanding of me, because neither of them were studious or had any interest in learning.

I walked around that entire day like a zombie, anxiously awaiting Sol Fine. I had no appetite and ate very little. I went down to Fordham Road and bought the *Yiddish Forward*. I read it, and I listened to WEVD. I was saddened by the news about the Holocaust survivors trying to sneak into Palestine on ramshackle boats, and I did not like the news coming out of the East European countries now totally controlled by the Soviet Union.

Finally, the house phone rang and the concierge announced that Sol Fine and a young lady were coming up. The door bell rang, and I let them in, inviting them into the living room.

Sol was a little on the short side, slim with black hair and a light complexion, and wearing a light beige suit with a tie. Goldie was 20 years old, of average height, with a nice hairdo, blue eyes, and a tiny nose. She was not at all bad looking. Sol was fluent in Yiddish, but Goldie, although she understood Yiddish, could not speak it. Sol's mother, who knew both my mother and my stepfather, had been born in Dynów, and she too had left for America in the early 1920s. Sol and his sister lived with their mother in the Bronx. Sol had graduated from CCNY as an engineer and now had a very good job. He had come to see if he could be of any help to me, so I told him about my hopes and goals.

Sol asked about our experiences in Europe and my future plans. When I completed my account and told him what I had in mind, he said, "I admire you, and I respect you for wishing to continue your education." Knowing that I had a rich uncle he continued, "Do you think that your uncle would subsidize you or lend you the money to go through school?" I told Sol that Uncle Irving was very good to us but did not believe that I should go school. He felt that I should get a good job and eventually go into some business. He also thought that law was not a very good profession.

"Larry, since you don't have anyone to subsidize your education, you must take a different route," Sol said. He suggested night school. "Our high schools in New York and CCNY have evening sessions. But you need to be aware that the teachers and professors in the night schools are not as good as those in the day schools. And it takes much, much longer to complete an education in the evening session than in the day session. The day sessions start at nine o'clock in the morning and continue through the afternoon. The evening sessions usually begin at seven and end at nine o'clock or occasionally ten o'clock. It is a long process, but if you are ambitious and determined, you can do it. It's a hard grind.

"You'll have to get a good job in order to earn some money to support yourself," Sol continued. "As for high school, not far from here on Fordham Road is Theodore Roosevelt High School, which is within walking distance of your building. After you graduate from high school with good grades, you can go to City College, which is tuition free."

Sol continued, "You'll have a hard time, especially since you don't know English." He suggested that I purchase a good Polish-English dictionary. "I am fully on your side and I have to give you credit for being so determined. Don't let anyone talk you out of it. We have quite a number of American-born people who got their education in evening schools and became very successful. Since you are a Zionist, you probably know what Theodor Herzl said: 'If you will it, it will be no dream.' "

Goldie interjected, "Listen to my brother. I completely agree with him." Sol said that the people I had been speaking to were uneducated workers and businessmen.

I began to feel a bit easier. Here was someone who agreed with my plan and was offering encouragement. Sol told me that I should not hesitate to call him; he and Goldie were ready to help. I thanked Sol and Goldie for their advice and their help. I could sense that even my mother felt a little better, because she had been very worried about me. On the other hand, my stepfather and even my sister Hella were not very excited about my going back to school. They felt that I should take Uncle Irving's advice and get a good job or go into business. They looked on Uncle Irving as God because of his accomplishments in America. Despite that, I felt as if a heavy stone had been lifted from my chest.

Mother served coffee and cake and thanked Sol and Goldie for coming to see us. I looked at Goldie, and I must say that she was a sweet, attractive girl. However, I was not ready to start a romance with anyone. I was poor, as poor as could be. I had in my pocket only the two dollar bills my uncle had given me upon our arrival.

Sol and Goldie bade us goodnight. They reminded us that their mother wanted very much to see us. We all kissed, and when I kissed Goldie we looked into each other's eyes. I felt much better, not because I had kissed her, but because I saw that somehow I would be able to continue my education, albeit by a very long and hard route. I slept much better that night.

The next day my cousin Rose Eiss, who was both attractive and single, called me. She said that she wanted to take me out the next Saturday. She would pick me up before noon and give me a tour of Manhattan. At last I would have a chance to get out and see the real New York City.

Rose arrived at our apartment just after ten. We walked the three blocks to the subway station on the corner of Fordham Road and the Grand Concourse. She deposited money in a turnstile, five cents per passenger, and said that she was going to pay for all our activities that day. She explained that the subway was the Sixth Avenue line, and the train we were on was the D train, which would take us to the center of Manhattan. This was my first subway ride. There were not many passengers and lots of empty seats. Rose said that the subway was not crowded because it was Saturday. On weekdays, however, when people were going to and from work, the subway was very crowded, and it was difficult to get a seat.

We disembarked at the 34th Street station in Manhattan. Rose took me to see the Empire State Building and as we walked along 34th Street, she pointed it out to me and said that it was the world's tallest building. I was amazed at its height, but I must confess that I had never even heard of the Empire State Building before.

Rose purchased two tickets for the guided tour. There were at least 20 people in the tour group, tourists from all over America. The guide was a fairly young man, and he told us about the history of the building and its construction, with Rose interpreting for me. The building had many elevators, and we took one all the way to the top. My head was spinning as the elevator shot upward at great speed. The view from the observation deck was simply breathtaking. For the first time I began to comprehend the power and might of America. Rose put some change in a coin-operated telescope so that I could view the vistas of Manhattan. When we finished the tour, we got on the down elevator, and that was one hell of a ride!

When we left the building, Rose took me to a restaurant called Horn & Hardart for lunch. I was amazed again when I saw customers inserting coins into slots and retrieving all kinds of sandwiches from the glass compartments. No wonder people in Europe are so awed by America, I said to myself. We both had tuna sandwiches and coffee.

After lunch Rose took me to Rockefeller Center. The name Rockefeller I had heard in Europe. Once again I was awed by the size and height of the buildings and by the garden, the sculptures, and the beautiful flowers. We took a long walk around the buildings and the garden. I was a bit tired, so we sat down on a bench in the garden. Rose told me that she was going to take me to a place called Radio City Music Hall. This was a movie theater in Rockefeller Center where we would see a movie and a dance show, but not for another hour or so.

I told Rose that I wanted to purchase a Polish-English dictionary, so we took a long walk and ended up at a bookstore called Barnes & Noble. It was a very large store, and there were a lot of people looking at the many books displayed on tables. Rose told one of the salesmen that she wanted to purchase a Polish-English dictionary. I asked Rose whether she could lend me money for it, but she replied that she would purchase it for me as a gift. I told Rose that was very nice of her, but she had been doing quite a lot for me that day, and I would like to purchase it myself if she would lend me the money. Rose responded, "Larry, today is your day, and the dictionary will be my gift to you."

The salesman came back with a large Polish-English dictionary. I glanced through it and found it more than sufficient. Rose paid for the dictionary and handed it to me, and I thanked her for this wonderful gift, kissing her on both cheeks.

Back at Radio City, Rose purchased two tickets. We walked into the theater and I was amazed by its splendor and size. We were obviously a few minutes late because the dancers and musicians were already performing. The dancers, whom Rose called the Rockettes, were beautiful young girls, twirling on the stage in their lovely skirts. It was a magnificent performance, and the audience did not stop applauding. The huge place was filled to capacity, and the audience consisted of a large number of young people.

The movie started soon after the show. Within minutes, I noticed that many young couples were hugging and kissing, rather than watching the movie. I had attended many movies in Poland, but I had never seen couples hugging and kissing during them. I asked myself, Is a movie house in America a place where young couples go to make love? Looking around me, I too developed an urge, and I grabbed Rose and started to hug and kiss her. Rose grabbed my hands and pulled them away from her face. "Hey, Larry, stop it! I'm your cousin, not your girlfriend," she said. "When I told you in the bookstore that today was your day, that did not include hugging and kissing. You have to learn how to behave. Don't copy these kids." I apologized to her, and explained that I was overtaken by an urge when I saw all those young couples hugging and kissing each other. It was all a little embarrassing.

When we got home, I told my parents and Hella where I had been and what I had seen. I also told them how kind Rose had been to me and about the money she had spent on me, including the purchase of the Polish-English dictionary. My parents thanked Rose for taking me out and my mother asked her to stay for supper, but Rose excused herself, saying she had to go home.

I told Hella she could look through the dictionary, told my mother that it had been a very productive and educational day, and told my family what a magnificent place Manhattan was. I asked Mother if I could have an early supper, as I was quite tired. I fell asleep very early that Saturday night because I was so exhausted from my Manhattan activities.

I got up early Sunday morning, looking forward to listening to WEVD because on Sundays it presented the excellent Yiddish commentator Shlomo Ben-Israel. (I also listened every day to the English stations in order to pick up English words and get a feel for the language.) That Sunday, Shlomo Ben-Israel gave an exhaustive report about the British blockade in the Mediterranean Sea, where the Royal Navy were stopping the ships on which survivors of the Holocaust were attempting to get to Palestine. He described old, dilapidated cargo vessels packed with men, women, and children eager to return to their ancient homeland, and how brutally they were treated when intercepted by the British. My heart ached. I simply could not understand how the civilized world could stand by and do nothing to help those unfortunate people.

Shlomo also told how Jewish organizations in America were organizing rallies and demonstrations against Great Britain, especially against its evil and anti-Semitic Foreign Minister, Ernest Bevin. In particular he mentioned the great Rabbi Abba Hillel Silver, the president of the Zionist Organization of America, who was in the forefront of the struggle.

He also spoke at great length about the activities of the Jewish underground organizations in Palestine. He specifically mentioned the Irgun Zvi Le'umi organization and its leader, Menachem Begin. The name Begin struck a bell, because I had met him in 1942 in Uzbekistan.

After Germany invaded the Soviet Union on June 22, 1941, the Polish government-in-exile in London, headed by General Wladyslaw Sikorski, entered into an agreement with the Soviet Union to cooperate in the fight against Hitler, the common enemy. Pursuant to the agreement, the Soviets agreed to release all Polish political prisoners and resettle them in the Muslim regions of Uzbekistan, Kazakhstan, Kirgyzstan, and Tajikistan. After our release, my family ended up in Fergana, Uzbekistan.

As part of the same agreement, a Polish army was organized from the released political prisoners under the leadership of General Wladyslaw Anders, who had also been a political prisoner in the Soviet Union. The Anders Army accepted very few Jewish volunteers. My older brother Shmulek volunteered, but was turned down. Menachem Begin, however, was accepted by the Anders Army, because he had been the leader of Beitar, the youth organization of the revisionist Zionist organization in Poland before the war.

In Fergana, where we had settled, my father dealt in the black market trade. One day he took me along to see his black market operations. We went to the house of his partner, another Polish Jew in Uzbekistan. My father's partner lived in a mud house like ours near Pioneer Street. There was a Polish soldier in the house, who was slim and on the short side. My father's partner introduced him as Menachem Begin, a friend from the Polish city of Wilno. His army camp was located in Margelany, not far from Fergana.

Once the Soviet Union began to prevail against Hitler's armies, it became concerned about the Anders Army. Stalin planned to make Poland a Communist state, so he wanted to get rid of the Anders Army, which could have opposed his plan. That is why the Anders Army was permitted to leave the Soviet Union, to fight alongside the British on the Italian front. After Begin left the Soviet Union with the Anders Army, he went to Palestine, where he became the leader of the Irgun Zvi Legume, the most aggressive Zionist underground. Years later he became the Prime Minister of Israel.

Later that morning Mrs. Flender called to say that her husband and her older son, Murray, wanted to meet me. She invited me up to their apartment. When I got there Mrs. Flender introduced me to her husband and Murray. Harold was also there. Mr. Flender had come from Poland many years before and had become a furrier, and Murray worked for his father. Mr. Flender was fluent in Yiddish, but his sons spoke no Yiddish at all.

Mr. Flender asked about my war experiences and was especially interested in our experiences with the Nazis and the Russians. He mentioned that he was currently importing mink and sable skins from the Soviet Union. He also asked about some Polish cities he had known. Murray was very attentive to everything I said.

At some point Harold asked whether I had decided to proceed with my education. I told them that I had no choice but to make a compromise, taking a job during the day and attending school at night. Harold was not happy about my compromise, saying that one could not get the same education in night school as in day school, and that it was going to take so much longer to graduate from college and law school. I replied that I had no choice, as nobody was willing to subsidize my education. Murray said that he gave me credit for being willing to undertake such a strenuous regimen, especially at the age of 22 and not knowing English.

Harold asked whether I knew about the upcoming Fourth of July holiday. I did, because I had studied American history back in Poland. He invited us to join him the following week for the big Fourth of July parade on the Grand Concourse.

July 4, 1946, was a beautiful sunny day. It was our third week in America, and we four new Americans, the Wenigs, met Harold Flender in the lobby of our building and walked over to the Grand Concourse to celebrate with our fellow Americans as free and new-born people, on this holiday so important to all Americans. No one who did not experience the Holocaust can truly appreciate or comprehend the meaning of my expression "new-born people"--we knew full well that our lives should have ended long ago, and so considered ourselves to be born again.

The Grand Concourse was a sea of people. We watched with pride and joy as columns of marchers of many ages and backgrounds passed by. The beautiful music warmed our hearts; I especially liked the bagpipes and the kilts. The Wenig family applauded enthusiastically as each new column passed by. It was a glorious holiday. We no longer had to worry about the evil SS or the KGB. We stayed until the very end of the parade, then we thanked

Harold for taking us, and together walked back to our building. It was a great day for us, the rebirth of our lives.

Chapter 3

SETTLING IN

When we returned to our apartment I lay down for little rest. My rest was interrupted by a telephone call from Peppi Mildwurf. A few days earlier she had been at the factory of L & D Jewelers and had asked if they might be interested in hiring me as an apprentice jeweler. As it happened, they were looking for a new apprentice so they wanted to meet me, but since they were going away for a two-week vacation they would see me after their return. Peppi said she would meet me at their place of business on the day of the interview. She told me that L&D stood for Liberty and Diamond. Mr. Liberty was an Italian American and Mr. Diamond was Jewish. The company was located on Maiden Lane in Manhattan, and Peppi gave me subway directions.

I was both happy and unhappy about this development, because I had dreamed of attending school full-time. My mother noticed my sad expression. She patted my head, "Lusiek," she said, "you'll see that everything will work out in your favor. Try to put a smile on your face."

The following morning the news on WEVD was unbelievable, so terrible that it turned my stomach upside down. While we had been celebrating the Fourth of July, there had been a pogrom in the Polish city of Kielce. The announcer said that 43 Jewish survivors were killed. I believe my heart stopped beating at its normal rate. How could this happen again, only one year after the end of the Holocaust perpetrated by Nazi Germany? I started to cry. I wanted to do something, but I had no idea what I could do. Here I was thinking about a job and school at the same time that my people were being murdered again. I practically pounded my fist on the kitchen table. The British were stopping Jewish survivors from entering their ancient homeland and the Poles were murdering Jewish survivors in the city of Kielce.

I recalled the silent oath I had taken on August 11, 1945, during the pogrom against the few Jews in Kraków. That day I swore that, because of what I just experienced, I would dedicate the rest of my life to the establishment of a Jewish state in our ancient Judean homeland. My parents and Hella were also very upset, but I was not just upset, I was angry, and I had guilt feelings. Mother asked me to sit down and have lunch. I told her that I could not eat. I just stood at the kitchen window and stared at the evil world we lived in.

Later, I lay down on my sofa bed and stared at the ceiling. Unanswerable questions bombarded my mind. Why did so Christians hate Jews so much? Where and when did it all start? Poland was a Catholic country. The Poles were very religious people. Cardinal Hlond, their highest ranking church official, was held in the same regard as the president of the country. Poland was neither rich nor industrialized; the bulk of the economy was agriculture. Most of the farming acreage was owned by the landed aristocracy and the Catholic Church. The bulk of the population consisted of poor peasants who tilled their small parcels of land or worked on land owned by the aristocracy and the Church. The peasantry was not educated, but they listened to and respected their priests. If the priests had told them not to do any harm to the Jews, they would have listened and complied.

However, in my experience, most of Poland's priests were virulent anti-Semites. Many of the death camps were located in Poland, as well as the biggest ghettos and the greatest number of Jewish victims. If the Pope had told the Polish priests to help the Jews, many Jews would have been saved. Therefore, I believe that Pope Pius XII must also have been a virulent anti-Semite. That is why there had been a pogrom in Kraków, and that is why there was now a pogrom in Kielce.

Lying on my sofa-bed, I asked myself a question. Many Christians believe in the second coming of Christ. If he were to come now, what would he say to them when he learned about the horrendous crimes Christians had been perpetrating against Jews for 2,000 years? I could see Christ pointing his finger at Europe's Christians: "You murdered them during the Crusades, you forced them to live in that hell, the ghetto of Venice, you burned them alive in the Inquisition, you drove them from your lands, you perpetrated forced conversions and massacres and pogroms against them, and every one of you was engaged in the most horrendous crime of all, the Holocaust; you even perpetrated pogroms against Jews after the Holocaust."

I am sure that Christ would have said, "How could you have done such horrendous and terrible deeds to my Jewish people? How can you call yourself Christians, after you have committed such atrocities against my Jewish people for over 2,000 years? Is this what I taught you? Don't you know that I, Jesus Christ, am a Jew! Don't you know that the Jewish people are my people!"

My thoughts were interrupted by a phone call. My father answered. "Harry Stelzer, of course I remember you. Of course you can come over today." Father told us that Harry Stelzer, once a very poor boy in Dynów, had become a rich ladies' belt manufacturer in New York and that he and his nephew were coming to visit.

Harry and his nephew arrived that evening. The concierge called to announce them, then the doorbell rang and my father opened the door. "Harry Stelzer, our landsman," Father said.

"Yoshe Wenig from Dynów, Itche Wenig's brother," responded Stelzer in excellent Yiddish. Harry introduced his nephew Bernie, who worked for him. Harry Stelzer was dressed in a very good suit, white shirt, and tie, and his black patent leather shoes were meticulously polished. He had a light complexion, a high forehead, small lips, and small blue eyes. He was very warm and friendly, and he spoke perfect Yiddish. He said, "I know what you went through during the war, but I want to hear from you personally about it, and also about our town, Dynów."

Once again my father appointed me to give a full account of our last days in Dynów and of our experiences in the Soviet Union. Harry was saddened and moved. I told him about the pogrom in Kielce. He shook his head. "It's hard to be a Jew," he said, "That's what Jews have said for the past 2,000 years. You are the lucky ones, you survived and you are here, the first Dynover Holocaust survivors in America." After a pause he continued, "America is a great and democratic country, and Americans are not like the evil anti-Semites in Europe. I know, Yoshe, that you have a very wealthy and good brother, but is there anything I can do for you?"

My father thanked him for his offer and said that he would soon start working for his brother, and Hella, being a young girl, would go to school during the day.

"How about you, Larry?" asked Harry. "What are your plans?"

I told him that I was 22 years old, and had to make a painful compromise. I told him that I had always been a student, and I had decided to attend school in the evening and work at a job during the day. I also told him that Peppi Mildwurf was arranging for me to get a job in a jewelry factory.

He asked what I wanted to study. I told him that I must first complete high school and then I would go to college and to law school, because I wanted to become a lawyer. I deliberately told him that I had been forced to make a painful compromise, hoping that he would come through with an offer to subsidize my education or extend a loan to make it possible for me to attend school in the daytime. However, he made no such offer. He expressed the same opinion as all our other landsmen, namely, that at age 22 I was too old to go to high school and college, that law was not such a great profession, and that I would be better off getting a good job or learning a trade and perhaps going into business. He told me that he had not finished elementary school, yet had become a very successful belt manufacturer. He even suggested that I should find myself a nice girl and get married. He pointed to his nephew and said, "Bernie, how about introducing Larry to some of your girlfriends?"

Bernie responded, "I'll look through my list and try to arrange a date for him."

At this time I was not interested in dating. I had other, more important problems on my mind. It was very characteristic that none of my landsmen, whether they were ordinary workers or successful businessmen and entrepreneurs, encouraged me to continue my schooling and become a lawyer. Since they themselves had never had much schooling, perhaps they felt it was arrogant or pretentious for a greenhorn to have such aspirations. Or perhaps the depression had skewed their attitude toward law as a profession. Either way, they felt that I would be wasting my time. Harry Stelzer was a nice man, but he did not lift my spirits.

Harry promised to keep in touch with us. After they left, my father remarked that he just could not believe how some people did so well in America. In Dynów, Harry had been as poor as poor could be. If it had not been for my mother's father, Harry would have starved to death. My mother's father had not only fed him but had provided him with clothing. Yet this poor boy had come to America and become a wealthy manufacturer. Perhaps my father thought that if he had come to America back then, he would not only have avoided the Holocaust but would now be a wealthy manufacturer as well.

We were still talking about Harry Stelzer when our doorbell rang again. My father opened the door, and in walked Uncle Irving, Aunt Ruthie, and my cousins Norman and Jerry. It was a wonderful surprise. They told us that they were returning from their summer home in Lake Mahopac because, although the factory was closed for vacation, my uncle had to take care of several matters in the city. Norman and Jerry were home from school, and the whole family had spent a few days at their summer home. This was the first we knew that they had one. Uncle Irving told my father that his job would begin the following Monday and that Sam Rund, who lived on the ground floor of our building, would drive him to and from the factory. Father said that he was happy to go to work, he had rested enough.

Then Uncle turned to me. "Greener, have you decided what you are going to do in America? You just can't stay home reading newspapers and listening to the radio."

I told him that Peppi Mildwurf had arranged for me to get a job at a jewelry factory in Manhattan. In addition, I would be going to school at night. Uncle said, "The jewelry job is a good idea, but going to school in the evening for so many years is just a waste of time."

He turned to Hella. "You are a young girl, you will have quite a nice rest at home, and will start school at the beginning of September, as that's when the semester starts." Uncle Irving said that he would take us out to his summer home the following weekend. I cannot deny that Uncle Irving and Aunt Ruthie were exceptionally nice to us but I would have been much happier if my good uncle had encouraged me to pursue my education, and perhaps subsidized me or lent me money so that I could attend school full-time.

Changing the subject, I mentioned the pogrom in Kielce. Uncle said that this kind of anti-Semitism was why he had left Poland so long ago and come to this golden country, America.

My cousins were on vacation from their private military high school in upstate New York until September. They said they would come by the next day and take me out to get better acquainted with the neighborhood. Aunt Ruthie told mother not to worry about anything, they would help us in any way they could. That certainly made us feel very relieved. Aunt Ruthie had again brought packages of food and cake. Uncle Irving took a wad of bills from his pocket and gave my father quite a few of them. He gave me a few one-dollar bills. After coffee and cake, Uncle Irving and his family bade us goodbye.

The next day I got up early and went to the newsstand on the corner of Fordham Road and the Grand Concourse where I bought all three Yiddish papers, the *Forward*, the *Morning Journal*, and the *Tag*. All three were full of news about the horrendous pogrom in Kielce. The papers reported that there would be rallies in synagogues, and perhaps a mass rally somewhere in Manhattan. I decided to go to one of the rallies in our neighborhood.

I turned on WEVD and heard the same news. There were calls for a mass rally, not only about the pogrom in Kielce, but also against England for preventing Holocaust survivors from the DP camps from going to Palestine. I turned on WCBS, for I was gradually beginning to learn English by listening to the radio as well to the people in my building, and by looking up words in my Polish-English dictionary. CBS too was reporting on the pogrom in Kielce. It is very difficult to describe my feelings, and even my guilt, about the pogrom. I was beside myself: What should I do now, what can I do now? In that state of mind I said to myself, I have to fight the enemies of Jews, the people who perpetrate such crimes against my people. But I had no idea how to do so.

My thoughts were interrupted by the doorbell. I looked through the peephole and saw my cousins Norman and Jerry. I opened the door and let them in. After we kissed each other, we went into the living room and sat down with Father, Mother, and Hella. We began to talk in broken English, using only the simplest words and phrases, because my young cousins did not know any Yiddish. They noticed that we were a bit downhearted, and I tried as best I could to explain that we were sad about the pogrom in Kielce.

Norman and Jerry were very nice, good-looking and friendly boys. They understood our mood that morning, but the news did not affect them as much as it did us. However, they wanted to cheer me up and suggested that I go down with them for a walk in the neighborhood. First they took me to St. James Park, which was just across the street from our building. It was an absolutely beautiful day, the sky was so clear and blue, and the sun spread its warm rays over us. The park had many long benches, and there were many young parents there with their children, some in strollers. The park had a nice playground and good tennis courts, and people were playing tennis there that morning. Norman and Jerry told me that they too played tennis.

Some other time, perhaps, I would have been very impressed, but that morning my mind was just not there. After St. James Park, my cousins took me to explore Kingsbridge Road, which was close to our building but in a different part of the Bronx. Kingsbridge Road was full of small stores, among them a kosher meat market and a good German bakery. From there they took me to a supermarket called A&P. My cousins explained that A&P had hundreds of stores throughout America. I was really very impressed by that huge food store. I had never before seen such a large store with so many food products. As we left the A&P supermarket, each of my cousins took out a ten-cent coin, which they called a dime, and gave it to me as a gift. From there, my cousins walked me back to Fordham Road and took me to a store called Woolworth. They explained that, like A&P, Woolworth was a chain store, and there were hundreds all over America. With my broken English I told my cousins that there were no such stores in Poland and certainly not in Stalin's workers' paradise. After that, my cousins took me to Krum's, that famous chocolate and ice cream store on the Grand Concourse. They treated me to a coffee sundae: coffee ice cream, nuts, and cream. This was the first time in my life that I experienced the delicious taste of such a delicacy; in fact, it was the first time I had even heard the words "ice cream sundae." A thought went through my mind: What a great country America is. In the Soviet Union we prayed that if only God gave us enough bread, we would be grateful, and would never ask for anything else. Here in America I was indulging myself in ice cream sundaes.

Norman and Jerry were such good kids, and they just could not do enough for me. We walked back to our apartment, and they kissed me good-bye after I thanked them for the wonderful day they had given me. I realized I had had too much activity that day, and I was so tired that I had to lie down. I was still physically weak and very emaciated. Lying on my sofa bed, resting from the day's good activities, my mind still could not reconcile the fact that I was indulging myself with all kinds of goodies while my people in Europe and the DP camps were living a miserable life with an uncertain future.

After we all had rested we had dinner, and after dinner we received a phone call from one of our neighbors, Mrs. Berman. As I mentioned previously, the Bermans had come to America from Poland shortly before World War II. Mrs. Berman told me that the following Thursday evening there would be a rally at the Schiff Center, a temple on Valentine Street, which was within walking distance of our building. The rally would deal with the Kielce pogrom and also with Great Britain's policy of stopping ships bringing Holocaust survivors to Palestine. She and her husband would be going, and she asked whether I would like to join them. I told her that it was my solemn duty and obligation to be there, and I would be very happy to go with them. She told me to meet her Thursday evening at seven in the lobby of our building. I told my parents and Hella that I would be going to the rally with the Bermans on Thursday. They indicated that they wanted to go too.

On Thursday we walked with the Bermans to the Schiff Center. I noticed that the seats in the temple were almost all filled and people were still coming in. The Bermans introduced us to some of them and when these new people learned that we were Holocaust survivors who had arrived in New

York only two weeks or so earlier, they shook our hands and said, "Thank God you survived." We were the first survivors they had met. I believe that we were on the third ship that brought survivors to America. Many of the people in the temple began gathering around and greeting us, although only a few of them spoke Yiddish.

Then, to my shock and dismay, I learned something I couldn't believe. Someone said in Yiddish, "That anti-Semite Roosevelt refused to bomb the railroad tracks to Auschwitz, which would have saved many Jews from the gas chambers. He just did not care that Jews were being gassed and cremated in Auschwitz."

I told this person that I did not know what he was talking about, for I considered President Roosevelt a great president and a friend of the Jewish people. His response to was, "Young man, you just came here a couple of weeks ago, and you don't know that President Roosevelt refused to do anything to help save European Jews during the war. Would you believe that he refused to permit the Jewish refugees on the *St. Louis* to enter America, and they ended up in Auschwitz!"

I asked him, "Please explain to me about the *St. Louis*. This is the first time I have heard the name." He told me that 900 German Jews on the ship *St. Louis* were trying find a refuge. They were first denied entry to Cuba, and when they reached the shores of America, American Jewish leaders pleaded with President Roosevelt to let them in. Roosevelt refused to give them permission to disembark, and that was a year after Kristallnacht.

I was so shocked that I almost could not believe it. I asked the same man to explain what he meant by the failure to bomb the railroad tracks to Auschwitz. He told me that the American government had always known about Auschwitz. When American Jewish leaders pleaded with President Roosevelt to bomb the tracks leading to Auschwitz, he had refused. I was devastated and could not believe what I had just heard. I remembered that when I was in the Soviet Union I had followed the war news diligently on a map. I remember reading in both Pravda and Izvestia that American planes were bombing the oil fields near the Romanian city of Ploesti. Why couldn't those planes have dropped a few bombs on the Auschwitz gas chambers and crematoria on their way to Ploesti? The news that I had just heard was so shocking to me that I lost all confidence in humanity. My life just continued to be in great turmoil.

The Schiff Center was filled to capacity, and there were a good many young people at the rally. There were many speakers, and most of them were

Zionists. They addressed us in English, which I did not fully understand at the time. Although they condemned the Polish people for the brutal pogrom in Kielce, they directed a major blast against England and its Foreign Minister, Ernest Bevin, for its brutality toward the Holocaust survivors who were trying to enter Palestine to rebuild their lives there. Of course the main thrust of the rally that night was that we must not cease working for the establishment of a Jewish state in Palestine. One of the speakers described the activities of the three Jewish underground organizations in Palestine, the Haganah, the Irgun, and the Stern organization. The last speaker pleaded with us to petition members of Congress and President Truman. He also spoke about our enemies in our State Department. He mentioned specifically the name Loy Henderson.

The rally ended with the singing of "Hatikvah", the Zionist anthem. I had tears in my eyes. The anthem speaks of the ancient Jewish hope of a national home for the Jewish people in their ancient homeland. Yet even as I sang, what I had heard about President Roosevelt's policies toward the unfortunate Jews in Europe during World War II was deeply engraved on my mind.

We walked back to our apartment with the Bermans. On the way my mother commented that it was about time that American Jews were finally waking up to the realities of life. I thanked the Bermans for taking us to the rally, and I asked them to keep in touch and inform me about any other activities in New York on behalf of the European Jews. I immediately went to bed and tried to fall asleep, but I could not, being especially troubled by what I had heard about President Roosevelt, who up till that evening had been my hero.

Friday morning Uncle Irving called my father to say that one of his employees would shortly come to our house to pick us up and drive us to his summer home in Lake Mahopac. Even I was excited by the news. Mother packed a few of our belongings, and the driver picked us up just a little before eleven and drove us to Uncle's summer home. It was a beautiful Friday morning and the sun shone brightly. We were driven along country roads with very little traffic. I looked at the beautiful trees on both sides of the peaceful country road.

Uncle Irving, Aunt Ruthie, and Norman and Jerry greeted us with kisses in front of their home. The house was located on a decent-sized plot of land on the shores of beautiful Lake Mahopac. The house looked to us like a beautiful castle. After mother unpacked our suitcase, they took us down to the lake, which was only a few yards from the house. There were speeding motorboats on the lake. What a beautiful sight it was, especially considering where we had been only a few weeks before. Uncle had his own dock, and he showed us his boat. It could seat as many as six people. Uncle pointed out a larger house to the left of the dock which was owned by his neighbor, a Mr. Warshaw, the owner of a paper factory.

Aunt Ruthie called us to come inside for lunch, and we sat down at a large table covered with a lovely white tablecloth. The table was set with porcelain dishes and silverware. Lunch was tuna salad and egg salad sandwiches with chocolate pie and coffee for dessert.

Uncle asked us what we had been doing lately, and we told him about the rally at the Schiff Center. After some talk, in which everybody participated, Uncle said, "Now, Greeners, I will take you on a boat ride."

We got into the boat. Father sat next to his brother, Mother and Hella sat in the next seat, and I was in the last seat. Uncle started the boat, the motor came to life with a loud, powerful roar, and we sped away. There were quite a number of boats here and there on the lake, and Uncle Irving greeted some of the other boaters as we passed them. Some of the boaters were fishing. This idyllic scene was so disconnected from our reality. I felt sure that the people on the lake in their boats lived in a different mental universe than I. Surely they did not have to think about going to night school with the help of a Polish dictionary. Nor was it likely that they were thinking about the Kielce pogrom or the Holocaust survivors trying to sneak into Palestine.

We were out on the lake for over an hour. Uncle Irving stopped from time to time to do some fishing, but he was not successful that Friday. We did quite a bit of talking, and Uncle asked my father about some of the people he had known in Dynów. He remembered some of the places in the town of our birth, and asked about a certain rabbi from the neighboring city of Blazon who had died before World War II, a rabbi whom he greatly respected.

Then Uncle switched topics, reminding Father that on Monday Sam Rund would be driving him to his first day of work. Father, who had always been a very active man, was happy about that, because he found sitting home and doing nothing quite boring.

Uncle Irving then asked me when I would be starting work. I told him that I was still waiting for the call from Peppi Mildwurf. I asked Uncle Irving whether he would object if I went along to the factory on Monday, as I wanted to see its operations in greater detail.

He responded, "Be my guest, and maybe you'll learn something."

When we tied up at the dock again, Uncle Irving pointed out something that looked like a little wooden shack, where he kept his supplies and also a freezer. As we walked toward the shack, which was close to the Warshaw house, he introduced us to Mrs. Warshaw, who did not speak any Yiddish.

Back at the house, Aunt Ruthie asked us how we liked the boat ride. Father told her that it was magnificent, and that he was very proud of his brother. Father was very much impressed with Uncle Irving, and I believe that he looked up to him as if he were God. I never disputed my uncle, and I told Hella that we should listen to him and look up to him. As for me, I regarded my uncle as a smart and successful businessman, but rather poorly educated. I had great respect for him because of his great kindness to us, and also because he was so very charitable, which is one of the important tenets of Judaism.

Cousin Norman said he would take us on the boat the next day. He invited Hella and me to go for a long walk along the lakefront that afternoon to see some of the fine houses. Jerry joined us.

Lake Mahopac was very large and beautiful, and I thought that I certainly would not object to having a house on a lake. Whether it is a lake or a river or the sea, being near water gives one a sense of tranquility and a good feeling about life. I recalled how I had once enjoyed taking walks in the summer on the banks of our river San in Dynów, and how I had always felt at ease when strolling on the riverside. I always felt that I could concentrate better and think more seriously there.

Our cousins told us about their private military high school, where they liked the discipline and the uniforms. I could not fully understand them, because of my limited knowledge of English, but I made some progress, especially when I used my dictionary. Our cousins spoke English to us, and sometimes used hand signs and gestures in order to get their meaning across. Both of my cousins were very nice to us, and they obviously knew what we had gone through during the war.

The next day, Sunday, Uncle Irving tried to take us for another boat ride, but he couldn't start the motor. He asked Norman to call the boat service company. Within a few minutes, a small airplane landed on the lake nearby and a man and a woman got out. Instead of wheels, the airplane had what looked like skis. The man from the airplane fixed the problem within a few minutes. When the boat started to move out onto the lake, I remarked that what had just happened was unbelievable, an airplane landing in the middle of the lake, and a repairman from the airplane fixing the boat. Uncle's response was, "Greener, don't forget that you are in America now, not in Poland."

He was certainly on the mark. Poland was so far behind America: in Poland a repairman would have arrived in a horse-drawn wagon. But I didn't like the constant digs, "Greener this, Greener that." I tried to understand what it was all about. Did he have a superiority complex, or was it because of his rich and lavish lifestyle, or was it simply a joke? I certainly respected and admired him, but was nonetheless troubled by his digs.

Still, it was a wonderful weekend, one I will never forget, especially because only three weeks before I had still been in that dump of a DP camp in Austria. Uncle drove us back to our apartment in the Bronx toward the end of that beautiful Sunday. Aunt Ruthie and the boys would be staying at their summer home during the week, and he would be in his Bronx home because he had a busy business schedule in the coming week. He also reminded father that starting tomorrow he would be working in the factory. We thanked him for the wonderful weekend and kissed him goodbye.

Mr. Rund called to tell my father to meet him at eight the next morning in the lobby and I told Mr. Rund that I would also be going to the factory. We met him in the morning as scheduled. He took us down to the underground garage of our building and got his car.

We reached the factory before nine, and Uncle Irving was already there. He introduced us to an Alex Saffer, who had an important job in the factory. Alex was related to Aunt Ruthie and was also the union representative in the factory. He too lived in the Bronx, not far from our building. He mentioned that he was a member of the Concourse Center of Israel, one of the largest synagogues in the Bronx. It was located on the Grand Concourse, a decent walk from our apartment. Alex Saffer spoke some Yiddish. He told us that there was a part-time synagogue closer to our building, on the Grand Concourse, above the Paradise Theater. He also told us to call him if we ever needed any help.

By nine all the workers were there. Alex walked my father into the factory and introduced him to the foreman. The foreman walked Father to a very large cutting machine and introduced him to one the workers who operated it. The foreman told Father that he would be working with this worker cutting large sheets of metal. With Alex as an interpreter, they explained how the machine worked. Father became very excited and he started to operate the machine together with this employee. Father became as exuberant as if he were back in his own business in Dynów. Alex and the foreman took me around the factory and pointed out to me the many machines, each with a different function. This really was a very busy and noisy place. There were machines doing cutting, bending, punching holes, and welding. It was a big operation. Alex Saffer said that during World War II the factory had manufactured ammunition boxes for the Army.

Impressed as I was, I knew that the factory was not my cup of tea. It was not that I refused to do manual work, but my mind was only on education. If I could, I would have attended school from early morning until late at night, seven days a week, all year round. After completing my tour of the factory for the second time, observing the operations of each and every machine, I walked back to the office. There Sam Rund told me that they had very large orders for their products because of the boom in the housing market.

Sandwiches were brought in for lunch. Uncle Irving was upstairs in his private office. At the end of the day, Father and I walked up there to say goodbye to him. Father told him that he was very happy with the work he was assigned, but I was surprised when Father told his brother that he should make some changes in a certain production area of the factory. I guess Father was still thinking like a man who owned his own business. There was no question in my mind that Uncle Irving had accomplished a great deal in America. He had arrived in New York as young boy in 1924. His first job had been as a dishwasher; now he was a substantial metal manufacturer.

Father and I were driven home by Sam Rund in his Chevrolet. Mother and Hella met us at the door. Father said he did not know what his weekly salary would be, but Uncle Irving was giving us the apartment rent-free. He said that the job was stressful, but he liked it. Mother had a good dinner ready for us.

The next morning, Father again left at eight to meet Sam Rund for the drive to the factory. I took out my Polish-English dictionary and began to study some English words. After breakfast I went down to the newsstand on the Grand Concourse to pick up the *Jewish Journal*. I learned that the Royal Navy was continuing to intercept boats carrying Holocaust survivors to Palestine. I also learned that the underground Jewish resistance organizations in Palestine were becoming more daring, not only attacking British military personnel but also fighting with Palestinian Arab terrorists. This all had a great effect on me. There were moments when I felt that I should pick up a rifle and go to Palestine and join the fight against the British colonial government. The events in Palestine were like a heavy stone lying on my heart.

In reading the news I also learned how the communization of the Eastern European countries was making great strides. I had learned about this process a long time ago when I was a political prisoner in the Soviet Union. I knew from attending Soviet schools that it is Soviet doctrine that communism must and would take over the world. When I mentioned this to the people who came to visit us now, they simply shrugged it off. They felt that the Soviet Union would not dare to do such a thing because it did not have the resources for such an undertaking. It had sustained great destruction during the war and had lost more than twenty million of its people.

I was eager to share my opinions with someone, so I grabbed the phone and called Harold Flender. I asked if we could meet and have a chat. My English was still limited, but I could communicate with Harold with my limited English vocabulary and some hand signs. Harold suggested that we go to St. James Park. A few minutes later I met him in the lobby of our building and we walked across the street to the park. We sat down on one of the benches and I asked Harold whether he had heard about the pogrom in Kielce. He responded off-handedly that he had read about it in the afternoon paper.

There was, and still is, a psychological difference between American Jews and Holocaust survivors. A secular American-born Jew could treat the Kielce pogrom as just another news item. He probably would consider it to be like a traffic accident in which some people were killed. To a Holocaust survivor like myself, a pogrom against other survivors in a Polish city only one year after World War II had ended was deeply shocking.

I then asked Harold whether he knew about the Royal Navy's interception of ships with Holocaust survivors trying to get to Palestine. Harold said this news was in the newspapers and on the radio. I told him that these events caused me sleepless nights and weighed heavily on me day and night. Harold responded that there was nothing I could do about it and I should go on with my life and build a future for myself. I must admit that I was shocked by his indifference to these horrifying events, even though I knew that Harold was a rather artistic person who hoped to become a writer.

Harold mentioned that he was doing research for a book he hoped to write one day about how the people of Denmark had saved their Jewish fellow citizens during World War II. Harold eventually did write such a book many years later, *Rescue in Denmark*, published in 1963.

Harold mentioned that he was no longer seeing Helen Meyerson, the sister of Bess Meyerson, who had been selected as Miss America in 1945. He told me that he had met a new girl named Enid, who was taking ballet lessons. He offered to introduce me to a Jewish American family of dedicated Zionists who thought the way I did and were fluent in Yiddish. They lived in Yonkers and had a very nice daughter named Linda.

Since I was planning to attend high school at night, Harold suggested that I start the application process. The next day I took a long walk along Fordham Road to Theodore Roosevelt High School. In my poor English, I explained to the woman at the desk that I wanted to attend the evening session. I told her that I had just arrived from Europe several weeks before, I was 22 years old, and had been a political prisoner in the Soviet Union during World War II. I also told her that I had attended high school in the Soviet Union. She said that I would probably be given credit for the courses I had taken there, but I would have to take Regents examinations in those subjects, and I would have to prepare an affidavit listing the courses I had completed in the Soviet Union. Since my English was so limited, I asked her to give me a sample of such an affidavit. She typed one out for me, and I thanked her very much for explaining what I needed to do and for typing the sample affidavit.

On the way home I decided to call Sol Fine, who had given me the initial idea of completing my high school education in the evening, and of doing it at nearby Theodore Roosevelt High School. I telephoned him that evening and explained to him what I had to do in order to be admitted. Sol told me that he had an electric typewriter and would gladly help with the affidavit. He suggested that I come to their apartment after one that Sunday, and suggested that my parents and sister should come as well, because his mother would like to see her Dynower landsmen. He gave me his address and instructions about how to get there by trolley.

Meanwhile, on Thursday evening Peppi Mildwurf called to tell me that she would meet me at Liberty & Diamond Jewelry Company a week from that coming Monday morning at about nine. She gave me the address of the company, which was located on Maiden Lane in Manhattan, and she told me how to get there by subway.

When Father returned from work, I told my parents about the invitation from Mrs. Fine for that coming Sunday and said that Sol Fine would help me with the documentation for my admission to the high school. I also told them about my date with Peppi Mildwurf the following Monday.

On Sunday we took a trolley on Fordham Road, transferred to another trolley, and arrived at the Fine apartment in the East Bronx. Sol's mother hugged and kissed my mother, and I greeted her and Sol, and handed him the document prepared by the secretary. Sol read it and said, "No problem at all. I will type out the affidavit for you." He took me to his room, and I sat down on a chair next to him. He turned on his electric typewriter and started to type, making a carbon copy. The affidavit simply asked for my name, place and date of birth, present address, and the name of the city in the Soviet Union where I had attended high school. I also had to list the subjects I had completed in the Russian and Polish high schools in Fergana, Soviet Republic of Uzbekistan. The Polish high school was run by the Union of Polish Patriots, a Communist organization. At the Russian high school the subjects I listed were: Russian literature, Russian history, world history, history of the Communist Party, algebra, and Communist songs. For the Polish high school I listed: Polish history, Polish literature I and II, geometry, biology, geography, and advanced algebra. Sol gave me both the original affidavit, which I had to give to the high school, and the copy for my own records. He told me that the affidavit would have to be signed and notarized, and he told me how I could find a notary and what it would cost.

Back in the dining room, we joined the conversation with Sol's mother and Goldie. Mrs. Fine was a very warm person, and she said that Sol and Goldie were ready to help me as much as they could. As I looked around the Fines' apartment, I realized what a magnificent apartment my uncle had given us. The difference between our apartment and theirs was like night and day. I now realized how kind my uncle and his family were. We had been in New York for just over three weeks and I did not have a job, yet I was enjoying a very nice lifestyle because I was being supported by my uncle. I told Goldie that once I was settled in school and in a job I would like to take her out on a date. She said she was looking forward to going out with me. We were served coffee and cake, and we bade goodbye to the Fine family with much hugging and kissing.

The following morning I went to a drug store about three blocks from our apartment. I asked the druggist whether he was a notary, and he responded that he was. I placed the original and the copy of the affidavit in front of him, and he read it. He asked me to sign it, and then he stamped it and signed it. He looked at me, and he probably noticed my pale and emaciated face. In any case, he kindly said that I did not have to pay any fee for the notarization of my affidavit. I went straight home.

I waited for awhile and then called the Flender residence. Harold answered and I told him about my visit to the high school office and about the affidavit. I told him that I would appreciate it very much if he would go with me to the high school and help me discuss my situation with the office clerk.

Harold said that he would gladly go with me and I should meet him in half an hour in the lobby. When Harold came down, I gave him the affidavit and asked him to explain to the high school officials the following problem: I was 22 years old and I intended not only to graduate from high school, but also to go to college and law school; I had a language problem, and I had to work during the day in order to support myself; I would be doing all my schooling in the evenings; and I would like to get my high school diploma as soon as possible.

I asked Sol to tell them that I would have gotten a high school diploma in the Soviet Union but was prevented from doing so because of the timing of our escape from the Soviet Union. I asked him to tell the officials that I believed that I had enough educational credits for a diploma because of the many subjects I had taken in the Soviet high schools.

We arrived at the high school and met the same woman I had talked to before. Harold explained to her that he was my friend and was trying to help me because of my language difficulties. He gave her my notarized affidavit, and he told her that he saw no reason why the high school couldn't give me full credit for the subjects I had studied in the Soviet Union. She said that they would give me credit for those subjects but I would have to take Regents exams for all of them. In addition, I would have to take a course in the English language, a course in English literature, a course in American history, and maybe some other subjects. She told Harold the Regents exams were given during the day, and the evening students had to take the Regents exams at the same time as the day students. I was shocked that I would have to take the Regents exams. Harold argued with the school official, but to no avail. She told Harold that the high school would inform me by letter when to come to the office and register for the required courses. She also told us that night school would start right after Labor Day weekend, and the courses were from seven to nine.

I now realized what a hard road lay ahead, but I was determined that no matter how difficult it was, and no matter how long it took, I would proceed with my high school education. I thanked Harold for his help and for his strong advocacy on my behalf. Harold said that he would try to help me, and that I should not hesitate to call upon him. I asked Harold what Labor Day was. Harold told me all about it. It was my first inkling of this holiday.

When I returned home I saw mother and Hella listening to WEVD. They told me that the news from Palestine was not good. Our people were not only being harassed by the British soldiers but also attacked by the Arabs. The news certainly did not cheer me up, it just added to my gloom. I told mother what I had learned at the high school office and the problems I would be facing. Mother, as usual, said, "Lusiek I have confidence in you, and I am sure that you will be able to handle it." I said to myself, "Now let's see what happens on Monday, when I meet Peppi Mildwurf at the jewelry factory in Manhattan."

Chapter 4

WORK

On Monday morning, I left our apartment before eight, picked up a Yiddish paper at the newsstand, and boarded the downtown D train. There were a number of passengers in my car, and we all had seats. At each stop more passengers got on, and soon practically all the seats were taken. When the doors opened at the next two stops, a torrent of people charged in, jostling each other for the few remaining seats. It looked like Pickett's charge at Gettysburg. Men pushed women away from the few available seats, young men pushed older men. It was a free-for-all in which the stronger and more brazen prevailed. What perplexed me was the disregard men had for women in this underground subway system. My upbringing had been totally different; I had been taught always to respect a woman. On this subway ride on my first day of work, I got up and gave my seat to a woman who was standing close by. I noticed that some of the other riders looked at me strangely, probably thinking there was something wrong with me. (For weeks I continued the practice of giving up my seat not only to women, but sometimes to elderly men. However, I admit that after some time I became "New Yorkized" and stopped giving up my seat.) By the time we reached 42nd Street the subway car was so packed with humanity that it looked like a sardine can.

After the 42nd Street station, passengers began getting off. I got off at the last stop, Chambers Street. From there it was only a few blocks to Maiden Lane, where the jewelry company was located. I entered the office of L. & D. Jewelry Co a few minutes before nine and found Peppi Mildwurf there already. Peppi introduced me to a beautiful young girl who was standing at the desk. This was Sonya, the daughter of Mr. Liberty, one of the partners. I must admit that I said to myself that I would not mind working for Sonya because she really looked zaftig (so sweet). Within a couple of minutes, another attractive woman arrived, and she was introduced to me as Mrs. Diamond, the wife of the other partner. Mrs. Diamond was probably in her late fifties and was very friendly. She even spoke a little Yiddish. I told myself that this was not a bad way to start the day. Both Sonya and Mrs. Diamond seemed to already know quite a bit about me, including the fact that I was determined to proceed with my education and become a lawyer. Both women looked at me with concern, for they obviously noticed my pale, emaciated face. Sonya went into the factory and called Mr. Liberty and Mr. Diamond. They both shook my hand and ushered me into the jewelry factory.

At first glance, I saw that there was a bench along the farthest wall and next to it were chairs on which workers were seated and working. Each worker had a set of tools that included a gas torch, an electric drill, tweezers, pliers, and hammers. Mr. Liberty and Mr. Diamond already knew everything about me from Peppi Mildwurf. The Mildwurfs were substantial customers of theirs. Mr. Diamond asked, "So, do you want to be a lawyer or a jewelry manufacturer?" I responded that I wanted to be a lawyer for the jewelry industry. They smiled, because they obviously liked my answer. They told me that I was hired and would be working on gold and silver chain repairs, as well as soldering charms onto gold and silver bracelets, charm bracelets being a very popular product at the time.

They introduced me to their employees, and I still remember the name of one, Kenneth Smith. Ken had been working for the company for several years. His father owned a jewelry store in Smithtown on Long Island.

I saw workers repairing rings, chains, earrings, and bracelets. Mr. Diamond's specialty was making new gold rings and complicated large earrings. There was a machine that polished items after they had been manufactured or repaired, in order to give them a nice bright shine. Mr. Diamond told me that the factory was open five days a week, and the workday ran from nine in the morning until five, with a lunch break from noon to one. As a jewelry apprentice, I would be paid 40 cents an hour, and my weekly salary would be $16, from which they would deduct only the social security tax. He said that Ken Smith would teach me how to solder broken chains and solder charms onto charm bracelets. I asked whether I would be able to take off if I had to take a school examination during the day. Mr. Diamond said yes. Mr. Liberty showed me my chair, bench, and tools, and told me to start working. I asked whether I could go into the office and say goodbye to Mrs. Mildwurf. He said, "Of course you can," and walked me into the office. Mr. Diamond said to Peppi, "We hired your friend." I thanked Peppi and kissed her goodbye

Returning to the factory, I sat down in my assigned chair next to Ken Smith. He explained how to hold a broken chain with a tweezers and a small pliers. Then he lit the gas torch, put a chemical compound on the broken chain and a piece of gold on the broken link, melting the gold piece and uniting the gold link with the chain. Ken explained that it would take a few such operations before I became an expert chain repairer. It was an interesting process, and it was not physically hard work, but my mind was somewhere else. The only exciting event in the jewelry factory was seeing and hearing Sonya. She came in quite often to ask her father about the prices she should quote to jewelry merchants for repairs on various items. Every time Sonya came into the factory, my head turned so that I could see her. So did Ken's, although he was a married man. When Ken saw me turn around he said, "Larry you are just too late, because Sonya is engaged to Jimmy." Ken explained that Jimmy was an Italian American diamond setter who had his own shop in the building. I met Jimmy two days later, as he came to visit Sonya frequently. Seeing them together I decided that they both had made a good choice. Jimmy was tall and very handsome. Compared to him, I was a little shrimp, very skinny with a pale, emaciated face, looking ripe for the undertaker.

That morning I made progress in soldering and joining gold links to chains or bracelets. Most of the workers, including the bosses, brought their lunch, which they kept in a refrigerator on the premises. I had no food with me, because I had not known whether I would be hired. Ken suggested that I go to the Horn & Hardart Automat a couple of blocks away on Broadway. This was the second time I had eaten at an automat since I came to New York

My workday ended at five, and I got a seat on the D train at Chambers Street, going back uptown to the Bronx. The crowding, shoving, and fighting for seats took place on the uptown train as well, but this time I did not give up my seat, because there were men passengers standing in front of my seat and I was very tired.

When I entered our apartment my mother grabbed me and kissed me. I had not called to tell her that I had been hired on the spot that morning. She was still operating on the Russian system. In the Soviet Union, if you did not return at the designated time, it was assumed that you had been hauled away by the KGB. In Russia one always told one's parents exactly when one would be back home. It took us a quite a while to get rid of that Soviet paranoia.

My parents were pleased that I had gotten the job. Mother said that she would call Peppi to thank her for her help. She also told me that our relative

Bernard Turner, who had visited us shortly after we arrived in New York, had sent father a large tallit (prayer shawl) and phylacteries, which had arrived at our house that afternoon. Father liked to pray, and obviously he had asked his relative to obtain these necessary ritual articles for him.

I told my parents that I would continue with my new job and would give most of my earnings to them in order to support our household. I also told mother that I had eaten at Horn & Hardart, but from now on would bring sandwiches to work. I told her about the refrigerator in the factory where the workers, including the bosses, kept their lunches. And I told my parents that since Peppi Mildwurf and Sol Fine had done so much for me, I had decided to take out Goldie Fine on a date.

As usual, Mother served us a good supper. She was not only a great cook, but she was also an excellent baker and that night she had baked a delicious nut cake for us. After supper I called the Fine residence and asked if I could speak to Goldie. When she came to the phone, I told her that I had gotten the job that day, thanks to her aunt Peppi. I asked Goldie whether she was free that coming Saturday evening, as I would like to take her out on a date. Goldie answered that she was looking forward to going out with me on Saturday.

On Saturday evening, I rang the doorbell of the Fine apartment, and Goldie opened the door. I did not kiss her, I just shook hands with her. I was wearing a nice summer suit my good Aunt Ruthie had bought me, a white shirt, new black shoes, and a tie. This was the first time in many years that I had worn a tie. In Stalin's country club you did not wear a tie. There you wore the worker's rubashka, a peasant's coarse linen shirt hanging outside over your trousers.

Goldie and I took the trolley to Fordham Road, where the action was. We went to the RKO theater there because Goldie wanted to see the movie they were showing. I do not recall the title, but I remember that it was a love story. There was lot of hugging and kissing going on in the movie house among the many young couples. Nearby there was a very young couple, and I saw the young boy place his hand under the girl's dress and heard the girl say, "Stop it, not here." I was beginning to learn why so many young people went to the movies in America. I was reminded of the passage in *My Universities,* a book by the Soviet writer Maxim Gorky, stating that life is always a university where you always learn new things. I did not kiss Goldie, nor did I hold hands with her in the movies. I simply watched the picture. We both enjoyed it because it was very romantic

After the movie I took Goldie to a pizza place: a worker who earns only $16 a week cannot take his date to some fancy eating establishment. As we waited for our pizza, I told Goldie, in both English and Yiddish, that I would definitely go through with my plan to work during the day and attend school in the evenings because I intended to become a lawyer no matter how long it might take. She just shook her head. I also told her that the situation in Palestine absorbed most of my thoughts. Despite all my personal problems, I said, I planned to get involved in activities that would speed the establishment of a Jewish state in Palestine. It seemed to me that Goldie had different interests. I am sure that she was interested in getting married, but this did not mean that she was interested in marrying me, she simply was looking for the man she wanted to marry. It was clear that Goldie and I were on different wavelengths.

Marriage was the last thing on my mind. It was not that I did not want to get married. If I had the financial means and were established in my profession, marriage would have been a wonderful idea. However, the realities of my life at that time were such that marriage for me was a no-no. What kind of marriage would it be for me or for my wife? I would be working all day, grabbing a quick bite somewhere for dinner and running to night school for many years. I would return at ten at the earliest, and then would have to do my homework until midnight or later. Nevertheless, that evening it felt good just to be out with a girl. We looked into each other's eyes, but there was no fire. We took the trolley back to Goldie's apartment. As she opened her door, I kissed her on the forehead and said good night. Out of respect for Goldie, I felt it was wrong for me to come into her apartment to kiss and neck.

When I returned to our apartment, everyone was sound asleep and they probably did not hear me come in. I undressed and fell into my sofa bed. I slept well that night. When I got up in the morning, the family was still sleeping. I pulled out the Polish dictionary, which was always near my sofa bed. I wanted to check some English words Goldie had used in our conversation. My mother came to my bed and asked about my date. Then she said quietly, "I have something to tell you that may surprise you." Mother told me that when she picked up the mail the day before she had found a letter that she had not wanted to give me in front of my stepfather or Hella.

"A letter from whom?" I asked.

"From your uncle Max Sarna in Palestine," she replied.

"Who is my uncle Max Sarna?" I asked.

Mother told me that Max Sarna was one of my natural father's brothers. I had never heard of Max Sarna, and I had never known that my natural father had brothers. In fact, I knew almost nothing about him, because my mother had always refused to talk about him. Mother gave me the unopened letter from Uncle Max.

I looked at the envelope, opened it, and took out the letter. It was written in Polish and was several pages long. It commenced with the words "Dear Eliezer," which is my Hebrew first name, as I was named after my natural father's father. The letter stated that Max Sarna was one of my father's three brothers. He too had been born in Poland, but now resided in Israel, in Tel Aviv. He had learned about me through some Jewish agency and had obtained my New York address from another Jewish organization.

The letter recounted Max Sarna's wartime experiences. Having been a political activist before the war, he had been arrested by the Soviet authorities when they took over eastern Poland, and he too had been sent to a gulag in Siberia. After Germany invaded the Soviet Union, the Polish government-in-exile, as I have already mentioned, entered into an agreement with the Soviet Union stipulating that all Polish citizens were to be released from the gulags and resettled in certain designated areas. Pursuant to this agreement, my uncle had been sent to Kazakhstan, and the Polish government in London had appointed him leader of the Polish exile community there with the rank of męż zaufania (literally "trusted person"), which is equivalent to consul. He tried but was unable to learn anything about the fate of his wife and his two sons.

In 1943 the Germans announced that they had discovered a huge burial ground in the Katyn forest near Smolensk with the bodies of around 10,000 Polish military officers. The Soviets blamed the massacre on the Nazis, but there was substantial evidence establishing that they, in fact, were the perpetrators. In the aftermath, the Soviet Union and the Polish government in London broke off diplomatic relations. Soon afterward the Soviets organized the so-called Union of Polish Patriots, a Communist front organization, under the leadership of the novelist Wanda Wasilewska, and a Polish volunteer army commanded by General Zygmunt Berling. When the Red Army advanced into Poland, the Union of Polish Patriots set up a Communist-oriented provisional government headed by Boleslaw Bierut, who became President. The Prime Minister was Edward Osóbka-Morawski.

This Communist front, known as the Lublin government, made a point of including people who were not Communists in order to mislead the West about its true political orientation. Thus, when my uncle returned to Poland in the early part of 1945, he was appointed an assistant to Osóbka-Morawski. He lasted only a few months. The Bierut-Morawski government decided that he could not be trusted because he was a known Zionist. They were about to arrest and perhaps even execute him, when he made a successful dash to the border and escaped.

He ended up in France, where he became a leader of the Zionist organization and the editor of a Zionist newspaper distributed in France, Holland, and Belgium. He soon discovered that his wife and two sons had also been imprisoned in a gulag, but had been able to leave the Soviet Union with the Anders Army and had gone to Palestine. In 1946, thanks to the intercession of the Jewish Agency, the de facto Jewish authority in Palestine, my uncle entered Palestine legally under the White Paper quota enacted by the British government in 1939. There he was reunited with his wife and sons, and became a leader of the General Zionist Organization.

The letter went on to state that I had a sister named Susi who lived in Sweden. My natural father, it seemed, had remarried in Switzerland, and Susi was the child of his second marriage. Max gave me her address and asked me to write to her. But the real bombshell came at the end of his letter. He asked me to change my last name from Wenig to Sarna, the reason being, he said, that I came from the famous Sarna family of scholars. Once again, my life was in turmoil.

My natural father had died when I was eight years old. Until that time, when my grandfather suddenly and unexpectedly called me in one day and told me to recite Kaddish, the Jewish mourner's prayer, I never knew that the man married to my mother was not my natural father. So far as I know, my natural father never tried to contact me. I was brought up by my stepfather, the man I considered to be my father. He saved my life during World War II. He brought me to America and gave me a new life. Would it be ethical or decent for me to change my last name from Wenig to Sarna? Yes, I was proud that my uncle was a great intellectual. Yes, I was proud that my uncle had been the Sikorski government's consul in Kazakhstan. Yes, I was proud that he had been an official in the Lublin government. Nevertheless, I decided not to change my last name.

To make sure that I had made the right decision, I decided to discuss it with someone I highly respected, our landsman Max Mildwurf. Max was very intelligent and well educated. I telephoned Max and told him my uncle's request. Max agreed with me on the spot, and said that it would be highly immoral for me to change my last name from Wenig to Sarna.

I did not mention my uncle's letter to either my father or Hella. After breakfast, Mother took me aside and asked me to tell her what Uncle Max had written. Mother knew Max, because he had been present at her wedding. I told her that he had asked me to change my name to Sarna, but that I had decided not to do it. She embraced me and kissed me on both cheeks.

It was very strange that Mother never wanted to discuss her marriage to my natural father. I had sometimes asked her about him when we were alone. Her answer was always that she'd rather not talk about it. However, I learned from my mother's sisters in Poland that her father had forced her to divorce him.

It was Sunday, and although I had made progress in English by speaking to people who corrected my mistakes and, of course, by studying the dictionary, on Sundays I was still drawn to WEVD, the Yiddish radio station. I was simply obsessed with the events in Palestine, especially the illegal transit of Holocaust survivors despite the British blockade. The radio commentator reported that there were several Jewish underground organizations in Palestine. Some of the more aggressive of them had assassinated Lord Moyne, the British official most responsible for closing the gates of Palestine to Jewish refugees. Other underground groups were blowing up the oil pipeline from Iraq to Haifa. According to the commentator, the entire Jewish population in Palestine was on the verge of a general uprising against the British colonial administration. All this information affected me greatly. Something inside me said that I had to do something. Part of my brain told me to join the Jews in Palestine and participate in their struggle against Great Britain. Another part of my brain said, "Larry, be realistic. What can you really do?"

I called WEVD and told the person answering the phone that I was a Holocaust survivor who had recently arrived in New York. I asked whether he knew of any place in New York City where recently arrived Holocaust survivors got together. He told me that there was indeed such a place. Some Jewish charitable organizations had rented part of the Marseille Hotel in Manhattan, on Broadway in the high 90s, where some Holocaust survivors who had no families in America were being housed temporarily. He gave me the address of the hotel and told me how to get there by subway.

I told my parents what I had heard on WEVD and also about the Marseille Hotel. I said that since I had nothing to do that day, I wanted to go there and perhaps find some people I knew. As my parents did not object, I took the subway and found the hotel. The main lobby was filled with young people speaking various foreign languages, including Polish and Yiddish. I introduced myself to two boys speaking Polish. I asked where in Poland they were from and when they had arrived in New York. They said that they had arrived only a few days before from a DP camp in Germany. They were the sole survivors of their families. They had been brought here by an American Jewish organization and were being housed at the hotel for the time being. Many of the other residents, they said, had also been brought to America by Jewish organizations.

I told them that I was in New York with my parents and a younger sister. They told me that I should count my blessings, because I had parents and was being helped by an uncle. They said they had wanted to go to Palestine, but because of the British blockade there was now a very long wait in the DP camps. They had become restless and decided to go to America instead, but they too felt guilty about betraying the Zionist cause.

I also met some older Holocaust survivors, and they had a quite different view of life. They had been so brutalized during the war and were so worn out that they simply wanted to rebuild their lives. All the survivors I talked to that day shared the same opinion, however: there had to be a Jewish state in Palestine if the Jewish people were to survive in this cruel, evil, anti-Semitic world.

As I walked around the lobby, I had no difficulty recognizing the Holocaust survivors. They all were pale, emaciated, and very shabbily dressed. One of the older men I spoke to in Yiddish told me that he had decided, along with some other residents of the hotel, to create an organization of Holocaust survivors. I told him that it was a good idea and we should start working toward the goal.

It was a good experience for me to visit with our people at the hotel. I decided that if I could find some time on the weekends before I started school, I would come back and even bring along my sister Hella.

Back home I shared my experiences at the hotel with my family. I told Hella that I would take her along on my next visit and perhaps we might find some of our friends from the Soviet Union and the DP camp in Austria. Mother served supper, and I reminded her to prepare lunch for me to take to my job the next day.

I left Monday morning on the same D train to Manhattan, carrying a Yiddish newspaper I had bought at the newsstand. I got a seat on the train and was reading my paper when, at one of the stations, a middle-aged couple got on and stood in front of my seat. It took me a while to notice them because I was so absorbed in my paper. Of course the news that absorbed me so much involved the activities of the Jewish underground in Palestine. I also read about events in the Soviet Union and in the newly communized East European countries. Lifting my head, I noticed that the couple in front of me were also reading the Yiddish paper. The woman spoke to me in broken Yiddish and said that she was surprised to see such a young fellow reading a Yiddish newspaper. She took a picture of a girl out of her pocketbook and showed it to me. The girl in the picture was young and very good looking. I returned the picture to the woman and got up and gave her my seat. I stood and continued to read the paper and was so absorbed that I did not notice them leaving the train.

I got off at Chambers Street and arrived at the factory a few minutes before 9. I was one of the first workers at the job. I put my bag of sandwiches in the refrigerator.

My work was the same as before, repairing chains. It was monotonous work which did not excite me at all. There was little talk between my tutor, Ken Smith, and me. We each attended to our own work. At noon we got up and took our lunch bags out of the refrigerator. I somehow did not want to eat my lunch with the rest of the people in the jewelry shop; I feared I would be embarrassed if they watched me and did not like my eating habits. Newcomers to a country always fear that everyone will look at them strangely and even disparage the way they eat. I took my lunch bag and walked to Horn & Hardart, where I bought a cup of coffee, opened my lunch bag, and took out my two sandwiches. One was a tuna salad sandwich, and the other an egg salad sandwich. My mother wanted to fatten me up, which is why she prepared two sandwiches. I was a little embarrassed, because I was the only one in that self-service restaurant who had brought his own lunch. Several customers gave me dirty looks. They probably thought me a miser. I gulped down my sandwiches in order to get out of there as quickly as possible. From that day on, I decided to eat with my co-workers in the factory.

I still had quite a bit of time because I had eaten so fast. I strolled about for a while and came across another very crowded eating establishment which had a sign that read "Chock-Full-of-Nuts." Looking inside, I noticed people eating muffins of many different kinds. I was beginning to learn more about New York City.

I returned to the jewelry factory and continued working on chains and bracelets. I got home that night a little tired and bored. It so happened that after dinner my friend and neighbor Harold Flender phoned. It was early and still light outside, so we met in the lobby and walked toward the Grand Concourse. Harold suggested that we walk to nearby Poe Park. He told me that the park was named after the famous American poet Edgar Allan Poe, and that people danced there.

Harold asked me what I had been doing in the last few days. I told him about my job. "So you're working in the exciting Wall Street area," Harold said. This was the first I knew that I was working "on Wall Street." I told him that my job was boring but I had no choice, as I had to earn some money to support myself. I also told him about the incident on the subway, when the middle-aged couple showed me the picture of their daughter. Harold asked, "What did the girl in the picture look like? Was she good looking?" I responded that she was young and had blonde hair, and she really was very good looking. "Did you take her name, and telephone number, and address?" Harold asked. I said that I just looked at the picture and returned it to the mother. "Larry, you're a real schmuck. Why do you think her mother showed you her daughter's picture?" Harold continued, "Larry, I am sorry to tell you again that you are a real schmuck. You missed an opportunity to meet a good-looking blonde girl."

I told Harold that I simply thought that the mother just wanted me to see a picture of her daughter.

"Larry, you have to become Americanized. In America, when a mother shows a boy a picture of her daughter, it is for one reason only, namely that the boy should meet her daughter. I want you to understand that."

I really felt embarrassed after Harold's lecture, and I decided that I was still quite obviously a greenhorn. I needed to forget about European customs and adapt to the American culture.

The next few days I traveled to work as usual with my Yiddish newspaper. Now, however, I ate my lunch with my bosses and my co-workers. My work did not change; I still worked on broken chains and charm bracelets.

Excitement came on July 22, 1946, when all the radio stations and newspaper headlines informed us about the bombing of the King David Hotel in Jerusalem. Even now I still remember the details. The King David Hotel housed the British military command and a branch of the Criminal Investigation Division. The bombing was carried out by members of the underground Irgun Zvi-Le'umi. The Irgun, headed by the same Menachem Begin I had met years earlier in Fergana, was more nationalistic and more aggressive than the Haganah. The attackers, disguised as milkmen, placed milk cans filled with explosives in the basement of the King David Hotel. Ninety-two people were killed.

The Jewish leadership immediately condemned the attack. The Jewish Agency expressed feelings of horror and blamed the attack on a gang of criminals. The Irgun organization claimed that they had telephoned the hotel with a warning, but the British had not taken the message seriously and did not evacuate the building. The same message had been given to the French consulate, which was next door, in order to prevent loss of life there. The King David bombing was a great tragedy because so many lives were lost. However, at the same time the British must also be blamed, because they failed to evacuate the building.

All this preoccupied my mind. I could see how the revolt against the British mandatory authority in Palestine was becoming more widespread and more deadly. In a way the British had brought these problems on themselves by behaving so cruelly toward Jews.

Before World War II they had enacted the White Paper, which limited entry to Palestine to only 1,800 Jews annually. A great many Jews wanted to emigrate to Palestine to save themselves from the Nazis. Among those who wanted to leave Poland was my own family. Probably hundreds of thousands of Jews could have been saved from Hitler's gas chambers and crematoria if Britain had opened the gates to Palestine. Now the war was over, but survivors of the Holocaust were being held in DP camps in Germany and Austria, and were still prevented from going to Palestine. Moreover, one must not forget that Britain had violated every provision of the League of Nations Mandate, which called for the creation of a Jewish state in the territory of the ancient kingdom of Judea. Events in Palestine occupied my mind more than my personal problems in New York

At the end of July, the Dynower Society sent out a letter to every member in New York and New Jersey, announcing an extraordinary meeting to take place in its office on the first Sunday of August at six o'clock. The highlight of the meeting would be a report on the last days of the Dynów Jewish community by Larry Wenig, the son of Yoshe Wenig, who had arrived in America in June.

We were escorted to the meeting via the IRT subway by Munia Waining, an officer of the society. The place was packed, and they had to bring in extra chairs. We were greeted very cordially. The president, Yankel Ores, asked me to take a seat on the dais. He whispered in my ear that this was largest gathering in the society's history. I noticed that all the Feldman brothers from

New Jersey were there, as were Max and Peppi Mildwurf. Harry Stelzer was there too. Uncle Irving and Aunt Ruthie arrived a little bit later, as they had an engagement in Manhattan.

Yankel Ores opened the meeting in Yiddish. In his opening remarks he stated that Yoshe Wenig's family, who had arrived only a few weeks before, were the first Dynover survivors to reach America. He introduced me and invited me up to the lectern.

I thanked the society's president and officers for giving me this opportunity. I spoke in Yiddish and I addressed members as my sisters and brothers: "I stand here before you in both joy and sadness. The joy that I am experiencing now is that I see before me so many from the town of our birth, those who had the wisdom and courage to leave the European continent many years ago to come to this blessed country. However, I also speak to you with great sadness, because some of your families, relatives, friends, and neighbors died a horrendous death."

I went on to recount the sad tale which I told years later, in the opening chapters of my book *From Nazi Inferno to Soviet Hell*. In 1939, Dynów had a large, vibrant, active, and proud Jewish community. Now the only Jews in Dynów were lying in its two Jewish cemeteries. Poland had always had anti-Semitism, but it became virulent after the death of Prime Minister Józef Pilsudski. In 1938, it became more virulent still when the Polish government foolishly joined with Hitler against Czechoslovakia because of Hitler's promise to give Poland some colonies in Africa and a part of Czech Silesia. The cries we heard then in Dynów, as well as all over Poland, were "Niech Żyje Wolna Polska bez Zydów: Long Live a Free Poland without Jews."

Germany invaded Poland on September 1, 1939, and within two weeks had occupied Dynów. Two days later, on the first day of Rosh Hashanah, the SS arrived. That afternoon they rounded up about 300 Jews and machine-gunned most of them in the nearby Uralic forest. All three synagogues were set on fire, and most of the Jewish refugees who were sleeping in the synagogues perished in the fire. Several days later some of the men, including my father and me and my two older brothers, escaped across the San River. We really did not know why we were escaping. It was simple panic that caused us to flee. A few hours later, the remainder of the town's Jewish populace was expelled by the Germans across the San, with only the clothing they had on their backs. In the villages on the other side of the river, to our surprise, we came across units of the Red Army. When we asked what they were doing there, they said they had been invited by the Polish workers and peasants. Of course the real truth was that Stalin had treacherously entered into a non-aggression agreement with Hitler to divide Poland between themselves. In my opinion, Stalin's treachery brought on World War II and the calamity it brought upon the world, as well as the Holocaust.

Meanwhile, the Soviets registered all the Polish refugees in the Soviet-occupied part of Poland. Professionals, Zionists, and businessmen like my father were classified as "capitalists and enemies of the people" and were exiled to gulags in Siberia. Some of our people perished there. Many of the others died in the gas chambers and the crematories in Auschwitz and the other concentration camps. Most of the families, relatives, neighbors, and friends of the people sitting in the audience, I said, had died brutal deaths. The flower of European Jewry had been turned into ashes, soap, rope, and lampshades. My family and I were among the very few lucky enough to survive.

"Now, my friends, I want you to look into my eyes, and into the eyes of my parents and my sister, and please tell me what you did to help your people who perished during this great calamity, the Holocaust?" Their eyes turned downwards, and there was silence in the room. "Many of our Holocaust survivors are languishing in DP camps in Germany and Austria. They are desperately trying to leave the DP camps and enter our ancient land of the kingdom of Judea, which has been renamed Palestine," I continued. "Europe is the cemetery of the Jewish people. We must spare no effort, and we must dedicate ourselves to bringing about the establishment of a Jewish state in Palestine where the rest of the European Jewish survivors want to go. Please promise me that this time American Jews will not fail their people." I was met with loud applause. I told them that I would entertain questions about their relatives or friends, or any other questions they might have about the Holocaust.

Quite a number of questions were asked, and I was able to answer them. Some people even asked specific questions about the Soviet Union. After I answered all the questions, practically everyone at the meeting came over to shake my hand and thank me for my report. The meeting ended at about nine, and my family and I were driven home by Uncle Irving.

When we returned to our apartment, Mother kissed me on the forehead. She whispered that I had spoken very well and the audience had been deeply moved. In bed that night, I asked myself whether I had been too tough on my Dynower landsmen. After debating with myself, I came to the conclusion that I had done the right thing. I asked myself whether any other American ethnic group would have sat by and done nothing when six million of their compatriots were being gassed and cremated the way the European Jews were.

CHAPTER 5

SCHOOL AT LAST

FOR THE NEXT few weeks in August I boarded the D train every morning and continued to work at the monotonous job of repairing chains. The only moments of excitement were when Sonya popped into the shop, several times a day, to get price quotations from her father or from Mr. Diamond. But all I could do was turn my head to take a look at Sonya's beautiful face and listen to her sweet voice.

On some of those August evenings in 1946, I strolled on the Grand Concourse with my friend and neighbor Harold Flender. Harold was always asking about the Soviet Union. On one occasion he wanted to know whether it was true that schoolchildren were asked by their teachers to spy on their parents.

I told Harold about the infamous Pavlik Morozov affair. Pavlik was a child in a village near Yekaterinburg in Russia. The teachers in his elementary school told the children to check and see whether their parents were hoarding grain. Pavlik turned in his parents, and they were executed as enemies of the Soviet state. Pavlik, in turn, was killed in revenge by relatives of his parents. The Soviet government put up a large statue of him in Moscow as a true hero and a good, dedicated communist, and the story of his martyrdom was recounted in textbooks and films. Not surprisingly, Harold was shocked by the story. Like most Americans, he knew very little about the Soviet Union except for its important role in defeating the Nazis.

Harold suggested that we spend a day at the beach. Since I didn't have a swim suit, he took me to Alexander's department store on Friday night to pick one out.

Saturday morning, with my new bathing suit, I went with Harold to Orchard Beach. This was my first visit to a beach since August 1939, when I had gone to Dynów's very tiny beach on the San River. By contrast, Orchard

Beach was very large, and on that beautiful, sunny Saturday morning, it was a mass of people, young and old. Some of them brought along beach chairs, and some spread their beach towels on the sand. Huge waves washed ashore. Harold and I just rushed into the water where we were hit by the large waves. This was a new experience for me, because now I was fighting huge waves of water rather than running from the KGB. For a few moments, I forgot all the problems that continually afflicted my mind.

When I returned home, there was a letter in the mail from the New York State Board of Regents informing me that I was eligible to study for a high school diploma. I registered at Theodore Roosevelt High School for evening session courses in English composition, English literature, American history, and science. I would have to attend evening school five days a week.

My classes at Theodore Roosevelt began in September, right after Labor Day. I will never forget my first day of school in America. I came home from my job, ate a fast dinner that my mother had prepared, grabbed my Polish dictionary, a pencil, and a notebook, and ran to Theodore Roosevelt High School, which was located on Fordham Road, a long walk from my building. I arrived at my assigned English class a little early, and there were several students already in the room. Some were young and some were much older, both males and females. I was really surprised to see the older students. It made me feel good to know that older people were also attending night school. I did not converse with any of the other students because I was embarrassed by my poor English. Sitting down at one of the desks, I opened my notebook, making believe that I was writing. I did that deliberately in order not to give the impression that I was unfriendly. The others were all talking to each other.

All of a sudden a student walked into the room and asked whether he was in the right class. I realized almost at once that he too was a Holocaust survivor. He was pale and emaciated, he spoke with a Polish accent, and his English was just as bad as mine. I walked over and asked in Polish his name and his city. He introduced himself in Polish as Wilek Serog, born in Bielsko, and said that his parents had perished. Bill Serog was twenty years old, two years younger than I. He was a bit shorter than I and had black hair and dark blue eyes. He too had arrived in New York in June 1946, brought over with the help of HIAS, the Hebrew Immigrant Aid Society, and with affidavits provided by his uncle. Our conversation was in Polish, and I am sure that our some of our classmates were listening to us.

The classroom began to fill up. A middle-aged woman came in and introduced herself as our English composition teacher. She was on the short side with blonde hair and small blue eyes. She took a roll call, explained what the course was about, and gave us the title of the textbook we had to purchase. She then called out my name and Bill Serog's and asked us to stand up, informing the class that the two of us had limited knowledge of English because we had just arrived from Europe a few months before. I felt somewhat ill at ease, perhaps a little embarrassed. She asked the two of us to sit down. I took out my Polish dictionary and my notebook. The teacher began her lecture. I took some notes, mostly in Polish but also in English. Thus began my first class in an American school.

Bill Serog and I sat next to each other and compared our notes after the teacher left the room. Then we went to another room for American history. The history teacher was a young man, and on the tall side. Bill and I went through the same procedure in this class: the teacher had us stand up to be introduced as new arrivals in America. I enjoyed the history lecture, because history has always been one of my favorite subjects. At nine o'clock, when the class ended, and Bill and I agreed to meet a little earlier the next evening to get to know each other better

I walked home by myself and told my family that had I met another Holocaust survivor who was taking the same subjects I was. I was a little tired and I asked Mother to give me a glass of chocolate milk. Hella wanted to tell me about her first day at Walton High School. I asked her to hold her story for the weekend because I was dead tired and wanted to go to sleep. I took a shower and tried to fall asleep, but I couldn't. Thinking about having to work all day and go to school five nights a week just boggled my mind. I eventually did fall asleep, however.

The next day, when I returned home from work, I just grabbed a sandwich and ran off to school to meet my new friend Bill Serog. Our class that second night was English literature. Bill was already in his seat and was holding the seat next to his for me. He began to tell me more about his life and his war experiences. He was an only child, and his parents were business people in Poland. He had been separated from them by the Nazis, and they had perished. Initially he was in a ghetto, but he ended up at Auschwitz after having been in seven other concentration camps.

Bill had an uncle, Dr. Julius Flamm, who had arrived in New York shortly before the outbreak of the war. Soon after his arrival, he was issued a license to practice family medicine in New York State. Dr. Flamm and his wife had an apartment on Allerton Avenue in the Bronx, which was not too far from our high school. Bill's uncle and aunt were childless and had adopted him unofficially as their son. I told Bill that it was my ambition to become a lawyer. Bill told me that he planned to go to medical school.

A new teacher walked into the room and introduced herself. Our English literature teacher was an older woman with a wide round face and graying hair. She told us that she liked poetry very much, and she gave us a quick introduction to English literature, including British and American writers and poets. Of course, she spoke quite a bit about Shakespeare and Poe. I found her to be an excellent teacher, and I enjoyed her class immensely. The next class that night was science. Our science teacher was an elderly man who was not very exciting. Bill and I were together in the science class, too.

As time went by, we began to make friends with our American-born fellow students. Bill and I decided to study together on weekends. And so we continued our high school courses five days a week from seven to nine during that fall semester. On Saturdays and Sundays, Bill would come to our apartment to study. My parents liked him very much, and even invited him to have lunch and supper with us. Bill and I studied very diligently in school, as well as on weekends together. Sometimes we studied together at his uncle's apartment on Allerton Avenue. We both received good grades in our first semester.

Winter break came, and with it the Hanukah holiday. It had been seven years since we had been able to celebrate the joy of the Hanukah festival of lights. We bought a Hanukah menorah, and the colored Hanukah candles burned for eight nights in our apartment. Each night after lighting the Hanukah candles, my father and I sang the beautiful Hanukah songs, especially "Ma'oz Tsur."

I now experienced my first winter in New York. There were, of course, some snowy days, but snow did not bother me at all. Compared to Siberia, a New York winter seemed tropical. Although we were now on school recess, Bill and I still had to study on Saturdays and Sundays for the Regents examinations for the courses we had taken before coming to America.

In the spring semester Bill and I had to separate. Bill was taking German, a course offered at Theodore Roosevelt, but I wanted to take Hebrew. The only night school in New York City that offered an advanced course in Hebrew was Washington Irving High School in lower Manhattan, so I registered there for the spring semester. In addition to Hebrew, I took courses in algebra, science, and European history.

Life became more difficult during the spring semester, because now I was unable to have supper with my family. I continued to work in the jewelry factory and had my lunch there--sandwiches Mother prepared for me. Right after work I took the IRT to 14th Street. In my briefcase, I had a "dinner" sandwich, also prepared by my mother, as well as some fruit. On the way I would buy a container of coffee at a luncheonette. Once at Washington Irving High School, I would sit down in any vacant classroom I could find and eat my cold sandwich with the hot coffee. Classes commenced at seven.

After my last class I had to take the Jerome Avenue IRT train to the Bronx, arriving home after ten, when my father and my sister Hella were already asleep. My mother was always up, anxiously awaiting my arrival. She served me hot cocoa and cookies and I worked on my homework, usually going to bed after midnight. That was the schedule I maintained every weekday during the entire 1947 spring semester. I did not have a single hot supper, except on Saturdays and Sundays.

I did most of my homework over the weekend, and continued to study on Saturdays and Sundays with Bill Serog. I had absolutely no social life. I did not date girls. I simply dedicated myself to studying, improving my English, and completing my high school education.

However, during this 1947 spring semester other very important events made demands on my time. Sometime in the early part of February, my mother noticed a whitish discharge from her left eye. At first she did not pay much attention to it, but she soon began to experience a continuous flow of the discharge. On a Saturday I took her to Dr. Vishner, a handsome, young, and very nice family practitioner who had an office in our building. He examined my mother's eye told me that he did not like what he was seeing. He said that she would have to see an eye specialist immediately. I asked Dr. Vishner whether he could recommend one. He looked through a book and recommended a Dr. Givner, whose office was located in Manhattan.

I asked Dr. Vishner whether he could call Dr. Givner and arrange an appointment. I listened as he told Dr. Givner that this was an emergency and asked him to see mother that coming Monday. Dr. Givner agreed to see her at nine on Monday morning. Dr. Vishner gave me Dr. Givner's address and told me how to get there by subway.

Now very concerned about my mother's eye, I called Uncle Irving. Aunt Ruthie answered the phone, and I told her the whole story. Aunt Ruthie told me not to worry about money, because Irving would pay all the expenses, and asked me to call on Monday to tell her Dr. Givner's diagnosis. Then she spoke to my mother, offering comfort and reiterating that we were not to worry about the medical expenses.

My mother and I arrived at Dr. Givner's office a few minutes before nine. I asked the nurse to let me make a phone call to the jewelry factory. She dialed the number, and I explained the situation to Mrs. Diamond. Then Dr. Givner called us into his office. I did all the talking, because at this point my mother had very little knowledge of English. Dr. Givner examined my mother's eye with various instruments and took a sample of the discharge. It was quite a long examination. Dr. Givner said that he would not have a complete diagnosis for a day or two, because he had to send the discharge and other samples to a laboratory, but he sounded quite pessimistic. I was very distressed. He did not prescribe any medication, but told us that Mother should stay in bed and not do any housework.

We returned home and I got Mother into bed. She started to cry. I tried to calm her down, telling her that she was in very good hands. I telephoned my father at the factory and told him what the doctor had said. I also telephoned Aunt Ruthie. She asked me for Dr. Givner's phone number. I was very upset, not knowing what to do. In about an hour Father came in, because Uncle Irving had told him to go home and stay with Mother.

I not only skipped work that day, but I also skipped school that evening. Father too was worried about Mother's condition. I gave her some tea and pleaded with her to sleep. When Hella returned from school in the afternoon, I told her that it looked very serious. My father said that he and Hella would stay home with Mother the next day, and I should go back to work and to school. I felt that it was wrong not to stay home with Mother, and I didn't know what to do. I did not care about my job, but school was very important to me, so at last I decided to listen to Father and go back to work and school.

On Wednesday, when I returned home from school around ten, I found Father very sad and Hella in tears. Dr. Givner had called to say that Mother's left eye was cancerous and must be taken out immediately. My mother lay listlessly in bed and just mumbled to me. I told Father and Hella that I would call Dr. Givner the next morning and then we would decide what to do.

I called Dr. Givner's office on Thursday a few minutes before nine. Dr. Givner was very friendly and very warm. He explained that Mother could be saved, because the cancer in her eye was localized and had not spread to other parts of her body, but the eye must be taken out immediately. It would be replaced with a glass eye. The surgery was not that difficult and he could perform it at Manhattan Eye and Ear Hospital, which was located in lower Manhattan. He said that she would have to take out the glass eye every night before she went to sleep and reinsert it in the morning. He promised that the color of the glass eye would match her right eye, and no one would be able to tell that it was a false eye. He assured me that we had nothing to worry about; the surgery would be successful and Mother would be able to live a normal life.

I repeated all this to Father, Hella, and Mother and then phoned Aunt Ruthie. She was shocked and surprised by the sad news. She said that she would come over to see us and discuss the problem. I phoned the jewelry factory and told Mrs. Diamond that I could not come in because of my mother's illness.

Aunt Ruthie arrived within the hour, and the first thing she did was to walk over to Mother's bed and try to calm her and make her comfortable. Then we sat down and discussed how to proceed. After a short discussion we decided to go ahead with the surgery. I called Dr. Givner and asked him to make the arrangements as soon as possible. Dr. Givner called back within the hour. She was to come the hospital the next morning, Friday, at seven.

At this point I argued with myself about what I should do and what my obligations were. As a son it was my duty to stay with my mother, and to heck with my job and my school. At the same time, I asked myself, how could I help her by staying home, since both Father and Hella had agreed to stay home with her? Father, Hella, and Aunt Ruthie all agreed that I should go back to work and school.

I took my briefcase and set out for the jewelry factory, arriving a few minutes before noon. I explained everything to my employers, and they were very supportive. I went to school that evening, and returned home after ten.

When I entered the apartment I found Uncle Irving and Aunt Ruthie and Cousin Lisa Eiss. I apologized to them for leaving Mother and going to work and school. They all understood that there was nothing I could have done for her, as my father and Hella had stayed home with her. Uncle Irving said that he would send one of his employees with a car the next morning at six to take Mother to the hospital. We thanked Uncle Irving and Aunt Ruthie for all the help they had been giving us. After they all left I had difficulty sleeping, because my conscience bothered me. I asked myself if I had been right to leave Mother and not stay with her.

The next day, Friday morning, we all got up around five and helped Mother get dressed. We had breakfast and waited for the car. The plan was that Father and I would take Mother to the hospital, and I would go school in the evening. The car and driver arrived at six, and Father and I carefully helped Mother into the car. We arrived at Manhattan Eye and Ear Hospital a few minutes before seven. Mother was taken in a wheelchair to one of the waiting rooms while I filled out all the necessary forms. The hospital staff told us that she would have to undergo the usual series of pre-operative tests, and one of the nurses told us that the surgery would not take place until the following Monday, so there was no reason for Father or me to stay in the hospital. Father decided to stay for a while and I went to work. I returned from school that Friday as usual after ten and found Father and Hella in the living room. Father told me that he had remained at the hospital till after 1 p.m.

All three of us decided to visit Mother the following day. We arrived at the hospital before noon and were directed to her room, which she shared with another woman patient. Mother was very gloomy, but we reassured her that she was in very good hands, since Dr. Givner was one of the best surgeons in the field. We went to visit her again on Sunday. Mother was in bed in a hospital gown and had a patch on her left eye. We were anxious about the operation, which a nurse told us would take place early in the morning.

Father and I arrived at the hospital around seven on Monday morning. We were ushered into a waiting room. It was a long wait. Dr. Givner came to see us just before eleven. The operation, he announced, had been a total success, and Mother would recover speedily. For the time being she was heavily sedated, and it would take a few hours for her to recover from the anesthesia. Father decided to stay in the hospital and I went to work. When I returned home from school after ten, I found Father and Hella more relaxed. Father had seen Mother late in the afternoon, and she was in a much better mood and not in much pain. She would have to stay in the hospital for at least a week, during which they would try to fit her for a glass eye. I decided to go visit her in the hospital early the next morning.

Mother was discharged from the hospital about seven days after her surgery, and was brought home in one of Uncle Irving's cars. She still had a patch over her left eye and had instructions to stay in bed and not to do any work at all. About two weeks later, Dr. Givner's office called and asked us to bring her in the next morning. Again one of Uncle Irving's employees drove us. Dr. Givner examined Mother and found the operation site fully healed. He then took a glass eye out of a little black box and inserted it, then showed Mother how to insert and remove it. We were so pleased. It was a perfect fit, and the color was a perfect match. From a distance one could not discern that she had a glass eye at all. Dr. Givner gave Mother full instructions about how to care for the glass eye. In addition, he told us that Uncle Irving had paid for the surgery and the hospital stay. I thanked Dr. Givner for all his help and concern. He responded that he felt he had a certain obligation to us as survivors who had been through so much during the war.

We were driven home by Uncle Irving's employee. We were so relieved; Mother was relaxed and at ease. I immediately telephoned Uncle Irving and Aunt Ruthie to thank them for their generosity and all the help they had given. At that moment I reminded myself what I had learned in my Jewish school in Dynów: "To save one person is to save the whole world." This is the dictum of the Jewish religion, and Uncle Irving and Ruthie certainly lived up to it. The nightmare of my mother's cancerous eye was now over. I was so relieved that she had been saved I felt that a heavy stone had been lifted from my chest.

I continued to go to work and school, with no further interruptions now, continuing to do my school work with Bill Serog, mostly on weekends and primarily in my apartment. Bill knew about Mother's eye replacement. When he saw Mother with her glass eye, he was surprised that the color was almost the same as that of her natural eye.

As Mother's crisis faded from my mind, the continuing crisis in Palestine and the Mediterranean again burdened me, especially the revolt against the British colonial government in Palestine. In New York City, there were rallies in various temples and synagogues in support of the Zionist cause, namely to stop British warships from intercepting vessels attempting to bring Holocaust survivors to Palestine and to fight for the establishment of a Jewish state in Palestine.

I decided one Sunday to attend a rally in a Manhattan temple where, according to WEVD, the main speaker would be Louis Lipsky, a man whose name I now heard for the first time. The temple was packed with men and women of all ages. The people sitting next to me told me that Lipsky was an important American Zionist leader.

Louis Lipsky was tall with a slim face and gray hair. He spoke about the treachery of the British Labour government and the brutality of its Minister of Foreign Affairs, Ernest Bevin. He denounced Bevin as the main force behind the policy of intercepting refugee ships headed for Palestine and opposing the establishment of a Jewish state. Lipsky compared Bevin to the Nazis. He said further that there were anti-Semitic elements in our own State Department that were opposed the establishment of a Jewish state. He mentioned Loy Henderson, an official in the State Department who was not only an anti-Semite but an Arabist. He urged everyone to write letters to President Harry Truman and to their senators and congressmen

It was at this rally that I first heard about the *Struma* affair. Many years later I made it my business to research the subject. It seems that in 1941, a group of Jews were trying to escape the anti-Semitic massacres in Romania. They fled to the port of Constanta and embarked on the *Struma*, a tiny vessel bound for Palestine. The *Struma* reached Istanbul with a defunct engine. It remained there for 70 days, but could not get British permission for the passengers to enter Palestine, or Turkish permission to repair the engine, disembark, or remain in Turkey. On the evening of February 23, 1942, Turkish police seized the ship and towed it out into the Black Sea. With no engine, she drifted during the night until, at first light, a Russian submarine sank her with a single torpedo. All told, 109 children, 269 women, and 406 men died. The tragedy ignited marches and uprisings in Palestine. In 1944 the Jewish underground assassinated Lord Moyne, the British official who had refused the *Struma* passengers visas to enter Palestine.

At the time of the *Struma* tragedy I was still in the Soviet Union. The newspapers and radio there never reported this horrible crime. As a matter of fact, the they never reported anything about the Jewish revolt in Warsaw, or about Auschwitz. When I learned about the *Struma* tragedy, I could feel my stomach drop. These events simply tormented my life. I left the rally very dispirited. I asked myself what I should do. Should I concentrate on my mother's recovery? Should I concentrate on school or my job? I just did not know what to do or even what to say.

I told my parents about the rally in the temple and the *Struma* affair. I picked up my briefcase and tried to do some homework. I glanced through some of the notes I had taken at school the previous week, but my mind could not absorb anything. I kept thinking about the helpless Jews from the *Struma* who were now at the bottom of the Black Sea. I put my notes back into my briefcase, and decided to lie down and rest. I thought that perhaps a snooze might calm me. But no matter how hard I tried, I just could not fall asleep.

As I lay there, suddenly reason took over, and I realized that if I wanted to help my people I must complete my schooling as soon as possible and acquire the communication skills to educate others about the injustices being done to the Jewish people. I got off the couch, grabbed my briefcase, opened my Polish dictionary, and began working on my English vocabulary.

Life went on much as before. I worked at the jewelry factory every day and went to class every night, five days a week. I studied with Bill Serog every weekend.

My family looked forward to the arrival of the Passover holiday. The last time we had celebrated Passover was in Poland in 1939. Now, in 1947, we would be able to celebrate the holiday in our new free country, America. Passover has always been a very important holiday for Orthodox Jews. It commemorates the liberation of the Jewish people from Egyptian slavery. We couldn't celebrate any religious holidays during our Communist slavery. My mother, despite her recent health problems, was looking forward to this first Passover holiday in New York. Despite her weakened health, she cleaned and scrubbed our entire apartment to make sure that there was not a single bread or cake crumb in it, in accordance with the ritual laws prohibiting any leavened products during the week of Passover.

On the Sunday before the holiday, my sister and I purchased all the required Passover foods: matzos, kosher wine, fish, meat, and kosher-for-Passover flour, nuts, vegetables, and honey. Mother made her own gefilte fish, baked a large Passover nut cake, and made chicken soup with matzo balls. She was an excellent cook and baker. We also purchased Passover Haggadah books. Uncle Irving and his entire family were invited to celebrate both nights of Passover with us, which fell on the 14th and 15th of April in 1947. Each family consisted of four members, totaling eight Wenigs.

The large dining room table was covered with a new white tablecloth. Porcelain Passover dishes were placed in front of each of us. A white cloth napkin was placed on the left side of the plate. On the white napkins were placed two forks, and to right of the plate, a knife, a soup spoon, and a teaspoon. In front of each plate were two glasses. One was a large water glass and the other a wine glass. At the center of the table were two silver candle holders containing candles. Next to the candle holders was a plate with matzos, covered by a special matzo cloth. Next to the matzo plate were some other plates, one containing a fresh green leaf. Next to that plate was another large glass plate which contained an egg, a shank bone, bitter herbs, parsley, and charoseth, a traditional mixture of chopped nuts, wine, and cinnamon. There was, of course, the large bottle of Manishevitz kosher wine. The reason I am mentioning all these details is because I had almost forgotten them during the previous seven years when we were not allowed to celebrate Passover.

When Uncle Irving and his family arrived, we all kissed each other. Uncle Irving and his family admired the settings on the dining table. We sat down to celebrate the Passover event, which is called the Seder.

My mother first lit the two candles and said the required prayer. Next my father poured wine into each wine glass. He recited the Kiddush prayer, the traditional blessing over the wine, with its reference to the exodus of the Jewish people from Egyptian slavery, and then asked me to recite the Kiddush. After the Kiddush, we all drank some of the wine in our glasses. I then recited the Four Questions, which ask why the night of Passover is different from all the other nights of the year. After that we all recited the Haggadah, the narrative that tells the history of the Jewish people as slaves in Egypt. It describes the brutality of their Egyptian slavemasters, their liberation by their leader, Moses, who took them out of Egypt, their wanderings in the desert, and finally their arrival in the Holy Land, as promised by God to Moses.

Father, Uncle Irving, and I recited the Haggadah in Hebrew, and the others recited it in English. After we finished reading the Haggadah, my mother served us a delicious Passover dinner. Uncle Irving told her that it had been a long time since he had eaten such a delicious kosher dinner.

This Seder was a very special event for our family. We had been unable to observe any Jewish holidays during our imprisonment in the Soviet Union. Moreover, at the time we never dared to imagine that we might survive, much less practice Judaism again someday. As I said at the table that night, I could write another Haggadah about our sojourn in the Soviet Union. This time the slavemaster was not the Pharaoh of Egypt but the evil Stalin. The people in the Soviet Union called this evil man "Genii Mira: World Genius" or "Otets Narodov: Father of all Peoples," but we Jews knew what he was really like.

During the Passover holidays I continued with the same daily routine, going to work and school, the only difference being that my sandwiches were made with matzos instead of bread. I ended the spring semester at Washington Irving in June with very good grades in all my subjects. I also got good marks on my Regents exams. At the end of the spring semester, I transferred back to Theodore Roosevelt High School for the 1947 fall semester. That made my life a little better, because I could eat supper every night in my parents' apartment.

My English had improved greatly, except that I could not get rid of my accent. One problem was that there were few opportunities for me to practice. At the jewelry factory there was very little conversation; you just did your work. At home we spoke only Polish and Yiddish. This continued until the day of my marriage to an American-born girl. Obviously, it is much different when you come to America as a child and attend school during the day, spending many hours speaking only English with your classmates and teachers. Night school is only two hours daily. It is also much more difficult to lose your accent when you arrive in America at age 22.

While I did not attend school in July and August, Bill and I occasionally spent some summer weekends studying for the Regents examinations. That summer I occasionally dated on Saturday night. I still recall a Greta and a Sonya from the Bronx. I also maintained my friendship with Harold Flender, who occasionally introduced me to girls. These were just Saturday night dates, not serious relationships. I simply could not at this juncture in my life think of having a serious relationship with a girl.

It was in the summer of 1947 that I made another visit to the Marseille Hotel on Broadway and 90th Street in Manhattan. There I learned from some young Holocaust survivors that they planned to rent a room on the Lower East Side that fall and winter, where young single Holocaust survivors could meet and do some dancing.

There were events in the spring and summer of 1947 that made me somewhat happy as well as unhappy. That spring the British Labour government of Clement Atlee finally realized that it could no longer handle the Palestinian Mandate awarded Great Britain by the League of Nations after World War I. In 1919, The League of Nations had given the British a mandate to establish a Jewish state in the entire territory of the ancient kingdom of Judea. Britain violated the mandate in 1922 by cutting off 77 percent of the territory, which they renamed Trans-Jordan, and giving it to Abdullah, a scion of the Hashemite family. Great Britain committed this treacherous act to further its colonial interests by reinforcing the frictions between the Hashemites and the rulers of Arabia.

Now, weakened both politically and economically after World War II and unable to put down the Jewish revolt in Palestine, Britain declared the mandate "unworkable" and referred the matter to the youthful United Nations. The UN created a special committee of eleven member states to study the issues and report its recommendations. The committee recommended an end to the mandate and a plan to partition Palestine between Jews and Arabs. However, the partition plan pertained only to the 23 percent of the original mandatory territory that remained after the British gave away 77 percent to create Trans-Jordan. Of the 23 percent that remained, 56 percent was allocated to a Jewish state, 42 percent to an Arab state, and Jerusalem was allocated 2 percent as an international zone for the holy places.

My relaxed and pleasant summer came to an end with the *Exodus* event on August 2, 1947. I have mentioned before that the British government had restricted the immigration of Jews to Palestine in order to appease the Arabs. The Royal Navy intercepted refugee ships and sent them back to their ports of origin in Europe.

The *Exodus* affair brought this terrible situation to the attention of the whole world, and as a result the *Exodus* became a symbol of the illegal immigration effort and the desperate effort of Holocaust survivors to reach their homeland. The *Exodus* left France with 4,515 passengers on July 11, 1947. As soon as it was outside French waters, British naval vessels began to follow it. When the *Exodus* reached the Palestine coast, it was rammed by a British vessel and boarded by British sailors and marines. During the boarding skirmish, two passengers and one crewman were killed and another 30 injured.

The *Exodus* was eventually towed into the port of Haifa and its passengers were herded onto deportation ships that would return them to France. When the ships reached France, the passengers from the *Exodus* refused to disembark. What ensued was a 24-day protest in extreme heat and with low food supplies and poor sanitary conditions. The French government refused to forcibly remove the protesters. Eventually, the British decided to move the ships to Germany. When they reached a port in the British occupation zone, the protesters were forced off and taken to detention camps surrounded by wire fences and guard towers that evoked images of Auschwitz. The media coverage of the *Exodus* incident became a public relations disaster for the British.

As the story played out, it showed the dramatic fight of immigrants seeking to flee anti-Semitism against the merciless and brutal British. Massive demonstrations took place in New York. One such demonstration took place in Madison Square Park. WEVD called for a massive show of Jewish strength, and we all turned out. The main speaker at the rally was the great American Jewish leader Rabbi Abba Hillel Silver, the president of the Zionist Organization of America. Rabbi Silver was not only a great leader but a great orator. I felt it was my sacred duty to go to the rally, and I also wanted to see and hear Rabbi Silver.

The rally began at two in the afternoon. I explained to my employers how important it was for me, as a Holocaust survivor, to attend the rally and protest against the heartless British policy. Without hesitation they gave me the afternoon off. When I arrived there, Madison Square Park was a sea of people. Many were carrying placards with the words "Let my people go" or denouncing Bevin, the British Foreign Minister, as a wicked person and a vicious anti-Semite. Still other placards called for the immediate establishment of a Jewish state in Palestine, the ancient homeland.

When Rabbi Silver was introduced, there was wild applause. This was the first time I saw and heard him. He was very distinguished looking, perhaps even aristocratic. He spoke with a powerful and moving voice. He moved us to tears when he described how the evil world had brutalized the Jews for centuries, and was still doing it today. He shredded Bevin to pieces, thrusting him onto the garbage heap of history. He called Bevin a brutal, heartless man, who had not one ounce of humanity in his body. He called for the immediate opening of the gates of Palestine and for allowing the wretched survivors of the Holocaust to empty the DP camps in Germany and Austria and settle in their ancient homeland.

All of us in the audience were profoundly moved. Rabbi Silver was one of the greatest orators I have ever heard. Great orators can inspire their listeners and move people to action. I heard Hitler speak several times on the radio in the 1930s, and he too had great oratorical skills. But what a difference between him and Abba Hillel Silver! Hitler called for death and destruction. Rabbi Silver called for compassion. He pleaded for justice and mercy. He spoke in the tradition of the ancient biblical prophets, urging the leaders of the world to make amends for the inhumanity of the last 2,000 years by permitting the establishment of a Jewish state in the Jews' ancient homeland.

I left the rally numbed and heartbroken. I wanted to do something, but I did not know what to do. I got on the subway to go home and found a seat. I closed my eyes, wanting to sleep, hoping that sleep would calm me. For two weeks I had been thinking that perhaps I finally would begin living a normal life. I had somehow adjusted to the fact that I would continue to work at my job and attend school for years to come. Yet the *Exodus* affair and the heartbreaking speech by Rabbi Silver put a wrench into my new life. With my eyes closed, I asked myself whether others felt as strongly as I did about the *Exodus* affair. I knew that my good friend and neighbor Harold Flender probably saw it as just another daily news item.

When I arrived home, I told my parents and Hella about the rally and the great speech delivered by Rabbi Silver. I urged them to go hear him at the next rally. Mother served dinner, but I just could not eat much. I said goodnight and went to bed, but I could not fall asleep.

Thinking about the *Exodus* ripped my heart apart. I was reminded of the popular Yiddish song "Vuhin Zol Ikh Geyn," translated into English as "Where Shall I Go?" The lyrics are as follows:

The Jew's always hounded and plagued,
Not sure of his hour or his day.
His life is in darkness enclosed,
His strivings are thwarted, opposed.
Deserted, no friends, only foe,
No safe place, no safe day to know.

Tell me where shall I go,
Who can answer my plea?
Tell me where shall I go,
Every door is barred to me?
Though the world's large enough,
There's no room for me I know,
What I see is not for me
Each road's closed for me,
Each road's closed, I'm not free
Tell me where shall I go.

It took me a long time that night to fall asleep after I remembered this song.

For the next few months my life continued in its normal rhythm: my job at the factory, high school, homework on the weekends with Bill Serog, and socializing with Harold Flender. I occasionally dated on Saturday nights. Sometimes I had a blind date. One of the girls was Vichna, a Holocaust survivor, a very attractive blonde girl but not too bright. Another one was Toby, who wrote poetry.

My father purchased tickets for the High Holidays, which began early that year. The first day of Rosh Hashanah was September 1st. The temple where my father purchased tickets was a temporary one located on the second floor of the Paradise Theater on the Grand Concourse. The premises of the temporary temple were owned by a rabbi whose name, I believe, was Friedman. It was actually a large hall where weddings and Bar Mitzvahs were held during the year. However, the rabbi used it as a temple for the High Holidays.

The temple was packed to capacity, with several hundred worshipers. The members of my family had seats next to each other. Next to us was an elderly man, and he asked my father who I was and why I was praying so fervently, My stepfather told him that I was his son. The man then struck up a conversation with me, asking who I was, where I lived, and many other questions. He showed me a photograph of Helene, his stepdaughter. He said that she was the personal secretary to Jacob Potofsky, the national president of the Amalgamated Clothing Workers of America. He asked me to take her out on a date, and he gave me her address and phone number. The picture showed Helene to be a very attractive brunette, and I told him that I would call her after the holidays.

After the Shaharit (morning) service the Torah scroll was taken out of the ark and certain selections from the Torah were read aloud. After this, Rabbi Friedman gave the sermon. It focused on the *Exodus*. Rabbi Friedman said that the British government wanted to give up the mandate. Perhaps the United Nations would agree to the establishment of a Jewish state.

I called Helene after the holidays. Her father, actually her stepfather, had already told her about me. I asked her for a date for the coming Saturday night, and Helene agreed. Saturday evening at about six I rang the bell at her apartment on Walton Avenue, which was within walking distance of my apartment, and Helene opened the door for me. Her stepfather and mother said hello. I sat down on one of the slip-covered chairs. Helene was an attractive girl, not slim but very sweet. She was at least five feet six inches tall, with a very smooth face, black eyes, and very nice curly hair. She wore a beige dress. I apologized for my thick Polish accent, and told her and her parents about some of my war experiences.

Helene and I went to see a movie at the Paradise Theater and then to a nearby Chinese restaurant. She was a very educated and intelligent girl. She wanted to know about the Soviet Union and its leaders, so that is what we spoke of most of the time.

I took Helene back home and she asked me in. We sat down and talked, but no necking was involved. Helene opened her heart to me. I had sensed all along that she had some problems. Her father had died quite a while before and her mother had remarried. She told me that for a long time she had been dating a young man with whom she had fallen in love, but he had broken off the relationship a few weeks before. I could see that she was still hurting over the breakup. I guess she needed to go out on a Saturday night to ease her pain. It was obvious that a date with anyone, even me, would be good enough.

I shook hands with Helene and said good night. It was quite an interesting experience. Helene's personal problems momentarily redirected my mind from international political events toward an individual's personal heartbreak.

My mother asked me in the morning about my date. I told her that Helene was a nice, good-looking girl, and that she was looking for the right man to marry. Mother asked me whether I would take her out again. I said that I was many years away from marriage, but I might ask her for another date.

However, I did not call her right away. I had learned in life that when you first date a girl you like, you should skip a week and not call her so that she thinks that you're not interested, which makes her eager to hear from you. Therefore, I did not call Helene the following week to ask for a date. I simply followed my theory not to show that I was eager to see her again,

My friend Bill Serog called me early Sunday morning to say he was coming over to do some homework with me. We studied our weekly assignments, as well as some of the subjects on the upcoming Regents examinations which would be given in the fall. I turned on WEVD to hear the commentary on the Palestinian situation by Shlomo Ben Israel. He said that the United Nations might decide to establish a Jewish state in Palestine.

The following week I called Helene and asked her out for the upcoming Saturday. I could sense that she sounded blah and something was bothering her. I got the impression that she would have been happier if it were her ex-boyfriend calling her for a date. Helene agreed to go out with me on Saturday, but she wanted to be picked up at seven.

When I arrived on Saturday exactly at seven, Helene was dressed rather shabbily in old dungarees and a sloppy pink blouse. Neither her mother nor her stepfather were in the apartment. We sat down on the sofa and talked a little about the latest news. I asked Helene whether she would like to go to see a war picture that was playing at the RKO movie house on Fordham Road. Helene said she would rather skip the movie and take a walk on the Grand Concourse, because the weather that evening was perfect for shpatsirn, a Yiddish expression meaning to stroll or promenade. At that time it was the habit for many young couples to shpatsirn on the Grand Concourse.

Of course I agreed. As we strolled back and forth on the Grand Concourse that Saturday evening, I asked Helene what kind of a week she had had. Helene told me that she was very happy with her job, and her boss, Jacob Potofsky, liked her very much. She seemed like a different person. After strolling back and forth for a long while on the Grand Concourse, Helene said she wanted to go home. I asked whether she would care to go to a restaurant. Helene indicated that she was in the mood for a shrimp cocktail. There was one restaurant on the corner of Fordham Road, close by Alexander's department store, which served lobster and shrimp. I must confess that I had never before eaten lobster or shrimp. I don't think lobster and shrimp were available in Poland when I lived there, and even if they had been, I would not have eaten them, because they are not kosher. In Poland my family was very religious and I would not have dared to eat non-kosher food. My parents also kept a kosher house in New York, but this Saturday night, I felt like tasting forbidden food. Helene and I had a shrimp cocktail, and I enjoyed it very much, hoping that God would forgive me for committing the sin.

I took Helene back to her apartment, and she invited me in. We sat down on the couch and began talking. There was no kissing on my second date with Helene either. There was a certain sadness that night about Helene. She thanked me for taking her out, and she told me that she was going to pour out her heart to me because I was a decent person. She told me that she still felt very hurt because the man she loved had broken up with her. In addition, Helene told me about her persistent health problems.

For the past few years, without warning, she would be afflicted by severe, unbearable pains in her gums. The pain was so severe that it made her scream. She had seen several doctors, but they all told her that the pain was probably caused by a virus, and they did not know how to cure it. Helene had experienced several such attacks recently, and had had a miserable week. I now understood why she seemed so different on this second date. I tried to console her by telling her that tremendous progress in medical science was being made, and I was sure that there would eventually be a cure for her sickness. She thanked me very much. I kissed her on the forehead and said goodbye.

I decided not to see Helene again. She wanted to get married soon, and she had too many problems, including a serious a health problem. I, on the other hand, could not possibly contemplate marriage. I was only interested in an occasional Saturday night date. The next morning my mother asked me about my date with Helene. I said that Helene had too many problems and I would not see her again.

That Sunday morning, after my last date with Helene, I turned on WEVD to learn more details about the proceedings at the United Nations. The announcer stated that sometime in November the report of the Special Committee on Palestine would come up for a vote by the General Assembly. It is difficult for me to describe my anxiety about the outcome.

On November 29th, the UN General Assembly, by a two-thirds vote (33 to 13, with Britain and nine others abstaining) passed Resolution 181, partitioning Palestine into two states, one Jewish and one Arab. I cannot possibly describe the tension in our apartment, where I was practically glued to the radio listening to the count as the voting took place. Huge tears flowed down my face. I told myself joyously that finally the Jews, like every other people, would have their own state. I was not happy about the tiny size of that state, but at least we would no longer be "Wandering Jews."

There was dancing and jubilation in the streets of New York and many other American cities. The Jewish community in Palestine, the Yishuv, jubilantly accepted partition despite the small size and strategic vulnerability of the proposed state. It not only did not include the regions we know today as the West Bank and the Gaza Strip, but Jerusalem was also excluded, along with most of the Galilee in the north and parts of the Negev desert in the south.

After the partition vote, the delegations from Iraq, Syria, Lebanon, Egypt, Saudi Arabia, and Yemen stormed out, threatening war and the annihilation of Palestinian Jewry. Pakistan's delegation followed suit. The Arab national movement in Palestine and the states of the Arab League angrily rejected partition. The Palestinian Arabs demanded the entire country for themselves and decided to resist partition by force. Had they accepted the UN proposal in 1947, a Palestinian Arab state covering an area much larger than Judea and Samaria (the West Bank) and Gaza would have been created along with Israel. Instead, they rejected the plan and launched a war to destroy the nascent Jewish state.

Almost immediately, Arab violence broke out against the Jews in Palestine. It is well described in the text that follows, which comes from a report by Robert Macatee, the American consul general in Jerusalem, published in the 1947 volume of the official State Department series Foreign Relations of the United States:

"It is tragic that many of the present casualties comprise innocent and harmless people going about their daily business. They are picked off while riding in buses, walking along the streets and stray shots even find them while asleep in their beds. A Jewish woman, mother of five children, was shot in Jerusalem while hanging out clothes on the roof. The ambulance rushing her to the hospital was machine gunned and finally the mourners following her to the funeral were attacked and one of them was stabbed to death.

"The Arabs started the war and were bluntly willing to take full responsibility. In an address to the UN Security Council on April 16, 1948, Jamal Husseini, the Arab Committee's spokesman, stated: 'The representative of the Jewish Agency told us yesterday that they were not the attackers, that the Arabs had begun the fighting. We told the whole world that we are going to fight.'

"The first large-scale assaults began on January 9, 1948, when approximately 1,000 Arabs attacked Jewish communities in northern Palestine. By February, so many Arab fighters had infiltrated Palestine that the British announced that they lacked the forces to turn them back. In fact, the British turned over bases and arms to Arab irregulars and to the Arab Legion, the British-commanded army of Trans-Jordan.

"On May 4, 1948, the Arab Legion attacked the kibbutz village of Kfar Etzion. The defenders drove them back, but the Legion returned a week later. After two days, the ill-equipped and outnumbered Jewish settlers were overwhelmed. Many of them were massacred after they surrendered. This took place before the invasion of Palestine by the armies of the Arab states after Israel issued its Declaration of Independence.

"The UN blamed the Arabs for the violence. The UN Palestine Commission was never permitted by the Arabs or the British to go to Palestine to implement the resolution. On February 16, 1948, the Commission reported to the Security Council: 'Powerful Arab interests both inside and outside Palestine are defying the resolution of the General Assembly, and are engaged in a deliberate effort to alter by force the settlement envisaged therein.'"

All these events took a great toll on my health. I could not sleep, I could not even eat. I discussed the Palestinian situation everywhere: with my coworkers, with my fellow students. Everyone else just treated the Palestinian situation as another news item. I, however, was tormented, and during my sleepless nights I felt that I should drop everything and join the fight in Palestine. I just could not believe that the world was standing by and doing absolutely nothing to enforce the United Nations resolution.

Then suddenly the situation in Palestine turned around, and the Jews began to make some progress in the war with the Arabs. Despite their disadvantages in numbers, organization, and weaponry, Jewish fighters began to take the initiative in the weeks from April 1 to the Declaration of Independence on May 14. The Haganah captured several major towns including Tiberias and Haifa and temporarily opened the road to Jerusalem.

Israel, the Jewish state in Palestine, was born on May 14, when the British finally left. Five Arab armies (Egypt, Syria, Trans-Jordan, Lebanon, and Iraq) immediately invaded the new state. Their intentions were declared by Azzam Pasha, Secretary-General of the Arab League: "This will be a war of extermination and a momentous massacre which will be spoken of like the Mongolian massacres and the Crusades."

The United States, the Soviet Union, and most other states recognized Israel soon after it declared independence on May 14, 1948, and immediately indicted the Arabs for their aggression. The United States urged a resolution charging the Arabs with breach of the peace. The Soviet delegate, Andrei Gromyko, told the Security Council on May 29: "This is not the first time that the Arab states, which organized the invasion of Palestine, have ignored a decision of the Security Council or of the General Assembly. The USSR delegation deems it essential that the council should states its opinion more clearly and more firmly with regard to this attitude of the Arab states toward decisions of the Security Council."

I was torn apart by these events. Part of my mind was occupied with the Israeli-Arab War, the other part had to concentrate on my final examinations and the Regents exams. Despite the emotional stress, I did very well on all my exams and graduated from Theodore Roosevelt High School in June, 1948. My parents and my sister came to the graduation. Bill Serog was also there with his uncle and aunt. The graduation and the high school diploma I received lifted my spirits a little bit.

Chapter 6

COLLEGE, LAW SCHOOL, AND THE HOTEL BUSINESS

Having finally obtained a high school diploma, I contacted City College to find out whether I was qualified to attend. Several days later, armed with my diploma and a transcript of my grades, I took some time off and went to the office of the registrar, which was located on Convent Avenue in Manhattan. I met with a friendly woman who counseled prospective students and showed her my documents. She told me right off that based on my grades I would have no problem being accepted for the evening session. This meant a great deal to me, because City College was tuition free.

The counselor, naturally, noticed my heavy accent. In response to her questions, I told her that I had arrived in America only two years before. She said that she admired my ambition and diligence, and asked about my future plans. I responded that I wanted to become a lawyer and said I was thinking of Brooklyn Law School because it was the only law school in the city with an evening session. She said that Brooklyn Law School accepted students with only 64 college credits, confirming what Sol Fine had told me. She registered me for the fall semester and recommended that my college program over the next field years should include courses in world history, philosophy, psychology, sociology, government, and English literature, subjects that had always been of great interest to me.

I left the registrar's office feeling very elated, and my parents and sister were delighted when I told them everything. Despite my personal good news, however, I continued to be preoccupied with the news from Palestine. My spirits lifted again when, toward the end of July, the Israeli defense forces stopped the Arab offensive and the fighting ended, at least for the time being. The Israelis won their War of Independence with minimal help from the

West. The United States supported the partition resolution, but did not want to provide the Jews with the means to defend themselves. On December 5, 1947, it imposed an arms embargo on the region.

The Arabs, of course, had no difficulty obtaining all the arms they needed. In fact, Jordan's Arab Legion was armed and trained by the British and led by a British officer. At the end of 1948 and the beginning of 1949, British RAF planes flew with Egyptian squadrons over the Israel-Egypt border. On January 7, 1949, Israeli planes shot down four of the British aircraft. The Jews, on the other hand, were forced to smuggle in weapons, principally from Czechoslovakia. When Israel declared independence in May, 1948, its army did not have a single cannon or tank. Its air force consisted of nine obsolete planes

Nonetheless, the Arab war to destroy Israel failed, and because of their aggression, the Arabs wound up with less territory than was offered them under the partition plan. The cost to Israel, however, was enormous. Many of its productive fields lay gutted and mined. Its citrus groves, the basis of the Jewish economy, were largely destroyed. Military expenditures totaled approximately $500 million. Worse still, 6,373 Israelis had been killed, nearly one percent of the Jewish population of 650,000.

The Arab countries signed armistice agreements with Israel in 1949, starting with Egypt on February 24. Lebanon followed on March 23, Jordan on April 3, and Syria on July 20. Iraq was the only country that did not sign an agreement with Israel, choosing instead to withdraw its troops. None of the Arab states was willing negotiate a peace agreement. The defeat of the Arab nations was a great relief to me. Nonetheless, I did not trust the Arabs. I recalled what a Russian Christian had told me in Uzbekistan, "These Muslims hate us so much; if they could, they would slaughter us all like sheep."

Meanwhile, life went on. Toward the end of July, my sister told me that she and some of her survivor friends planned to meet one Sunday at Bay 5 of Brighton Beach in Brooklyn. She asked me to come along. I really didn't feel like it. Beside, I had a prior engagement to meet Harold Flender to discuss the courses I had just registered for.

Harold and I once again met in the lobby and crossed the street to St. James Park. Harold approved of the courses I was taking. We discussed the Arab-Israeli War and the developing Cold War with the Soviet Union. As I explained to Harold that day, in my view the Truman Doctrine and the Marshall Plan were excellent ideas. I had always known that we would soon face serious problems with the Soviet Union, although many Americans were skeptical. I told Harold that our financial help in rebuilding the West European countries, especially West Germany, would irk the Soviets. I added that I was not thrilled by the notion of rebuilding West Germany after what it had done to the world, but it was necessary because of the Soviet menace.

On her return from the Brighton Beach outing, Hella was in a very bubbly mood. She told me that I had made a big mistake by not coming, because there had been many friendly young people there, all of them Holocaust survivors. Some of the girls, she said, were quite nice and attractive, and I would have enjoyed meeting them. She had met a good-looking fellow named Sol Wexler who lived in Brooklyn. He had taken down her telephone number and promised to call soon to ask her out.

Hella had learned that a couple of young Holocaust survivors had hired Hannington Hall on Delancey Street for Saturday evenings, so that unmarried young Holocaust survivors could meet, dance, and get acquainted. She said that I should go because it was about time I learned how to dance. It's true that I was not much of a dancer.

Later that week Sol called Hella and arranged a date for Saturday night. My parents and I were very curious to meet him. He arrived at our apartment on Saturday after 6 p.m. I imagine he was very impressed with the building and our apartment He was of medium height with black hair and nice facial features. He too was a Holocaust survivor, and he told us about his war experiences.

Sol's father had come to America about a year before the beginning of the war, brought here by his brother, who had been living in New York for many years. Meanwhile, Sol, his mother, and a younger brother remained in their hometown of Bilcze Zloty in eastern Poland near the borders with Romania and Russia. The area had a large Ukrainian population. When the Nazis invaded the Soviet Union on June 22, 1941, they immediately began to round up the Jewish population. The Wexlers and another family, the Stermers, who were relatives, as well as some other Jews, took refuge in a large cavern. They lived there until the Red Army finally liberated the area. Sol told us that conditions in the cave were unbearably horrendous. His mother and his younger brother both died there. After the war Sol was brought to New York by his father and got a job in a factory that manufactured leather briefcases. He dated Hella steadily, and they got married on December 3, 1950. Hella always called him "Cookie," and said he was a good dancer.

I started classes at City College in September, shortly after Labor Day weekend, and of course I continued as usual at the jewelry factory, where I received a $2 raise, making my gross weekly salary $18. I loved all the subjects I was taking.

I attended class five nights a week and my schedule was as follows: I left my job at 5 p.m., taking from the refrigerator in the factory the sandwich my mother had prepared for my supper. I took the Eighth Avenue subway to 145th Street in Manhattan and walked the few blocks to City College. On the way I picked up a container of coffee. Just as in high school, I ate in a vacant classroom. During my years at the college I never had a hot evening meal.

Classes began at 7 and ended at 9 p.m. I returned home about 10. Once again, mother would prepare a cup of hot chocolate and some cake for me. I did some of my homework in the subway and continued it upon returning home in the evening, sometimes until midnight. I did most of my homework on the weekend, all weekend. However, no matter how difficult the schedule, and despite the lack of a decent supper, I just loved college and the courses I was taking.

The classes at CCNY were co-ed, and most of my fellow students were very serious. In my first semester, I was the only foreign-born student and I spoke with a very heavy accent. But I was a very good student, and I asked most of the questions in my classes. I also frequently volunteered to answer the questions asked by our professors.

On September 3, 1948, I received a registration notice from the Selective Service System. I reported as required and registered for the draft. On October 29 I received a card classifying me as 1-A. In November, I was called for a medical examination. I was examined by three doctors, one of whom, I believe, was a psychologist. Although I had now been in the United States for more than two years, I was still very emaciated, pale, and weak, but I was really looking forward to serving in the army of my new country. To my shock and disappointment, I was now classified as 4-F, which meant that I was not eligible for the draft. I was quite embarrassed, and I shared this information only with my parents.

We celebrated the High Holidays that year by again attending Rabbi Friedman's service in the Paradise Theater. The first day of Rosh Hashanah fell on October 1. Uncle Irving and Aunt Ruthie came to visit us a few days before the holidays to wish us a happy and healthy new year.

Although I had little time or inclination for dating, I attended a couple of meetings at a house plan at City College. This was a social gathering where male and female students could meet. Sometimes there was dancing, but I was never much of a dancer. The girls I met were not very exciting, and I noticed that the American-born girls tended to keep away from the foreign-born male students. At one of these gatherings I met a fellow student named Julius Reiner, also a survivor. He agreed with my impression about American-born girls. We decided that these American-born girls, themselves the children of immigrants, were influenced by their parents' view that new immigrants were ignorant greenhorns.

I must admit that all my contacts were with Jewish girls. I felt strongly that if I were ever to marry, it would be with a Jewish girl. Not that I did not like non-Jewish girls, but my parents would have been heartbroken. At college I met some lovely Christian girls who would have made wonderful wives. After the Holocaust, however, in which a third of the world's Jewish population was annihilated, Jews couldn't afford to lose any more of their numbers. My friend Julius Reiner, who had lost his entire family in the Holocaust, was of the same opinion,

Hella was now going out with Sol Wexler every week, and on Saturdays they often went to the gatherings and dances at Hannington Hall. I preferred to spend my time with Harold Flender and his friends.

My father was acquainted with a Mr. Zalc, whom he had met in the DP camp in Austria. Mr. Zalc, who had lost his wife and children in the Holocaust, was brought to the United States by his sister, who had come to New York many years earlier. Mr. Zalc occasionally called my father and came to visit us. He was a very nervous person. I believe it was sometime around the end of November that he called to say that he had a fantastic business proposition. My father agreed to meet with him on the following Sunday afternoon.

Mr. Zalc arrived at the scheduled time and seemed very upbeat. My father and I sat down in our living room to listen to this fantastic business proposition. Zalc addressed my father formally as Herr Wenig. In his loud, high-pitched voice he said: "You were a rich and successful merchant in Poland, and now you work in a factory fifty weeks a year. I am coming to you now with a business proposition where you will work at most ten or twelve weeks a year and make a lot of money. The business I am talking about is buying and running a hotel in the Catskill Mountains in Sullivan County, upstate New York.

"The hotel business in the Catskills is a summer resort business. The season runs from the Memorial Day weekend until after the High Holidays. I have just been offered an opportunity to purchase the Oliver Country Club in

Woodbourne. We can get it for a song. It has more than a hundred rooms, a swimming pool, and a little forest behind the hotel building, and we can pick it up very cheaply for only $20,000."

My father asked why the owners were willing to sell the hotel for so little if it was really such a good business. Zalc responded that the owner was very ill and could no longer run the hotel. "The beautiful part of the deal," he said, "is that I know the hotel business. I owned a hotel in the Carpathian Mountains in Poland."

Zalc said that luck was really with us, because Rabbi Parneth wanted to become a partner. Rabbi Parneth had a large following in the Orthodox Jewish community in Manhattan and Brooklyn, and he would be able to fill the hotel to capacity with his followers during the summer season. My father asked Zalc about Rabbi Parneth. Zalc responded that he was a very distinguished and aristocratic rabbi who lived in Manhattan.

Father said he would have to think about whether he should go into the hotel business. One reason was that he did not have $5,000 for his share of the partnership and he would have to ask his brother to lend it to him. The other reason was that he had a friend, Marek Chasin, and he would like him to become a partner too. Chasin was a fellow Holocaust survivor and a good friend. More important, he was an interior decorator and had a large clientele of young people who would want to come to the hotel. If that was the case, Zalc said, he would have no objections to making Marek Chasin a partner.

Zalc said, "Wenig, I want you to know not only that I want to buy this hotel, but if this deal is a success, I plan to buy a whole string of hotels in the Catskills." Listening to Zalc, I grew a few inches taller. I saw myself as a future Hilton. At the same time I wondered whether he was for real or just living in a dreamland.

The meeting ended with my father promising to ask Uncle Irving about the money and Marek Chasin about the partnership. He said he would get back to Zalc in a few days. Zalc bid us goodbye and told Father, "Wenig, you're going to be a very rich man."

We were all very excited about the hotel, but I had my doubts. After Zalc left, my father told us that he had less than $2,000 in his savings account. The next day, he spoke to Uncle Irving about the hotel proposition, and Uncle Irving said he would give him $5,000 as gift. Uncle Irving was truly a beautiful person. That evening Father called Marek Chasin and outlined the proposition. Marek Chasin agreed on the spot, but he suggested that a meeting be arranged so that the prospective partners could get to know one other and discuss all the details. He added that we should arrange a visit to the hotel as soon as possible. My father telephoned Mr. Zalc with the news and arranged a meeting for the following Sunday morning at ten o'clock.

I had a lot of homework that weekend, in particular a great deal of reading for my philosophy course, but I decided to be present at the meeting. The three prospective partners arrived at the scheduled time to meet with Rabbi Parneth. He too was a Holocaust survivor. He was tall and distinguished looking with broad shoulders and a little goatee. He told us that he had a large following who would definitely come to the hotel if he recommended it, provided that the hotel was strictly kosher and employed a mashgiach to supervise the kitchen and the food purchases.

Mr. Zalc said that the hotel had a steady clientele and the present owners would give us a list of names, addresses, and telephone numbers. Marek Chasin commented that all that was fine, but one must not rely only on one set group of prospective guests. Chasin said that he had a large following of young singles whom he could persuade to spend their vacations at the hotel. He said that it was very important to have a mix of people. He suggested that we should place some beds and lounges in the forest behind the hotel building so that the single boys and girls could have a good time. Even Rabbi Parneth laughed, but he had no objections to the idea. I sat and listened to the conversation, but decided to mind my own business and not butt in.

The other part of the meeting dealt with the functions of each partner. Father knew absolutely nothing about the hotel business, but Zalc suggested that he could see to it that the physical aspects of the hotel were in good working order (the plumbing, electricity, kitchen equipment, lawn, swimming pool, etc.) and keep an eye on the employees to make sure they did their jobs properly.

Chasin said that as an interior decorator he would see to it that the hotel lobby was nicely decorated, the guest rooms properly painted, and the amenities in good order. He wanted to be the one to hire the orchestra for the summer, as well as the weekly entertainers.

Zalc said that he would oversee the kitchen and would hire the kitchen help, the waiters, the office help, the busboys, and the bellhops. Rabbi Parneth said that the only thing he could do was to bring the guests and mingle with them during their stay in the hotel. My father suggested that Mother and Mrs. Chasin could help out in the kitchen.

The four prospective partners arrived at this agreement that morning, but they wanted to visit the hotel before making a final decision. The four decided that Zalc should set up a visit as soon as possible. They wished each other good luck and agreed to meet again at the hotel.

Mr. Zalc made arrangements for the four of them to drive to Woodbourne the following Sunday to meet the sellers at the hotel. When father returned he said he was very impressed by what he had seen. He had always been a businessman, and he really believed that buying the hotel was a good idea. Father said that all four agreed that the purchase of the hotel was an excellent idea. Father brought along a number of colored postcards from the hotel and I must say that it looked good.

Uncle Irving gave my father the $5,000. Mr. Zalc's sister retained an attorney to do the closing. The lawyer suggested that the partners incorporate in order to avoid any personal liability, so they did, and the corporation bought the hotel. The closing took place in January 1950.

Although the Oliver Country Club was now a corporate entity, the four stockholders still called themselves partners. They met again in our apartment in mid-February. Mr. Zalc brought along the names and addresses of the hotel's former guests, as well as announcement cards he'd had printed. The partners decided that sometime in March or April my father would go to the hotel to see whether any damage had occurred during the winter. Since he had some understanding of plumbing, he would visit each and every room to check for leaks.

The list of former guests had several hundred names. The partners divided it up and sent them cards announcing that the hotel was under a new ownership. My father assigned me his share of the list, and I addressed the cards and mailed them out.

Zalc told the partners that he had persuaded the hotel's former chef to stay on. He had checked and she was a very good cook. He had also persuaded the bookkeeper-secretary to stay on. Marek Chasin announced that he had hired a salad chef with whom he was acquainted.

Zalc then turned to me. "Lusiek, why are you wasting your time in the jewelry factory? This is going to be a big business, we're going to own lots of hotels, and as a lawyer you could be an important officer in our corporation." Zalc urged me to work in the hotel as a busboy that summer. He said I would earn more than in the jewelry factory, especially with the tips I would be getting from the guests. I told him that I would think about it.

Around this time Hella became engaged to Sol Wexler, and their wedding was planned for the end of the year. My sister also landed a job as a bookkeeper in the office of the Zale jewelry company, which owned stores throughout the United States. I kept my job in the jewelry factory and continued at City College, but I gave serious thought to Mr. Zalc's idea that I should take an interest in the hotel, especially if his plans to buy several hotels came to fruition.

I finally decided that it made no sense to stay in the jewelry factory for only $18 a week. I'd make more at the hotel, and furthermore, since I had been working so hard for so long, I was entitled to spend the summer in the Catskills and breathe the pure country air. The idea of being a top executive in Zalc's hotel conglomerate was very appealing, but since the conglomerate did not yet exist, and anyway I had to learn the hotel business, I would start at the bottom as a busboy. I told my father of my decision, and asked him to tell the partners.

Around the end of March in 1950, my father went up to the hotel to make a thorough inspection, room by room. Sol Wexler accompanied him. Before long they called with a very bleak report. The hotel had apparently been flooded. There were broken, leaking water pipes everywhere; even the water tanks in many of the toilets were leaking. The walls and ceilings were peeling. Father was heartbroken: the hotel was supposed to open for business on the Memorial Day weekend, and it was flooded.

Obviously neither Mr. Zalc, who claimed to have owned a hotel in the Carpathians, nor any of the other three partners knew enough to hire an experienced professional to check out the plumbing, the electrical system, and the heating system, as well as each and every room, before they took title. During the one pre-purchase visit to the hotel, the partners were so impressed with the overall structure that they hadn't bothered with the particulars. The conniving sellers had shown them the few rooms that were in good condition.

Now the nascent hotel conglomerate was facing a serious problem. Did they have enough time or money to make all the necessary repairs before Memorial Day? My father called the others, told them the bad news, and asked them immediately come up to the hotel immediately. They went up the next day. After inspecting the damage, they hired a local contractor to get the place ready to open for business on Memorial Day weekend. Marek Chasin took the measurements for new drapes and new covers for the couches and sofas. They decided that father and Sol would remain at the hotel with the contractors until the work was completed.

I ended the spring semester with excellent grades. The partners and their families went up to the hotel a week before the crucial Memorial Day weekend, which was the official opening of the summer vacation season, and the repairs were completed just in time.

I told my employers that I would be taking off the two days before Memorial Day because I needed a long rest after the exhausting examinations I had just completed. I traveled to the hotel by bus, a hard, bumpy ride on two-lane Route 17 that took more than six hours. The bus stop was about two blocks from the hotel. I noticed a large sign on the left side on the road: "Welcome to The Oliver Country Club, Where Boy Meets Girl." The sign had been put up long before by the former owners. I wondered how it was going to strike the Orthodox crowd delivered by Rabbi Parneth.

This was my first visit to the hotel, and it was certainly an impressive building. As I walked into the lobby I saw my mother and Hella sitting on a sofa talking to Mrs. Chasin. They introduced me to Mrs. Parneth, Rabbi Parneth's wife, who was sitting nearby with her young son Tully. Mrs. Parneth was an attractive young woman with a blond sheytl (wig). Tully had a skullcap and long blond side curls on each side of his face. The partners' wives were all happy with the hotel and looking forward to a successful season.

The Oliver Country Club was strictly a summer resort. It did not have a golf course, tennis courts, or basketball or volleyball courts. The dining room was large, with nice tables and chairs. I walked into the big kitchen. All four partners were there along with my future brother-in-law, Sol, and some other people I didn't know. I was introduced to the chef and her two male assistants, and to Henry, the salad chef, who was also the maitre d'.

Henry was talking to some waiters and busboys, but he said, "Larry, wait here for a minute and I'll teach you how to carry plates away from the table on a tray and make a good busboy out of you." Henry picked up an empty tray, asked me to put some dishes on it, and showed me how to carry the tray filled with dishes. After a few loadings and unloadings, I learned how to pick up the tray, balance it on my hand, and walk with it loaded with dishes. I had acquired a new trade.

The waiters and busboys were all college students. Some of them had worked for the former owner, but most were new. There were also two bellhops.

The hotel was not completely filled for that first weekend, the Memorial Day weekend of 1950. Most of the guests had been there before, but there were also some of Marek Chasin's young singles, who spent the weekend hugging and kissing on the beds and lounges in the forest behind the hotel. The religious Orthodox followers of Rabbi Parneth did not come for the three-day weekend.

I believe that my performance as a busboy did not disappoint the guests, my waiter, or the partners. I did not tell the guests that I was the son of one of the owners. The waiter I worked with warned me to keep that information under my hat. If the people at my tables knew I was an owner's son, they probably would not tip me, or would give me only a small tip. I ended up that three-day Memorial Day weekend with over $20 in tips, which was more than the $18 I made in a week at the jewelry factory. In addition, I did not have to pay for the three huge meals I ate at the hotel every day.

The Memorial Day weekend was not as good as the owners had expected, but it was not a bad weekend either. The owners had hoped the hotel would be booked to capacity, but 80 percent was not so bad. The guests seemed to be quite satisfied with the food, the orchestra, and the two evening shows, which were excellent. Most of them assured the management that they would book their summer vacations at the hotel.

By late Monday afternoon the hotel was empty, and only the owners stayed around until the next day. One of the waiters drove Hella, Sol, and me home late Monday afternoon. He dropped Hella and me off at our building in the Bronx and then went on to Brooklyn, where he and Sol both lived.

On Tuesday morning, Hella and I went back to work as usual. When I picked up an English papers at the newsstand, a bold headline informed me about the trouble brewing on the Korean peninsula. Toward the end of World War II, the United States and the Soviet Union had agreed to maintain separate occupation zones in Korea. In the next few years the two parts of Korea grew apart. The Soviet Union sponsored a Communist state in the north, the People's Republic of Korea, headed by Kim Il Sung, who had spent many years in the Soviet Union and was an officer in the Red Army. In the south the United States sponsored free elections. Syngman Rhee, a conservative nationalist, won 80 percent of the votes and became President of the democratic Republic of Korea. Both states looked forward to the eventual reunification of the Korean peninsula.

The Communist victory in China and the first Soviet nuclear tests in 1949 resulted in a new U.S. policy of containment in Asia. The containment policy was to be primarily non-military, with economic and military aid given to non-communist Asian governments. On January 5, 1950, Secretary of State Dean Acheson, speaking at the National Press Club, named the countries the United States would defend with force against Communist aggression. He did not mention Korea.

Meanwhile, the last American occupation forces withdrew from South Korea. Certain that the United States would not intervene, Kim Il Sung decided to reunite North and South Korea by force. The Soviet Union led by Stalin and the Chinese led by Mao concurred with his judgment about the United States and his plans to unify the country by force. In June 1950, Kim's army struck.

Once again I began to worry about world events. I hoped and prayed that our government would take the Soviet threat seriously and prepare our people for the real challenges that lay ahead. I now had to worry not only about my job and school but about the menace posed by the upsurge of world communism. Most people went on with their daily lives, but my mind was tormented by the upcoming struggle with the communists on the European and Asiatic continents. When I spoke about the communist menace, people told me I was a perpetual worrier and pessimist. As it turned out, the history of the Cold War proved me to be right. My friends spent their time dating girls and going out to movies and dances. I, on the other hand, would spend whatever free time I had listening to news of world events. I scrutinized the Soviet tank production, and counted how many MiGs and Tupolov aircraft were manufactured annually. I studied maps, trying to deduce where the next conflict might arise.

In the middle of the last week of June 1950, I told my employers that I had to quit because my father had become a partner in the Oliver Country Club and wanted me to work there full-time. I apologized for not giving more notice, but explained that my father's partnership in the hotel was a last-minute deal. I showed them a postcard of the hotel and said goodbye.

Father, Mother, Hella, and I packed our summer things and set out for the hotel at the end of June. My parents and Hella checked into a room in the main building. I was assigned a room in one of the small houses where the hotel staff resided. I was to share my room with one of the waiters or busboys. The hotel had several such houses for the staff.

Mr. Zalc and Marek Chasin and his wife were already there. The staff began to arrive a couple of days later. In the days that followed we were busy every minute getting things ready. The partners gave full instructions to all the employees. The swimming pool was filled with water, and the lifeguard added the proper chemicals. The food supplies and linens began arriving daily. Father inspected the rooms every day to make sure there were no more leaks.

The bookkeeper and the secretary were in the office checking the reservations for the first weeks of July. I helped out in the office, even taking calls from prospective guests, some of whom booked vacations for two weeks. The partners were in touch with agents who booked shows for the summer season. I checked the playhouse, where the shows were to be held, going around with the electricians to make sure that the various lights, especially the stage lights, were all in good working order. The rooms for card players were readied. The grounds were made meticulous with neatly mowed grass and lovely flowers. I sat in with the partners when they discussed last-minute details. A meeting was held with the chef and the kitchen staff about the menu for the Fourth of July weekend. The maitre d' assigned tables to the guests who had made reservations for the Fourth of July weekend, those who made reservations for the entire week that included the Fourth of July, and those who made reservations for the two weeks including the Fourth. I couldn't help believing that the hotel would be a successful enterprise.

Guests began to check in on the first day of July. Most of them had been brought in by Rabbi Parneth, and they were very Orthodox, some with beards and side curls. They were both young and old. The other guests included former guests of the hotel and the young singles brought in by Marek Chasin. The hotel was almost filled to capacity for the Fourth of July weekend, which made the partners and me very happy.

The food was very good, but problems developed almost immediately. The mashgiach, the Orthodox supervisor who made sure that everything in the kitchen and the dining room was strictly kosher, would run into the kitchen and scream if he found a meat spoon next to a dairy spoon. He yelled at the waiters and the busboys in the dining room not to mix the utensils.

The shows were also very good. Most of them included a comedian and a singer. The guests liked the singer and the orchestra. Some of the songs were old-time Yiddish songs. Problems arose, however when the young people and the former guests got up to dance--ordinary ballroom dancing. The Orthodox guests complained that modern dancing and songs were not in conformity with the culture of Orthodox Judaism.

The Orthodox tried to shout down the orchestra, demanding that they stop playing modern dance tunes. The young people shouted for the orchestra to continue with the modern dance music. The Orthodox guests stormed out of the clubhouse in a rage. The young people angrily complained to the management. They stated that they would not put up with Orthodox restrictions. The friction brought about a crisis that management was unable to resolve. I could sense big trouble ahead. All of a sudden my dream of becoming a future Hilton began to fade away.

Meanwhile, one of the waiters told me that the store in the village that sold ice cream and sandwiches had a young waitress from Canada who, like me, was fluent in Yiddish, and he suggested that I should go meet her. I took the waiter's advice and walked over to the store, which was near the hotel. There were no customers, and I saw the Canadian waitress sitting all by herself reading a book.

I asked whether I could sit down with her. I introduced myself and told her that I was the son of one of the owners of the hotel. She put aside her book. We spoke Yiddish as well as English. She told me that her name was Nina and she was from Winnipeg. The city had just sustained a tremendous flood when the Red River overflowed its banks and flooded the entire city, so her parents had made arrangements for her to spend the summer with their cousins, who owned this store. She was the only waitress.

Nina was an attractive girl, about five feet two inches, with a very smooth face, dark eyes, and curly black hair, some of which curled down over her forehead. She was wearing a rather shabby beige dress. She told me that she was 18 years old and had just graduated from high school. I told her that I was a college student. She asked me about my interests, and I told her about my law school plans and my interest in world politics. I invited her to come hotel the next day and take a swim in our pool.

Nina came the following afternoon, as we had arranged, and swam for almost an hour. After she got out of the pool she sat down on one on the chairs around the pool. After some talk, I asked her for a date the following evening. I told her that I wanted to take her to a restaurant in the nearby hamlet of South Fallsburg.

I picked Nina up the next evening by taxi and we went to the restaurant. We had a complete three-course meat dinner, and returned to the hotel by taxi. I suggested to Nina that we sit for a while on one of the benches outside the hotel. After a few minutes of talk, Nina invited me to kiss her breasts. I was shocked, because nothing like this had ever happened to me before. At most on a first date, I might give the girl a kiss on the forehead or the hand. Nevertheless, I enjoyed very much kissing her nice breasts.

I couldn't help remembering, however, that when I was a young, religious boy in Dynów, we made blessings for everything we did. I remembered practically all the daily blessings in Hebrew. For instance, before I ate bread, or any food made of flour, I said the blessing for bread: Hamotzi lechem min ha'aretz

("Blessed art Thou, Lord our God, Ruler of the universe, who bringest forth food from the earth").

Another blessing I remembered was the one before eating food other than bread, food made from wheat, barley, rye, oats, or spelt: "Blessed art Thou, Lord our God, Ruler of the universe, who createst all kinds of food." The blessing before drinking wine was "Blessed art Thou, Lord our God, Ruler of the universe, who createst the fruit of the vine."

I don't recall whether I ever saw or read in any prayer book of a blessing one has to make before kissing a woman's breast. At this exciting moment, I thought that perhaps I should say the Hamotzi blessing while kissing Nina's breasts, but that would clearly have been improper since it is the blessing for anything made from flour. So I decided to create my own blessing for this moment of great pleasure. Therefore, at this blissful moment of kissing Nina's nice breasts, I composed a special blessing: "Blessed art Thou, Lord our God, Ruler of the universe, who created women's breasts in order for men to have the joy and pleasure of kissing them."

After this beautiful, pleasurable evening I walked Nina home and said goodnight by kissing her passionately on her lips. The following week, I asked Nina out on a date again. I told her that I wanted to take her to the movies in the local theater. Nina accepted, but did not sound that warm.

We went to see a movie about a woman ballet dancer, *The Red Shoes*. After the movie we walked over to her cousin's store for some ice cream. I ordered sundaes for both of us. I could tell from Nina's mood that something was not right. When we finished our ice cream, Nina said, "Larry, I am sorry about what I am about to tell you. I met a boy named Joey, who is very good-looking. He works as a waiter at the Aladdin Hotel, he is a college student, he owns a car, and he asked me to be his girlfriend. So I'm sorry, but I won't be able to see you any more." She continued, "Larry, I hate to tell you this, but you look so pale and your face is so emaciated that I feel you may be sick, so I can't be your girlfriend."

I was shocked and heartbroken. As I walked back to the hotel, I tried to analyze why Nina had broken off with me. The Aladdin hotel, where Nina's new boyfriend Joey worked, was much bigger and more modern than ours. Joey was a waiter, and I was only a busboy, and perhaps a waiter had more status than a busboy. The next thing that went through my mind was that I still looked emaciated and pale, and Joey was very handsome. Joey had a car, and I did not. Then something else went through my mind, something Nina had probably asked herself: "What kind of shmegegge is Larry? I asked him to kiss my breasts, and he stopped right there. Why didn't Larry keep on going to the lower and more pleasurable part of my body? There must be something wrong with him."

Of course I was disappointed that Nina had broken up with me, but at the same time I was not ready to ask any girl to be my steady girlfriend. At the end of the season, Nina went to New York City to stay with her aunt in Brooklyn until she could arrange a flight to Winnipeg. Joey invited her to his house to introduce her to his parents. After a long conversation, Joey's mother asked Nina when she was going back home. That was the end of the Nina/Joey relationship. I received that information from Nina's cousin who was the owner of the little restaurant where Nina had lived and worked as a waitress for the two summer months. Her cousin felt bad that Nina broke off with me. Her cousin liked me very much.

I continued to work as a busboy. The hotel was busy in its first season, but it was not difficult to see the evolving problems. There was a major conflict between the Orthodox and secular guests, especially the young singles. I did not think the hotel venture would last much longer. I decided that this was probably its first and last season. I would continue working there until the end of the summer and then return to New York City for good.

Like most of the hotels in the Catskills, our hotel closed up after the Labor Day weekend. We returned to the Bronx. My parents were still optimistic that the problems would straighten themselves out. I decided to look for another job, one that would be closer to home so that I would not have so much traveling between job, college, and home.

I looked at the want ads and found that K & B Jewelry Manufacturing Corporation was looking for experienced jewelry workers. It was located on 47th Street in Manhattan between Sixth and Seventh Avenues, much closer to my home and college. I responded to the ad and made an appointment for an interview.

K & B was a very big jewelry company that manufactured all kinds of gold rings. It had more than 30 employees, all of whom were members of the jewelry union. The initials K and B stood for Karlin and Bleicher. Karlin was Jewish, Bleicher was Christian.

I was offered a job as a filer of rings. A ring began its manufacture when melted gold was poured into a mold. After the ring cooled off, it was a raw ring. My job was to file the raw ring, both inside and out, to make it glossy and shiny. After that, the ring went to the stone-setting department where the ring was set with a diamond or some other precious stone. After the stone was set, the ring went to the polishing department, where it was polished.

I was interviewed by Bill Bleicher, the son of Mrs. Bleicher, one of the partners who owned the firm. Bill supervised the operations in the factory. Bill offered me a job at $35 a week, twice what I had made at L & D Jewelry. I accepted on the spot and began working almost immediately, and, of course, I joined the jewelry union.

The new semester commenced soon after Labor Day. I again signed up for a full schedule, five days a week. My courses were history, political science, and government. I was one of the most active students in my classes. The professors almost always called on me during the question-and-answer periods.

My father continued to work at the metal factory, but still had hopes for the hotel. The partners kept in constant touch with each other and talked enthusiastically about how good the next season would be. The only help I could render was to talk up the hotel to everyone I met. For this purpose I always carried along a few hotel postcards wherever I went.

Although I did most of my studying and homework on the weekend, I still sometimes found it necessary to take a leisurely walk in order to give my mind a little rest. One Sunday afternoon, I called Harold Flender and asked him to join me. Harold said I had called him at the right time, because he was just about to go to the Grand Concourse to meet a girl. We walked over together. On the way Harold told me that the girl we were meeting was named Lucille, and she was a philosophy tutor in the day session at CCNY. Harold explained that her title was tutor, but her academic rank was equivalent to assistant professor.

Harold introduced me to Lucille without mentioning her last name. The three of us walked side by side, with Lucille in the middle. She was a tall, attractive brunette, with dark eyes and thick black hair. She had a tiny nose and wore heavy, dark red lipstick. She was unusually bright and very intelligent. I had never before come across such a young faculty member at City College. Although she taught philosophy, she was also very well versed in history.

As we strolled, Lucille picked my brain about the Soviet Union, especially its present leaders. I tried to explain why communism was a total failure and would never work. I said that according to Marxist philosophy, the Communist leaders should be idealists working for the welfare of their people, but in reality they were cruel and evil monsters. Unfortunately many people in our country knew nothing about the evils of communism. I also spoke of my concern about the Korean war and about the possible conflict with the Soviet Union in Germany.

Although I very much enjoyed meeting Lucille, I gave up much too much of my time that Sunday, time I could not afford to take away from my studies. The following Tuesday evening the telephone rang in our apartment. Hella answered it and told me that a Lucille wanted to speak to me. I picked up the receiver and recognized Lucille's voice. After an exchange of pleasantries, Lucille said that she wanted to take me out on a date that coming Saturday. I was not only surprised, I was shocked. I had never heard of a girl calling a boy to ask him for a date. Of course I agreed. She asked me to meet her at seven at her apartment, and she gave me her address, which was near Mosholu Parkway in the Bronx. As I put down the telephone, I was aghast. I just could not believe that a girl who was a tutor at a college would call a mere undergraduate student and ask him for date. I put away my books, because I just could not study any more that evening. I told my family what had just happened. My mother said that she was very proud.

I felt obliged to tell Harold. I wasn't sure what his relationship with Lucille was, and I did not want to lose his friendship. Harold thanked me for calling and said that he already knew, because Lucille had called him to get my phone number. Harold assured me that Lucille was not his girlfriend. He was serious about Enid, who was now attending ballet school.

At seven on Saturday I rang the doorbell at Lucille's apartment, and she opened the door. I walked into the apartment and shook hands with her. She was dressed in a nice pink dress, a much nicer dress than she had worn the previous week. Lucille told me that her parents had gone to visit some of their relatives. I sat down in an armchair. She asked me about my week, and I told her about my usual activities, working at the jewelry factory and going to class in the evening. After some conversation, I asked Lucille whether she would like to see any particular movie that night. Lucille said that she was not interested in a movie, she just wanted to pick my brain. She suggested that we go for a stroll in the Grand Concourse and Fordham Road area, and then perhaps we would have a bite in some restaurant.

The Grand Concourse and Fordham Road area was the Times Square of the Bronx. I do not recall whether we took the bus or trolley car, but we arrived at the intersection of Grand Concourse and Fordham Road. The sidewalks were packed with people. In those days walking the Grand Concourse and Fordham Road was a major activity on Saturday and Sunday evenings. People did not yet have air-conditioners or televisions.

As we walked, Lucille and I discussed Spinoza and Kant. We also discussed the war in Korea. I brought up the subject of Israel. I told Lucille of my disappointment that American Jewry had done absolutely nothing to help save the Jews of Europe during the Holocaust. It was imperative now to make sure that Israel survived as a Jewish state. I told her about my experiences with the Muslims in Uzbekistan and about the hatred Muslims have for Christians and Jews. Lucille admitted that she was very surprised to hear that the Koran preached hatred against people of other religions.

Lucille then said bluntly that she was very interested in getting married. She continued that the man she wanted to marry must be well educated and intelligent. I told Lucille that at this stage in my life, when I was still at college and looking forward to a few more years of law school, I could not contemplate marriage. I could not make out whether Lucille meant to marry me, or was just making a general statement about wanting to get married.

After the end of our discussion of marriage, I suggested that we go to a nearby restaurant. Lucille said that she had already eaten supper, and would be just as happy to have some ice cream. We walked over to the famous Krum's ice cream store for the usual sundae. I must admit that Lucille was the type of girl I would have wanted to marry if marriage had not been out of the question at this time of my life. We rode back to Lucille's apartment. I dropped her off at the door of her apartment, and I bade her good night with a kiss on the forehead.

I did quite a great deal of thinking as I rode back home. Here was a girl with whom I had quite a bit in common, yet my circumstances were such that I could not undertake a serious relationship. I had great respect for Lucille, and I felt that it would be wrong for me to waste her time by dating her just for the pleasure of her company on a weekend night.

Harold called me early Sunday morning and asked about our date. I told him exactly what Lucille had told me. Harold said, "Larry, I think Lucille wants to marry you. Are you ready to marry Lucille?" I responded, "I am not ready to get married for another few years." Harold continued, "Larry, I think you are making a mistake, because Lucille is the type of girl you would want to marry." That ended another chapter in my life. I was somehow in that Hamlet-like dilemma, "To be, or not to be." My life was just in a continuous turmoil.

One Saturday evening in the fall I decided to make my first visit to Hannington Hall, the place where unmarried young Holocaust survivors would meet to socialize and dance on Saturday nights.

I arrived there rather late that evening. The place was packed, and the musicians were playing dance tunes of all kinds, including the cha-cha and the samba, dances that were not familiar to me. I walked around the packed hall and recognized only a few of the people I had met the year before at the Hotel Marseille.

Most of the people there spoke very little English, and very few of them were attending school. The languages I heard were Yiddish, Polish, Hungarian, and German. The hall was supposed to be a place where young people met and did some dancing, but I did not do any dancing that Saturday evening--my mission was to talk up the Oliver Country Club and line up prospective guests for the summer. I introduced myself to some of the people and handed out the large, colorful business cards that showed the hotel to great advantage. Many of them were impressed with the pictures and indicated that they might be interested. Some of the boys who saw the cards asked whether I had a sister. They obviously wanted to meet the daughter of a rich hotel owner. I made sure to mention that lots of young single people came to the hotel. I also mentioned that since the owners of the hotel were Holocaust survivors, they would make special accommodations for other Holocaust survivors. They might even put on special shows and entertainment of interest to survivors.

I met some nice, good-looking girls at Hannington Hall. Few of them were attending school, but all of them were looking for someone to marry. As I have already stated, I was not interested in marriage at that time. I do not want to leave the impression that I am snobbish. I was only interested in occasional casual dates with girls who had intellectual interests similar to mine. I did not meet any such girls in the dancing establishment that evening.

On the job at K & B I developed very friendly relationship with my co-workers. The foreman, whose name I no longer recall, took a liking to me. He liked my political views and my hatred of the Soviet Union and world communism. Our nation was now engaged in a war against communism in Korea. Many of our young men had been drafted, yet I, who would have been happy to volunteer in that fight, had been classified 4F. This was a source of some bitterness to me.

On December 3, 1950, Hella and Sol Wexler got married in Rabbi Friedman's wedding hall above the Paradise Theater. All our relatives and friends and all Sol's family and friends were invited. It was the first time in my life that I rented a tuxedo. The ceremony was very nice, and I did some dancing at the wedding. Hella moved out, and she and Sol rented an apartment nearby, on Walton Avenue.

I ended up the fall semester of 1950 with very good grades again, and registered immediately for the spring semester of 1951. My father and the hotel partners met constantly throughout the spring. Most of the meetings took place on Sundays in our apartment. The partners really believed that the hotel would one day be a success. I kept out of it. I knew by now that the enterprise was doomed; there was no way you could mix the religious, Orthodox crowd with the secular crowd, especially the young singles.

The hotel opened again for the Memorial Day weekend, and then for the summer season on July 4th. I came up for only one weekend to see my parents. The hotel was far from fully occupied that summer. The partners ended up with a tiny profit for the 1951 season. But all of them, and especially Mr. Zalc, still saw a very good future in the hotel.

At the end of the fall semester in 1951, again with very good grades, I had completed the necessary courses and credits to apply to Brooklyn Law School. I was accepted for the evening session, and began my first semester on February 4, 1952.

The law school was located on Joralemon Street in Brooklyn, which created a difficult transit problem for me. Our apartment was at the far end of the Bronx. I had to travel early in the morning to the jewelry factory on 47th Street in Manhattan. I left work at 5 p.m. and took the D train to the West 4th Street station in Manhattan; there I transferred to the A train and took it to the Borough Hall subway station in Brooklyn, which was near the law school. Classes began at seven and ended at 9 p.m.

To return home, I took the A train at Borough Hall to West 4th Street where I took the D train to Fordham Road. The trip home took almost one and a half hours. I usually arrived home after 10:30 p.m. I did some of my homework on the long subway ride and continued to do my homework after I arrived home until after midnight, and of course throughout the weekend.

During my attendance at Brooklyn Law School, as was true also of my years at City College and before that in high school, I never had the pleasure of a decent hot meal on weeknights. My supper consisted of a sandwich and some fruit that mother prepared for me every morning. I kept my supper sandwich in the refrigerator at the jewelry factory. The only hot item on those five work/school days was a container of coffee purchased on the way to school.

Life was not easy for me, but I was determined and I persevered in order to achieve my goal. I wanted to prove to everyone--my family, my landsmen, everyone who kept telling me that I was wasting my time and would never make it--that they were wrong. The school experience steeled me for later life. I learned that if I made a decision to do something and pursued it vigorously, I would attain my goal. Life, after all, is a struggle from the day we are born. Some of us, when we meet difficulties in pursuing our goal, give up easily. My life experience taught me that if you persevere, you can achieve your goal.

My law school classmates were of various ages. Some were younger than I, and some older. One student, Charlie, was a grandfather. Many were married, others were single. Most of them already had a profession. Quite a few of my classmates were CPAs. Some were insurance brokers or real estate brokers. Most of them owned their own businesses. I believe that we even had a couple of high school teachers. A couple of students had been in some of the classes at City College. The bulk of the students were men, but there were a few girls. There was even one Israeli student, whose name was Simcha Mandelbaum. I was the only student working on a jewelry bench.

I had very little social life while at law school. I simply had no time to socialize. If I dated, it was only occasionally on a Saturday night. While in law school I was introduced to a couple of girls. One of them was a Laurie from Manhattan, and the other, a Rita, from Brooklyn.

As much as I had to concentrate on law school, which after all was my lifelong dream, the world political situation absorbed a great deal of my attention. On March 5, 1953, the media trumpeted the news that the evil, ruthless barbarian Stalin had died. In my school days in the Soviet Union, our teachers taught us that Stalin was the Otets Narodov ("Father of All Peoples") and Genii Mira ("World Genius"). Ordinarily, we feel sad when someone dies. By nature I am a warm and compassionate person. But when Stalin died I felt a sense of relief, and I said to myself, too bad he lived so long.

Law school was much harder than college. Although my English had greatly improved, I came across many words in my law books that I did not know, and I had to make frequent use of my Polish dictionary. My teachers were real legal scholars. One of them, Professor Glasser, was a federal judge. I had to take advantage of every minute of the day. I even studied my law books in the jewelry factory while eating my lunch sandwich at my bench. Occasionally some of the workers in the factory would come to discuss their legal problems with me.

Chapter 7

SELMA

One Saturday in August 1953, my sister Hella invited me over for lunch. As we sat at the table, I was struck by a photograph on a nearby table. It showed two couples, Hella and Sol, and next to them Sol's best friend, Morris Siegelstein, and a beautiful girl. I picked up the photograph, and on the back it stated that it had been taken at Zimmerman's Hungarian nightclub in midtown Manhattan. I held up the photograph and took a closer look at the beautiful girl. There was something about her that attracted me very strongly. I once read about profile psychology. It is not an exact science, but it suggests that one can tell something about another person just by looking at his or her face. Supposedly, intelligence agencies use profile psychology to analyze people they have an interest in.

Hella asked what interested me about the photograph. I told her that I was looking at a girl I would like to meet. My sister said, "Selma will never go out with you!" There were several reasons why she responded this way. First, she was my stepsister, and she treated me like a stepbrother. Also, she knew that Morris Siegelstein was her husband's best friend, and she did not want to upset her husband. Finally, my sister was a jealous person and probably did not want to have competition.

I am by nature very determined and persevering. If I want something, I will pursue and get it. At that moment, all I knew about this girl was that she had a beautiful face and her name was Selma. I put the photograph down and deliberately changed the subject in order to throw my sister off the track. After a few minutes of gabbing, I asked, "Is this girl a Polish refugee?" Hella responded, "No, Selma is an American; her parents are Hungarian Jews, and their last name is Werber."

Now I had before me the picture of a girl named Selma Werber. I needed one more piece of information, namely, the borough of New York City where

Selma Werber lived. I again changed the subject in order to keep my sister in the dark. I gabbed a little more and then I said, "Hella, I don't date very much because I am so busy studying. As you know, I have never gone out on a double date, and I've been wondering, if you double date, like you did this time with Morris, did you meet at your house or at the girl's house or at the night club?" Hella responded, "I live in the Bronx, and Selma lives in Long Island City, so we met at the night club."

I now had all the information I needed. I thanked my sister for the lunch, and I ran to the nearest candy store on Jerome Avenue, where I knew there was a coin telephone and telephone books for all five boroughs. I took out the directory for Queens. My hand was trembling as I flipped the pages until I got to the W's. I located three listings under Werber. The first Werber name looked right because of the address.

I wrote down the phone number and address on a piece of paper. I paused for a few seconds, in order to decide what to do and what I could say to Selma. I had learned in American history about a famous Civil War general who said that to win, "Git thar fustest with the mostest."

I dialed the number, and a young female voice answered. "Hello," I said, "I would like to speak to Selma Werber?" The sweet female voice answered, "I am Selma Werber." My heart was pumping very fast, and I said, "Let me tell you why I am calling you. My name is Larry and I am the brother of Hella Wexler. Hella invited me to her house for lunch today, because my parents are away at the hotel they own in the Catskill Mountains. The reason that I am not with my parents at their hotel is because I am attending law school." I continued, "As I was eating lunch, Hella showed me a photograph of you both at Zimmerman's Hungarian night club, and Hella said to me, 'Larry,' pointing her finger at your picture, 'it would mean an awful lot to me if you would take this girl out on a date.' Hella gave me your name, your address, and your telephone number, and that is why I am calling you."

I continued, "Selma, I would like to take you out next Saturday evening to Lewisohn Stadium to a concert by José Greco." Selma responded, "I will gladly go out with you to the José Greco concert." I told Selma that the concert started at seven, and I would pick her up before six. I asked Selma how to get to her house by subway, and she gave me all the train information. "I am looking forward to seeing you next Saturday," I said.

Here is what I did to impress Selma. I told her that my parents owned a hotel in the Catskills. Selma probably thought to herself, "I am being asked for a date by the son of the owner of a hotel." I mentioned that I was going to law school. Selma probably thought to herself, "I am being asked for a date by a future lawyer." And, even though it was not true, I told her that my sister had asked me to take her out on a date. That's what our famous Civil War general meant by "fustest with the mostest."

I felt very good as I boarded the train to Lewisohn Stadium in Manhattan to get two tickets for the José Greco concert. Of course I didn't mention anything to anyone about my date with Selma.

The next Saturday I took the Jerome Avenue IRT to Grand Central Station in Manhattan and changed downstairs for the Flushing line to Sunnyside, Queens, where I got off at the Lowery station. This was the first time I had ever been in Queens. I walked about two blocks to reach Selma's house, which was located on 41st Street. Selma's parents were tenants in a two-family house and they lived on the second floor.

I rang the Werbers' doorbell, and after I identified myself, the door was opened. I walked upstairs, and Selma opened the door of the Werbers' apartment. She was a stunning beauty, even prettier than the photograph. She was dressed in a beautiful blue dress with white circles in the blue material. She had beautiful tiny dark brown eyes. Her lovely face was smooth as alabaster and surrounded by beautiful curly black hair. She was the most beautiful girl I had ever dated. She was there alone. She told me that her parents were on a trip to California, and her older sister was now on her honeymoon somewhere in one of the Western states. Her younger brother was also away. I was stunned just to see her.

Looking at her face I could tell that she was an entirely different American Jewish girl. I mentioned earlier that American Jewish girls born to immigrant parents tended to look down on new immigrants. Their parents considered themselves superior, smarter than the newcomers to America. Some of them, I found, were really quite ignorant. They simply had a superiority complex because they had arrived in America many years earlier. Their children, though, were influenced by this mentality, and considered new immigrants to be people of a lower order, "Greenhorns."

Speaking to Selma on the train, I could see that she was not that type of person. I asked whether she was bothered by my heavy accent. She responded that it did not bother her at all. She also told me she had friends who were newly arrived immigrants, both boys and girls. Considering that she was physically so beautiful, she was not conceited at all. I had met many good-looking girls who were conceited simply because of their good looks.

Selma was also a very warm person. She told me that she was a teacher and taught at a nearby public school.

We arrived at Lewisohn stadium a few minutes before the program began. José Greco was magnificent. And as a bonus, there was a performance of part of the Swan Lake ballet. Throughout the entire show, I held hands with Selma, which I had never done with any girl on a first date. From time to time I looked directly into Selma's eyes, because I was so attracted to her. I want to emphasize that it was not so much her very good looks, but her nice personality, and her good, compassionate heart that attracted me. I fell in love with Selma that evening, and resolved to marry her.

After the concert I took Selma home. When we turned onto 41st Street, we noticed a middle-aged man on the same sidewalk, weaving back and forth and obviously drunk. I was very concerned about Selma's safety, because her family was out of town. We walked upstairs to her apartment and Selma opened the door. I wanted to show her respect because she was alone, so I decided not to go in with her. In the doorway I asked her to double-lock the door because of the drunk outside on the street. I told her that I had enjoyed very much being with her that night. I kissed her on the forehead, and said good night.

On the subway returning home, I could not stop thinking about Selma. She had stolen my heart, and I was determined to marry her. When I got home, I woke up Bernie Berger, a friend from City College who was spending the night with us. I told Bernie that I had been out on a blind date, and I had fallen in love with the girl and decided to marry her. Bernie said, "Larry, are you out of your mind? You take out a girl for the first time, and you fall in love with her, and you decide to marry her?" I nodded that this was indeed so. Bernie continued, "I've never heard of anything like it. How much do you know about her from one date? Please control yourself, and take some time to learn more about this girl." I did not respond, because my mind was made up. I was going to marry Selma.

The next morning I called her. "Selma, I am just calling to find out whether you're safe, because I was concerned about the drunk on your street last night." Selma thanked me for calling and showing concern about her safety. I then said goodbye, without saying anything else to her.

I decided not to mention anything to anyone about Selma. As much as I wanted to see her the following week, I decided not to call and ask her for a date. As I've said before, it's a good policy for men not to show the girl that you are so anxious to see her right away. It's better to let her wonder whether you are interested. I must admit that it was very difficult not to be with Selma that week.

A week later, on Tuesday evening, I called Selma. Her mother answered, and I identified myself and asked how she had liked her California trip, and how she and her husband felt after such a long trip. I then asked to speak to Selma. She got on, and after a short conversation I asked her for a date for the coming Saturday night, and she accepted.

I rang the bell at the Werber residence that Saturday evening. Selma opened the door and let me in. She introduced me to her parents. I sat down on one of the upholstered chairs and asked Selma to sit next to me. Selma was again dressed in a very nice pink dress. We all started to converse, and here is what I learned about the Werber family: Sol Werber had come to the United States from Hungary many years before. His first job in New York was driving a taxi. He met Selma's mother at a meeting of the Hungarian Jewish landsmanshaften society. Selma's mother's parents had come from Hungary, and Selma's mother had been born in New York. Selma's mother was a very warm person, and she regularly deferred to her husband, who had a loud voice and was very opinionated. I got the impression on the first meeting that Selma's mother was afraid of her husband. She never contradicted him and she spoke very little. Selma's mother probably had an inferiority complex, although she was better educated than her husband. On the other hand, Selma's father, despite his limited education, had a superiority complex. After their marriage they went into the grocery business in a store on Second Avenue near 28th Street. They had lived at first in a walkup apartment above the grocery store.

Selma's parents--or perhaps I should say Selma's father--asked me about my job and my school and about my family's hotel in the Catskills. At this point Selma asked her mother to help her insert earrings into her pierced ears. Her mother was very clumsy at this, and Selma screamed, "Ouch, mother, you're hurting me!" I then intervened and said, "Mrs. Werber, please let me do it, because I don't want you to hurt Selma." I indeed was successful in putting in Selma's earrings without hurting her. I think that my gesture made a very good impression on Selma's parents.

I took Selma to a neighborhood movie that night. This was my second date with her, and because I couldn't help it, I kissed her several times that night in the movie house. After the movie I took Selma to a nearby Greek seafood restaurant.

When we returned home to Selma's apartment, her parents were already asleep. We sat down on the couch and embraced each other, and I knew this was it, that Selma would be my wife. From then on I dated Selma every Saturday night. I was very aware of how much in love I was with Selma, and I treated her with great respect and behaved toward her as a true gentleman.

My parents returned from the hotel, now closed for the winter, after the Labor Day weekend of 1953. They told me that it had not been a very good season, but they still felt that business would get better. I said nothing at all about Selma.

However, as my romance with Selma grew stronger and stronger, along with my determination to marry her, I realized that I would have to let my parents in on what was happening. Selma's birthday was coming up on December 28, and I decided that it would be the perfect occasion to propose to her. Therefore, I decided to invite Selma before then to meet my parents.

I had already mentioned to Selma that my parents kept a kosher home, and that we observed the Sabbath and all the Jewish holidays as holy. Friday evenings we always had a real Sabbath dinner, with gefilte fish, chicken soup, chicken, flanken, and cakes and tea.

I decided to invite Selma to meet my parents for a Friday night dinner in the middle of December, 1953. Only after she accepted the invitation did I tell my parents that I was dating a girl and had invited her to have dinner with us that Friday night. I didn't tell my parents anything about her or even her name, and I asked them to invite Hella and Sol, and just to tell them that I was bringing a girl to dinner.

Friday night arrived. Selma was more beautiful than ever. When I introduced her to my parents, a big smile came over my mother's face. We walked into our large, sunken living room, part of which also served as a dining room. The table was covered with a pure white linen tablecloth and was very nicely set as usual. Two upholstered chairs were on either side of the table, and a similar chair was at each end. In front of each chair was a large white porcelain plate with a small white porcelain plate resting on it. At the end of the table was a very nicely embroidered challah cloth, under which were a round challah and a braided challah. Behind the challahs were two tall silver Sabbath candlesticks, each one holding a large candle.

The four of us sat down in the other part of the living room and chatted for a while. Selma had only a very vague knowledge of Yiddish. She knew just a few Yiddish words, and my parents knew just a few English words, so I had to do some interpreting. After a few minutes, the doorbell rang, and mother opened the door. Hella and Sol walked in. When Hella saw Selma, her face almost turned green. Sol's face was ashen. Mother introduced Selma to Hella and Sol as Larry's girlfriend. She had no idea that Hella and Sol already knew her.

As I have already mentioned, I first saw Selma's picture in Hella's apartment. When I told Hella I wanted to meet her, she said that Selma would never go out with me, so I had obtained Selma's last name and address by clever trickery. Hella was a jealous person, and obviously did not want me to meet such a nice girl. Moreover, she knew that Selma had gone out a couple of times with Morris Siegelstein, Sol's best friend. And of course, like the other members of the family, she regarded me as a stepbrother, not a real brother. Like many other members of my father's family, she didn't feel that I was truly kin, but only a stepson, only a stepbrother. I felt this hurt very deeply, because I could not say or do anything about it. It was a major element in the turmoil of my life. My good mother felt my hurt and she tried to make it up to me by giving me her special attention

Mother asked us to take our seats. My father sat down at the head of the table and my mother at the foot. Hella and Sol sat on one side of the table, and Selma and I on the other side, facing them. Mother lit the two candles. Moving her hands in a circle three times in front of the candles, she intoned the usual Friday night prayer.

Father poured kosher Manishevitz wine into the glasses in front of our plates. We all stood up, and father lifted his wine glass and intoned the Kiddush over the wine. After father finished, I too lifted my wine glass and recited the same Kiddush. Then father said the Hamotzi blessing over the challah. He sliced it and gave each of us a piece.

Mother served the usual Friday night dinner, and we ended the meal with delicious cake she had baked. Our Friday celebration on that Sabbath made a very fine impression on Selma. After dinner, she insisted on helping my mother clear the table and also wash the dishes. In the kitchen Selma and my mother carried on a conversation somehow, in mixed English and Yiddish.

Selma made a very good impression on my parents. My mother whispered into my ear that she liked her very much. Selma thanked my parents for the invitation and the good Sabbath dinner, and said good night.

I took Selma home by subway. When we got there, her parents were already in bed. As Selma and I sat down on the couch, there were twinkles in our eyes. I was more convinced than ever that Selma would be my wife. As

I sat there, hugging and kissing her, I wondered whether I should propose marriage to her at that moment. Then I hesitated, reasoning with myself that perhaps I should give Selma a chance to tell her parents about the evening at my parent's apartment.

I returned home quite late, but my parents were still up. Mother said that she had really liked Selma, and she was definitely the girl for me.

I went to bed, but instead of sleeping, I started to plan when and how to propose to Selma. I knew that her birthday was coming up in a few weeks, and I decided that would be the right time to pop the question.

I telephoned Selma and told her that I would be taking her out on December 28 to the Copacabana nightclub to celebrate her birthday.

I walked into Selma's house the evening of December 28, 1953, dressed in a new suit and carrying a box which contained a large orchid. Selma was dressed in a very beautiful dress with a flowing skirt. I kissed her on the forehead. I took out the orchid and pinned it on her dress, wishing her a happy birthday. I also kissed her mother, and we left her house.

I had reserved a table at the Copacabana nightclub. Once we were seated, the club photographer took a picture of us, delivering the photograph within the hour. We ordered drinks, and a large chocolate cake with candles was placed before us. The writing on the cake said, "Happy Birthday Dear Selma." Several waiters came over. One of them lit the candles, and all of them sang "Happy birthday, dear Selma," accompanied by three musicians who had joined them. I kissed and hugged Selma. That was the moment when I proposed, and Selma said yes. A few minutes later we telephoned our respective parents to tell them that we had become engaged. At this moment I felt so good that all my worries about Israel and all my personal worries flew out of my mind.

When I got home, my parents were sitting in the living room waiting for me. I told them how happy I was that Selma had agreed to marry me. My mother embraced and kissed me. She told me that she had been waiting for this for a long time. My mother and my stepfather both liked Selma very much. We had many things to discuss, but we decided to wait until the next day, as the hour was late.

The next morning, my father called Uncle Irving. My father and mother spoke to both Irving and Ruthie, informing them about my engagement to a very fine American girl named Selma. They were both delighted by the good news and offered me their warmest congratulations.

The day was December 29, and I returned to work at the jewelry factory. I was now on my winter break from law school, so I went directly home after work. When I got there, my mother told me that Aunt Ruthie had called and proposed that we have an engagement party at our apartment in about two weeks, which would be in the middle of January. Father returned home a bit later, and he said that he had discussed my engagement with Uncle Irving.

After supper we began planning the engagement party. First we talked about contacting one of the jewelers Father knew on 47th Street, the diamond district in Manhattan, and purchasing a diamond engagement ring. We discussed our finances. I had less than $500 in my savings account, and my father had about $2,000 in his. We knew that the bride's parents traditionally arranged and paid for the wedding, and the groom's parents paid for the orchestra, the flowers, and the liquor. The total amount of cash in our savings bank was less than $2,500, which could pay for only a small part of the engagement ring and the wedding.

The other problem that came up was my jewelry job, which gave me a weekly salary of only $45. And I still had two and half more years of law school ahead.

Next we discussed the question of where Selma and I would live. In 1954 it was very difficult to obtain an apartment in a rent-controlled building. The last item on our agenda was where I would get the money for a honeymoon.

Father said that he would speak to Uncle Irving about the expenses of the wedding. He advised me to leave my job in the jewelry factory and get a new job that would pay enough to support Selma. A thought went through my mind: why not approach Harry Stelzer, our landsman from Dynów? Harry Stelzer was supposedly the biggest ladies' belt manufacturer in New York. Father agreed that it would indeed be a good idea to see if he could offer me a job.

We set the date for the engagement party as the Sunday after the following Sunday. I telephoned my future in-laws and introduced my parents to them over the phone. My mother told them about the engagement party and asked whether the date we had chosen was all right. It was. Selma's parents told my mother that they wanted to bring along their older, married daughter, Dorothy, and her husband, Abe. They added that their son, Seymour, would not be there because he was in the army, stationed in Germany. My mother and Selma's parents ended their conversation by wishing each other mazal tov, which is Hebrew for "good luck."

The same evening my father telephoned his diamond merchant friend.

He asked whether we could come to his place of business the following afternoon and purchase a ring. The friend was agreeable. The diamond merchant's office was located about a block away from the place where I worked.

I met my father at the diamond merchant's office the next afternoon. He told me that he had discussed our monetary problems with Uncle Irving, and Irving had agreed to share some of the wedding expenses.

The diamond merchant, whose name I don't recall, opened his vault and took out a tray with diamonds of all shapes and sizes. We looked at the many diamonds, and we liked each and every one of them. The diamond merchant, who knew father very well, asked, "Yoshu, how much are you willing to spend for a diamond engagement ring?" Father responded that he was willing to spend up to $1,000. The diamond merchant picked a nicely cut diamond, more than one carat in size and a nice blue color. The price of the diamond set in a platinum ring was $850. The diamond merchant, who also resided in the Bronx, told us that he would bring it to our house one evening that week.

I took $200 out of my savings account and gave it to my father toward the payment for the ring. It was delivered in the evening a few days later by the diamond merchant, and my father gave him $850. To my eyes the engagement ring looked very sparkly and very nice.

I took Selma out that Saturday evening to a local restaurant near her house in order to discuss the engagement party and our wedding plans. I didn't mention a word to her about the ring. I told her that we had invited Uncle Irving and Aunt Ruthie to the party, as well as their sons, Norman and Jerry, and their wives, Delores and Renee.

I told Selma that my law school semester would end in May, making the middle of June a good time for our wedding. Selma's beautiful face was beaming, and she said that her semester as a teacher would end at the beginning of June, so mid-June would indeed be a good time.

I also explained the hardships she would have to endure while I was still attending law school over the next two years. Selma responded that she was willing to endure it. I also explained that my jewelry job paid only $45 a week, which was not enough to support her in a decent life-style for the next two years. Selma told me not to be concerned, because she would be working full-time as a teacher and getting a good salary. I continued that by June I might have less than $1,000 in my savings account. Selma responded that she had some money in the bank, and expected to get a nice monetary wedding gift from her parents. I said that I too expected some nice monetary gifts from some of the people my parents were inviting to our wedding. I also told her that we should not have a problem getting a rent-controlled apartment, as my uncle's building manager handled many buildings in the Bronx and would be able to get us one.

I was relieved and happy that Selma was so understanding, so practical, and not at all demanding. I grabbed her face with both hands and kissed her uncontrollably in the restaurant.

I walked Selma home from the restaurant on that cold, wintry Saturday night. I didn't stay long, and returned home as usual on the elevated subway.

I woke up my parents when I got home to tell them how sweet and understanding Selma was. Father told me that he would call Harry Stelzer and set up an appointment for me. Mother told me that she and Aunt Ruthie had been planning the menu for the engagement party.

I didn't say a word to my coworkers about my engagement. She was a beautiful and very fine girl, but many of them routinely used foul language and spoke disrespectfully about women. I certainly had no intention of bringing Selma to the jewelry factory and introducing her to any of the lowlifes there.

Plate 1: This is the picture I saw in my sister Hella's apartment. It was taken in Zimmerman's Hungarian Nightclub in Manhattan. From left to right: Morris Siegelstein (a friend of Hella's husband, who was on a date with Selma that night), Selma, Hella and her husband, Sol. c. 1953

Plate 2: Our wedding picture. June 13, 1954

Plate 3: Wedding picture, l. to r. - Selma's father, her mother, Selma, me, my mother and my father.

Plate 4: Wedding picture, l. to r. - Sol, Hella, Selma, me, my mother and father.

Plate 5: center - My uncle Irving with his sons, my cousins Jerry (l.) and Norman.

Plate 6: Aunt Ruthie, my uncle Irving's wife.

Good grandchildren and students:

Plate 7: Phyllis (my daughter) and Albert's children, Matthew, Michelle and Elena.

Plate 8: Alan (my son) and Debra's children, Alex and Arielle.

Plate 9: A meeting of the board of the North Shore Zionist district where I was President. Selma and I are in the center.

Plate 10: The Israeli Day Parade in Manhattan. I am in the center, holding the banner.

Plate 11: The Israeli Day Parade in Manhattan. I am on the right, holding the banner.

Plate 12: Addressing the Brandeis Award Dinner, and thanking them for bestowing upon Selma and me the prestigious Justice Louis Brandeis Award.

THE LONG ISLAND REGION
ZIONIST ORGANIZATION OF AMERICA

cordially invites you to attend the

BRANDEIS AWARD DINNER

honoring

LARRY and SELMA WENIG

SUNDAY, MAY 4th, 1986, 7:00 p.m.
TEMPLE BETH SHOLOM
OSLYN ROAD, ROSLYN HEIGHTS, NEW YORK

Guest Artist

MISHA RAITZIN

"The Golden Voice of His People"

nternationally Acclaimed Metropolitan Opera Tenor
Soviet Jewish Emigre to Israel

uvert $150. per person

Kindly respond

Plate 13 & 14: The invitation to the dinner and the Brandeis statue.

Plate 14: With the defense Minister of Israel, Ariel Sharon, at the Zionist Convention in Jerusalem.

Plate 15: Headline in Egyptian government-owned newspaper, Al-Akhbar.

THE NEW YORK TIMES, WEDNESDAY, MAY

The Big Lie Is Still Aliv

"Thanks to Hitler, of blessed memory, who, on behalf of the Palestinians, revenged in advance against the most vile criminals on the face of the earth. Although we do have a complaint against him for his revenge on them was not enough."

– *Al-Akhbar*, Egyptian government-sponsored newspaper, April 18, 2001*

THE WHITE HOUSE
WASHINGTON

July 30, 2003

Mr. Larry Wenig
Number 1606
2450 Presidential Way
West Palm Beach, Florida 33401-1329

Dear Mr. Wenig:

Thank you for your kind words and the materials you sent. I appreciate your concerns and welcome your suggestions.

During this time of great consequence, I am grateful for your support as my Administration continues to reform domestic programs, secure our homeland, and work to create opportunities for all Americans. Again, thank you for taking the time to write.

Sincerely,

George W. Bush

Plate 16: Response from President Bush for my letter addressing my dismay at our allies who did not join us in the war against Sadaam Hussein in Iraq. He also thanks me for a copy of my book, *From Nazi Inferno to Soviet Hell.*

THE SECRETARY OF STATE
WASHINGTON

April 30, 2001

Dear Mr. Wenig:

Thank you for your thoughtful letter and for the copy of your book, *From Nazi Inferno to Soviet Hell*. I regret that the first copy you sent was not received during the transition period. I look forward to reading your book at the earliest opportunity.

Thank you for thinking of me.

Sincerely,

Colin L. Powell

Mr. Larry Wenig,
Wenig & Wenig,
150 Broadway, Suite 911,
New York, NY 10038.

JOSEPH I. LIEBERMAN
CONNECTICUT

UNITED STATES SENATE
WASHINGTON, D. C. 20510

January 16, 2001

Larry Wenig, Esq.
Wenig & Wenig
Attorneys At Law
150 Broadway, Suite 911
New York, NY 10038

Dear Mr. Wenig:

Thank you for your letter and congratulations on your book. It must have been painful to document the story of your family's suffering in the Soviet Union. You can be proud that you have helped to educate the public on aspects of Soviet repression during World War II that are not widely known in the U.S.

I appreciated your observations on several issues, as well as your op-ed on Jerusalem. I will continue to keep a very close eye on the situation in the Middle East and on the efforts of the new Administration. I continue to hope that a just and peaceful solution can be found.

Best personal regards.

Sincerely,

Joseph I. Lieberman

JIL:sh

Plate 17 & 18: I received thank you letters from Secretary of State, Colin Powell and Senator Joseph Leiberman for copies of *From Nazi Inferno to Soviet Hell.*

Plate 19 & 20: Letters from the White House and Condeleezza Rice.

THE WHITE HOUSE

WASHINGTON

July 10, 1996

Mr. Larry Wenig
12637 White Coral Drive
Wellington, Florida 33414

Dear Larry:

Thanks for sharing your views with me. The historic progress we have witnessed since September 1993 holds forth the promise of hope for all the people of the Middle East. For too long, conflict has robbed that region of its resources, its potential, and, most important, the lives of so many of its sons and daughters. Now there is an opportunity to define the future of the Middle East in terms of reconciliation and coexistence rather than confrontation and violence.

The leaders of Israel and its Arab neighbors have been charting a new course toward a brighter future. Implementation of the historic Israeli-Palestinian Declaration of Principles is underway, and both sides are facing the challenge of overcoming old sorrows and antagonisms to realize a shared vision of peace. Israel and Jordan have signed a peace treaty and are committed to building a warm relationship with enduring ties of cooperation between their countries. There are no limits to what can be done if the region's energy and talents can be channeled into creating new opportunities and building a land as bountiful and peaceful as it is holy. I have pledged the active support of the United States toward this goal.

The path ahead will not be easy. Difficult issues must be discussed and resolved. And the enemies of peace, whose weapon is terror and whose mission is to destroy, will not be silent. But they cannot be allowed to succeed, and the United States will work actively to ensure that they do not. The progress already made in peace negotiations is substantial, and we will do everything possible to facilitate further advances on the Syrian and Lebanese negotiating tracks. The United States will continue to be a full and active partner in these negotiations.

Our success will mean a brighter future for the region and the world.

Sincerely,

Bill Clinton

JOHN McCAIN
UNITED STATES SENATOR
WASHINGTON, DC 20510

October 16, 2000

Mr. Larry Wenig
Wenig & Wenig
150 Broadway, Suite 911
New York, NY 10038

Dear Larry,

Thank you for sending me an autographed copy of your book, From Nazi Inferno to Soviet Hell. I look forward to reading your book and I am sure to find it poignant and insightful.

Again, thank you, and I wish you the best in all your future endeavors.

Sincerely,

John McCain
United States Senator

NOT PRINTED AT GOVERNMENT EXPENSE

THE WHITE HOUSE

WASHINGTON

July 25, 2001

Mr. Larry Wenig
150 Broadway
Suite 911
New York, New York 10038-4302

Dear Mr. Wenig:

On behalf of Condoleezza Rice, thank you for the copy of your book.

However, restrictions on the receipt of gifts by White House staff result in our returning it to you. We appreciate your thoughtfulness and your understanding.

With best wishes,

Christa J. Bailey

Christa J. Bailey
Director
White House Gift Office

Enclosure

Plate 21: Thank you letter from John McCain for a copy of *From Nazi Inferno to Soviet Hell.*

COMMITTEES:

INTERNATIONAL RELATIONS

GOVERNMENT REFORM

SUBCOMMITTEE ON MIDDLE EAST AND CENTRAL ASIA

SUBCOMMITTEE ON WESTERN HEMISPHERE

SUBCOMMITTEE ON WELLNESS AND HUMAN RIGHTS

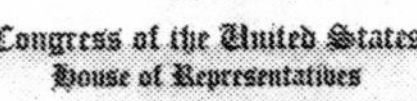

Congress of the United States
House of Representatives
ILEANA ROS-LEHTINEN

September 27, 2005

Mr. Larry Wenig
Wenig & Wenig
150 Broadway, Suite 911
New York, NY 10038

Dear Mr. Wenig:

Let me take this opportunity to thank you for giving me a copy of your book, *From Nazi Inferno to Soviet Hell*. As an attorney and leader of the ZOA, your work is very beneficial to the Jewish community.

I can only imagine what your experiences in Europe must have been like. Your escape to America was amazingly courageous and ensured your survival. Despite coming to New York without speaking English and with little financial security, your tenaciousness and drive for success are truly inspirational. Your are blessed to have family members in America who took you in and guided you in an unfamiliar country.

Once again, thank you very much for the gift of your book. It was a pleasure meeting you.

With Best Wishes,

Ileana Ros-Lehtinen
Member of Congress

Plate 22: I met Congress-Woman Ileana Ros-Lehtinen in Washington and gave her a copy of *From Nazi Inferno to Soviet Hell.*

Plate 23: Letter from John Shalikashvili, Chairman of the Joint Chief of Staff whom I met at a meeting of the Conference of Presidents of Major Jewish Organizations. I told him about my experience as a five year political prisoner in the Soviet Union and Uzbekistan.

CHAIRMAN OF THE JOINT CHIEFS OF STAFF
WASHINGTON, D.C. 20318-9999

9 June 1997

Mr. Larry Wenig
Suite 911
150 Broadway
New York, NY 10038

Dear Mr. Wenig,

I enjoyed meeting you at the luncheon hosted by the Conference of Presidents of Major Jewish Organizations. The story of how you overcame such terrible obstacles to come to America was a harrowing one.

Your story epitomizes the American Dream – building a new life and taking advantage of the many opportunities our Nation offers. You have much of which to be proud.

With best wishes for all your future endeavors.

Sincerely,

JOHN M. SHALIKASHVILI
Chairman
of the Joint Chiefs of Staff

Mr. Larry Wenig
With best wishes,

THE WHITE HOUSE
WASHINGTON

April 2, 2002

Mr. Larry Wenig
2450 Presidential Way
Apartment 1606
West Palm Beach, Florida 33401

Dear Mr. Wenig:

On behalf of President Bush, I want to thank you for taking the time to write.

The President appreciates your sharing with him your comments and suggestions. Many difficult challenges lie ahead, and President Bush believes the views of individual Americans can play an invaluable role in guiding his Administration's efforts to meet those challenges.

You were good to write the President, and we appreciate your words of support.

With the President's best wishes,

Sincerely,

Kenneth B. Mehlman
Deputy Assistant to the President and
Director of Political Affairs

Plate 24: Thank you letter from Kenneth B. Melchman, deputy Assistant to the President, for sending the President copies of my op-eds published in the Sun-Sentinel of Florida, about the problems we are facing in the Arab-Muslim world.

Plate 25: Thank you letter from Elie Wiesel for *From Nazi Inferno to Soviet Hell.*

Boston University
ELIE WIESEL
University Professor and
Andrew W. Mellon Professor in the Humanities

147 Bay State Road
Boston, Massachusetts 02215
617-353-4561 Fax: 617-353-4024

September 6, 2005

Mr. Larry Wenig
270-10 Grand Central Parkway, Apt. 27E
Floral Park, NY 11005-1127

Dear Larry Wenig,

Thanks for your letter, and the kind words it contained. I do remember meeting you, and so it was good to hear from you. I just hope you'll forgive this delay in replying!

Thanks, also, for such thoughtfulness in sending your book. As you suggest, a book such as yours is most welcome as we seek to learn everything we can about those dark times. Naturally, I shall read it with the interest it deserves—

With every good wish,

Elie Wiesel

EW/ros

Edward I. Koch

1290 Avenue of the Americas
37th Floor
New York, New York 10104

Tel: (212) 541-2100
Fax: (212) 541-1321
E-Mail: eikoch@bryancave.com

May 5, 2004

Larry Wenig LLB
270-27E Grand Central Parkway
Floral Park, NY 11005

Dear Mr. Wenig:

Thanks very much for your April 29th letter. I appreciate your sharing your insights with me.

All the best.

Sincerely,

Edward I. Koch

NY/300069/112/494.3

Plate 26: Thank you letter from Mayor Edward Koch.

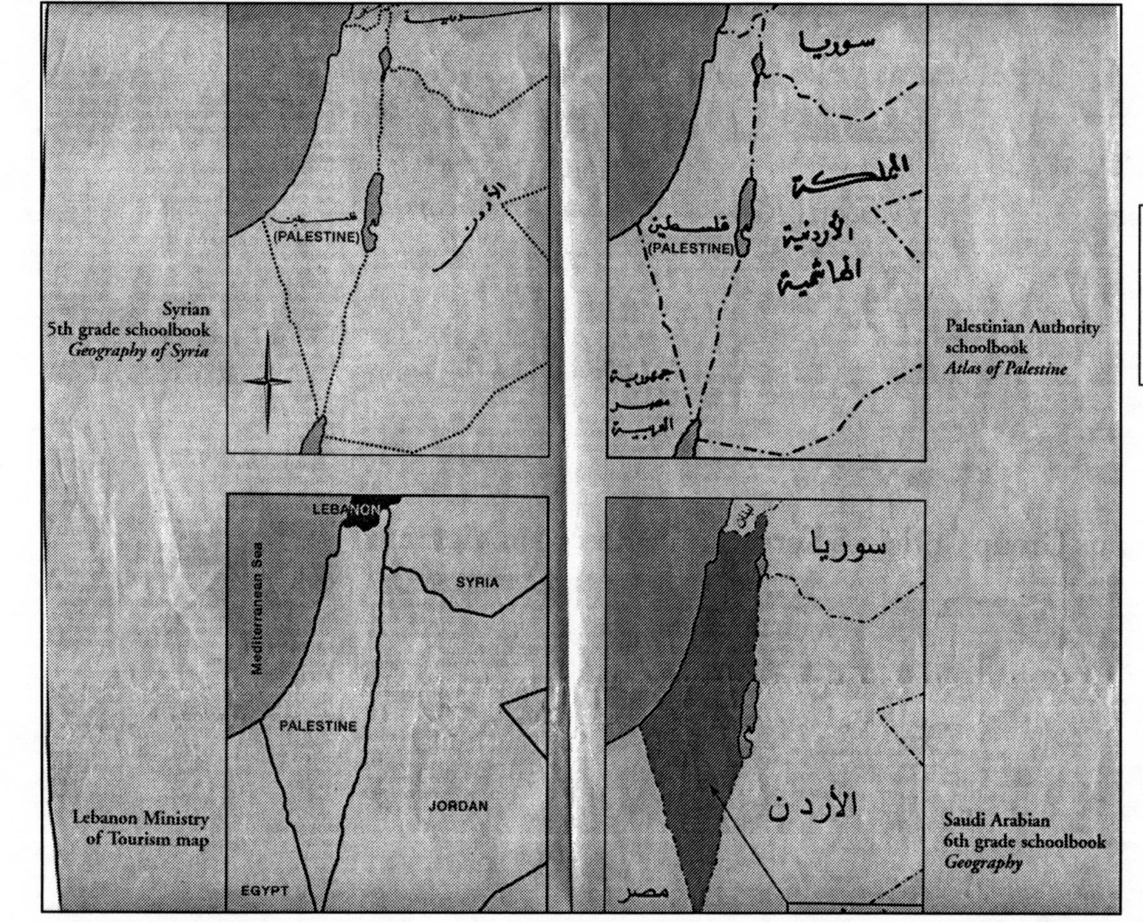

Plate 27: Map from a school textbook in an Arab Muslim country showing no country of Israel.

Plate 28: Another textbook map showing the Muslim Arab countries and Israel, which includes the provinces of Judea, Samaria and Gaza, as a tiny speck.

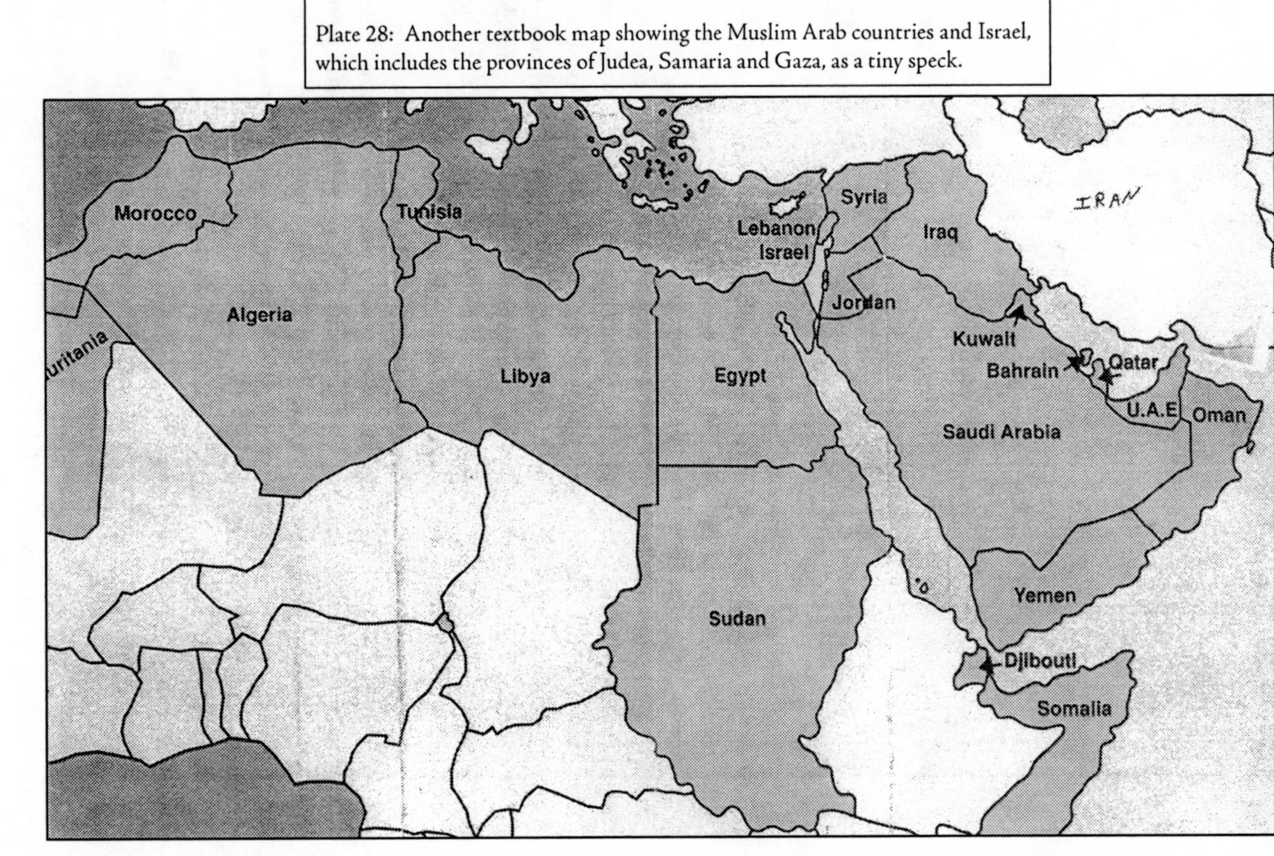

Chapter 8

SALES JOB AND MARRIAGE

When I returned home from work the next day, my father told me that Harry Stelzer had agreed to see the two of us at his factory the following Monday afternoon.

At the appointed time, we arrived at the office of Harry Stelzer Ladies' Belts, Inc. The office and the adjoining factory together occupied the entire third floor of 270 West 38th Street in Manhattan.

Mr. Kuhn, the office manager, led us in to Harry's office. Harry was dressed in a good-quality navy suit with a white handkerchief in his breast pocket. His light blue tie went perfectly with the suit, the sleeves of his white shirt were fastened with large gold cufflinks, and his fingernails were manicured. Harry was sitting in a high-backed leather chair behind a large, nicely carved wooden desk. Father and I sat down in comfortable leather chairs on the other side of his desk. Harry's strong cologne hit my nostrils.

Harry started the conversation by asking what I was doing with myself. He and I spoke in English, while my father spoke to him in Yiddish. I told him about my job and law school. "Larry," he said, "I am impressed with your persistence in continuing your education. I give you credit for sticking to your guns and not listening to my advice, or our Dynower landsmen's advice, not to waste your time in night school."

He said that my father had told him about my engagement, and I took the opportunity to say a few words about how wonderful Selma was. "When will the wedding take place?" Harry asked. I responded that although I still had two years of law school, we had decided to get married this year. Harry asked how much I was earning. When I told him, he snapped back, "You can't support a wife on a $45 a week." Harry looked at me for a moment. "I'll give you a job as a belt salesman, and your weekly salary will be $100." I almost fell off my chair.

Harry showed us around the factory. It was an amazing sight. There were at least a hundred workers: women working the electric sawing machines, sawing cloth and plastic ladies' belts; men using cutting presses to cut out plastic and leather belts; other men stapling metal buckles onto belts, or using punching machines to punch five holes in the belts. Awed by the huge factory with its many employees, I said to myself, "Only in America!" Harry Stelzer had been a poor, starving, uneducated orphan in Poland. Here in America he was a wealthy manufacturer.

Back in his office, Harry called in Mr. Kuhn and the sales manager, Harry Ross. He told them that he was hiring me as a salesman. He told Mr. Ross to train me and assign me some dress manufacturers as my exclusive territory. Harry said that my starting salary would be $100, and he directed Mr. Ross to treat me well. He told him that after I learned the art of salesmanship and developed a good relationship with some manufacturers, they might one day become my law clients. Harry Ross said that he would do everything he could and would personally take me around to all the dress manufacturers in the territory assigned to me and tell them about my background as a Holocaust survivor. Mr. Ross introduced me to the firm's other two salesmen, Danny Weiner and Al Bushell.

Harry Stelzer was very nice to me and my father. He took out a bottle of Chivas Regal and poured some of it into small whiskey glasses. We raised our glasses and toasted each other with the words Le-Chayim, which in English means "To Life." Harry Stelzer said that I was to start the following Monday at nine o'clock sharp. I couldn't believe what had just happened. My weekly salary had jumped from $45 to $100. In 1954, $100 was a decent salary.

I didn't tell my jewelry employers or co-workers that this would be my last week with them. That evening I did not even share the news with my law school classmates. It was either Wednesday or Thursday of that week that I gave notice to Mr. Bleicher that I would be quitting on Friday. Mr. Bleicher had always treated me well, and he was always satisfied with my work. I didn't want him to feel bad, so I said that I was quitting because my courses were now so difficult that I would have to devote all my time to my homework for the next two years. Mr. Bleicher said that he was sorry to lose me but he could understand my problem. I told the same thing to my coworkers in the factory.

On Friday, my last day of work, Mr. Bleicher handed me my weekly paycheck during the lunch break, as he always did, and told me that I could leave early. I used this gift of a free afternoon to go straight to the lounge at Brooklyn Law School to do some homework. And for the first time in a long while I had a decent hot dinner before class.

Monday, the big day, Harry Ross assigned me a desk, sat down next to me, and gave a detailed lecture on the New York garment industry. There were quite a few ladies' belt manufacturers in the city, Harry said, but Stelzer was the largest and most highly respected.

All of the dress manufacturers were within walking distance of our factory. Harry opened his sample case and showed me some belt samples. As a salesman I would be calling on the dress designers almost every day. Most of the designers were women, and they were constantly designing dresses, many of which needed belts. It wasn't necessary to make appointments. Since the dress designers were already our clients, we could just walk into their work rooms and ask whether they had any new dresses that needed belts.

After a new dress was selected for manufacture, the trimming buyer or the boss himself would call, giving us an order for the belt the designer had selected at a price agreed upon by Stelzer and the manufacturer. If any of the new dresses made a hit in the stores, we would get many reorders for that particular belt, which would be given a style number. It was a rather long lecture, and it opened my eyes to a whole new world I had never known about before. Harry explained that his territory included the biggest dress manufacturers in the country: Jonathan Logan, R & K Dress Manufacturers, Taylor Junior, Parade, and McKettrick Williams.

Our visits to clients began with the designer at R & K Dresses, about two blocks away at 1400 Broadway. When we got there, Harry introduced me to the famous dress designer Miss Fraccia. He told her I was a new salesman and recounted my background as a Holocaust survivor and law student. From their conversation I could tell that Miss Fraccia was very close to Mr. Ross. She appeared to be about 60 years old, and was considered to be one of the best designers in New York. Miss Fraccia was of medium height, rather slim, and spoke with a very soft, melodic voice. She showed Harry a new dress she had just designed, for which she wanted a black patent leather belt, one and a half inches wide. She wanted the buckle to be made of black plastic. Harry told her that he would have a sample belt, size 12, made for the dress.

We went back to the factory. A sample belt was made to Miss Fraccia's specifications, and we took it back to show her. Harry Ross emphasized to me that fast service made for good business relationships with the dress manufacturers. After a new dress was designed, he said, it was exhibited to dress buyers from various stores and department stores. If the buyers liked the new dress, they placed orders for it the same day. That was when Stelzer got its orders from the trimming buyer of the dress manufacturer. The same procedure applied to all dress manufacturers. The important thing was to keep in constant contact with the designers.

Harry added that sometimes the Stelzer Company designed new belts and made up samples in both genuine leather and plastic with various new metal buckles. A number of such newly designed belts were exhibited to the dress designers. Sometimes a designer would design a new dress to complement the new belt.

It was all very interesting and challenging. The job would be exciting, and it would give me the opportunity to meet people and learn the art of doing business. It seemed especially exciting after all those boring months on a jewelry bench.

Harry took me out for lunch that day at the Dubrow cafeteria, which was located nearby on Seventh Avenue. He said that he and the other salesmen usually brought sandwiches from home and ate in the sales office.

Back at Stelzer, Harry sat down at my desk to go over the visit with Miss Fraccia. He emphasized that it was very important to cultivate the dress designers and maintain a close, friendly relationship with them. He asked whether I found our interchange with Miss Fraccia interesting. I told him that I liked it very much indeed, and I found it quite exciting.

Harry then prepared a list of the dress manufacturers he was assigning to me as my territory. There were three accounts in the building at 1400 Broadway: Westover Fashions, Parade Dress, and Lido Fashions. Westover Fashions was the largest of them. Its showroom and sales office were at 1400 Broadway, but the designing, manufacturing, and shipping operations were all in Pennsylvania.

He also assigned me Nelly DeGrab, at 1407 Broadway, across the street from 1400 Broadway; Dan Keller Dress Company, at 498 Seventh Avenue; and Sportwhirl Skirt Manufacturing, on 35th Street, close to Seventh Avenue. The final customer assigned me was Borgenicht Brothers, a ladies' coat manufacturer on Eighth Avenue. All these places were within walking distance of our factory. Harry promised to take me to all of them the next day. Then he showed me how to write out orders and explained the various belt sizes and styles. It was a very good and thorough lecture, and I was eager to visit the firms.

The next day, Tuesday, I arrived at the office a few minutes before nine. Harry Ross came in a few minutes later and packed his sample case with belts and buckles. We left the office at about ten and walked over to the famous dress-manufacturing building at 1400 Broadway. Our first stop was Westower Fashions. Harry introduced me to the owners as the new salesman who would be handling their account and told them a bit about my background. I remember the names of only two of the owners, Mr. Schor and Mr. Weinberg. Both of them seemed to me to be college educated; they were very elegantly dressed and well spoken. They told me that they had never met a former gulag inmate before.

Then Harry started to talk business. He opened his sample case and displayed the new belts. They were interested in a couple and asked us to send them some samples. We shook hands, and they wished me good luck on my new job. I enjoyed meeting the bosses of this large dress-manufacturing company.

Our next stop in the 1400 Broadway building was Parade Dress. Harry introduced me to the dress designer and the trimming buyer. Our last stop there was Lido Fashions, where we went through the same routine.

We left 1400 and walked over to 1407 Broadway and Nelly DeGrab. It was a newer building than 1400 Broadway, and the tenants were all ladies' dress manufacturers. One of the other companies in the building was Jonathan Logan, and Harry personally handled that account. The trimming buyer at Nelly DeGrab was named Sonny. He was a very nice, friendly young man. As usual Harry gave a brief account of my background. Sonny commented that I would be better off as a lawyer than as a salesman in the cutthroat garment business. He ordered some of the belt samples Harry displayed to him.

We now went on to the Dan Keller Dress Company at 498 Seventh Avenue--another building full of dress-manufacturing companies. Then, as our last stop, we visited the Sportwhirl Skirt Manufacturing Company, on 35th Street, between Broadway and Seventh Avenue. In the showroom Harry introduced me to David Saporta, the owner. When he learned that I was Holocaust survivor, Mr. Saporta put his arms around me in a warm embrace. He was a Sephardic Jew whose family had come to America from Greece. In the past, he said, he had sometimes bought belts from other firms, but from now on he would get all his belts from me.

It was now late in the afternoon and we returned to the office. Harry gave an account of our activities to Mr. Stelzer and then to Danny Weiner and Al Bushel, the other two salesmen. The egg salad sandwich my mother had prepared for my lunch tasted especially good. I was happy and felt great. I called my future in-laws to tell them about my day and to ask how they and

Selma were. I think it's a good policy to always maintain a good relationship with your in-laws.

After lunch, Harry took me into the factory and collected some new sample belts from Richie, the belt designer. He brought the belts into the sales office and attached them to pieces of cardboard, each of which had rubber strings that held three belts. He put several of these cardboards into a small sample case for me. From now on, he explained, whenever I visited the customers we had met today, I was to show them new samples. In addition, I was free to visit other manufacturers and try to develop new accounts on my own. The New York garment industry was huge, he said, and new companies were opening for business almost every day.

I was all charged up and ready to start selling belts. As of tomorrow, Harry said, I would be on my own. Later in the week he would take me to McKettrick Williams and Borgenicht Ladies Coats, which he had also assigned to my territory.

The next day I went to see my accounts, and I also checked in the directories of some of the buildings along Broadway and Seventh Avenue for the names of dress manufacturers that hadn't so far been approached by Stelzer salesmen. I continued doing this all week and even got orders from some of the new firms I approached on my own.

My first Friday on the job was very exciting. I received my first weekly pay check for $100, more than double what I had earned in the jewelry factory. I had such a good feeling on that first Friday, not only because of my greatly increased income, but also because I had met some wealthy dress manufacturers and they had all taken a liking to me. I couldn't help thinking that some day some of them might be law clients. For the moment my happiness overcame my worries about Israel. I called Selma to tell her my news, and again spoke to my future in-laws.

I returned home that evening after ten. My parents were already in bed, but I awakened them to share my good news. I didn't go to sleep right away, because I had to study for two exams. I studied all weekend, except for Saturday night, when I went to see Selma. When she opened the door and I saw her beautiful face, my heart melted. I kissed her, as well as her mother. We went to a local restaurant in Long Island City, where we discussed our wedding plans. I had never been to Florida, and I asked whether she would agree to go there for our honeymoon. I told her to take her time and think about it.

That whole week my mother shopped for the food and other goodies for the engagement party. She cooked and baked all week. On Sunday morning, Father and I put together two tables in our dining room to accommodate all the people who had been invited to the party. We borrowed some chairs from our neighbor, Mrs. Berman. I helped mother by placing white tablecloths on the tables and arranging the plates, the white cloth napkins, and the cutlery.

Hella and Sol arrived about an hour early. Selma and her family arrived around noontime. Selma was stunning in a new pink dress. Her beautiful face was shining like alabaster. There was hugging and kissing by the members of our two families, all wishing each other mazal tov. A few minutes later Uncle Irving, Aunt Ruthie, and their married sons and their wives arrived. After everyone was introduced, my mother asked us to take our seats at the dining room tables. Uncle Irving whispered in my ear that I was very lucky and had shown very good taste in picking Selma

Wine was served first, in wine glasses mother had purchased only a few days before. When the wine glasses were lifted, we all exclaimed in Hebrew, "Le-Chayim--To Life." Vegetable soup was served and then salad, followed by minute steak and vegetables. The food was just delicious.

My mother was not only a very good cook, she was an excellent baker. She brought in a big nut cake she had baked and set it in the center of the table. At that point, I took the diamond engagement ring from the little box in my pocket and put it on Selma's finger. I told her how much I loved her, and how happy I was that she was going to be my wonderful wife. Selma responded that she was very happy, and that she loved me very much. I grabbed her face, and we kissed each other for a couple of minutes. A loud mazal tov reverberated in the dining room, and then the cake was served with tea.

Uncle Irving asked when the wedding would be. We told him that we planned on that coming June. Had we selected a hall? When we said no, he recommended the Park River Terrace, near Yankee Stadium. We thanked him for the suggestion and said we would contact the hall the following week.

The engagement party was really beautiful, and I was so happy that everything went so smoothly. Our families got along very well. The party ended around four in the afternoon.

After the party I called the manager of Park River Terrace, who suggested that we come by the following Sunday around noon. A wedding would be in progress and we could see if we liked the way it was handled.

The following Sunday, Selma and I and both sets of parents went to the Park River Terrace. We saw a wedding in progress and liked what we saw. The manager said that June was a very heavy wedding month, but Sunday noon, June 13th, was available, and so that was the date we chose. Our parents told the manager exactly what we wanted in respect to food and other matters. In particular they wanted the same rabbi and choir boy we had just seen. Everything was settled, including the price, and they signed the contract right there and then.

The following Monday I went to work as usual. I didn't say anything to Mr. Stelzer or to anyone else about my engagement party or wedding plans. I went as usual to school that night, and again I didn't mention anything about my engagement or my forthcoming wedding.

When I returned home that Monday, Father told me that Uncle Irving was very taken with Selma and had offered to help with the wedding expenses. As if this wasn't kind enough, he had asked his real estate management agent to find us a rent-controlled apartment in the Bronx.

The next few months flew by. In May, Selma and I made reservations at the Nautilus Hotel in Miami Beach for our honeymoon and purchased the plane tickets. Mr. Abramson, Uncle Irving's real estate agent, found us a one-bedroom apartment in a rent-controlled apartment building at 2608 Creston Avenue, about a block and a half from my parents' building and two blocks from Kingsbridge Road with its many stores.

Selma and I met Mr. Abramson and went to see the apartment on Saturday morning. It was an elevator building, and the apartment was on the second floor. It had a kitchen with all the necessary appliances, including a refrigerator. The one bathroom had a tub as well as a shower, the living room was of a decent size, and the bedroom window faced St. James Park. The monthly rent was $73.

We decided to take the apartment. Unfortunately, it would not be available until September, because after the present tenant vacated around the beginning of July, the landlord would need time to make some repairs and paint the apartment. Meanwhile, Mr. Abramson said, he would mail me the lease and both of us had to sign it.

After we left the building, Selma and I sat down on a bench in St. James Park to talk about our future life. I told her how lucky we were to be getting a decent apartment in a rent-controlled building in a good area, and how grateful we should be to Uncle Irving. Even in those days, it was very difficult to find a rent-controlled apartment, especially in a good location.

Then I had to tell her something very embarrassing. I did not have $73 to pay our first month's rent, which was due on June 1st along with the signed lease. I explained that I had to pay the tuition for the summer session, I had purchased some new clothing for our honeymoon, and I had to make my regular contribution to my parents. And finally, I had to pay for our airline flight to Miami. I told Selma that I expected some nice wedding gifts from the relatives and friends who would attend our wedding. My good Selma told me not to worry: she would pay the first month's rent. As a teacher, she said, she was earning a nice salary, and she didn't have to contribute any money to her parents. I thanked her for being so understanding.

Selma wanted her sister Dorothy and my sister Hella to be the maids of honor. I selected Sol, my sister's husband, as my best man, and four of my cousins, Norman and Jerry, Uncle Irving's sons, and Norbert and Nathan Turner, as ushers. Selma asked whether her cousins Morris Stern and Jack Werber could also be ushers, and I agreed. I walked Selma to the Jerome Avenue subway station and then went home to prepare for the upcoming examinations.

When I got home, I told my parents that Selma and I were going to take the apartment on Creston Avenue, and that Selma would pay the first month's rent because I was out of cash. My parents felt bad about my not paying the first month's rent, but they too were short of cash, because they planned to give us a nice monetary wedding gift.

I telephoned Hella and told her we wanted her as a maid of honor and Sol as my best man. Hella thanked me for the double honor. About two hours later, however, she arrived at our apartment with some unpleasant news. Sol refused to come to the wedding unless I invited his best friend, Morris Siegelstein--the same Morris Siegelstein who had dated Selma before I came into the picture. If Sol did not come to the wedding, Hella said, she couldn't come either.

I felt as if someone had jabbed a knife through my heart. This was one of the most unpleasant moments in my life. This was the kind of unpleasant jab I have always experienced in life, not only from my stepsister, but also from my stepfather's family, both in Poland and in America. The pain of these jabs often kept me up at night, wondering why my mother had to go and divorce my natural father.

My parents were beside themselves when I told them about Hella's ultimatum. I didn't tell my stepsister my decision right away; I said I would think about it and let her know later on. Then I continued with my school work, totally ignoring her presence in the apartment.

That Saturday night, as usual, I went to see Selma. We went to a local Chinese restaurant again, because Selma liked Chinese food. I told about the nasty trick Hella had sprung upon me. Selma said that as unpleasant it might be, I had no choice but to comply with Hella's request. This was all so painful. At a time when I should have been overcome by happiness over marrying such a wonderful and beautiful girl, stones were being thrown at me. But I had no choice. Not wanting to make a scene at the wedding, I had to swallow the poison pill.

Sunday morning, I told my parents that Hella and Sol had hurt me deeply, but I had no choice but to comply with their request, and Selma had agreed to invite Morris Siegelstein. I telephoned Hella and asked for his address so that I could send him an invitation. Hella asked whether I still wanted her as a maid of honor and Sol as the best man. I told her yes.

Sunday, June 13, 1954, finally arrived, and it was a beautiful, sunny day. My father dressed up in a very nice tuxedo and bow tie. My mother put on the lovely blue cocktail dress she had purchased for my wedding. I, on the other hand, put on an ordinary business suit, and was carrying a special bag containing my rented tuxedo, my dress shirt and studs, and the black bow tie. This was because Selma and I would be leaving for Miami Beach after the wedding: I would need the ordinary suit to travel in, and the tuxedo would have to be returned to the rental establishment.

We arrived by taxi at the Park River Terrace wedding hall at about ten. In the dressing room there I changed into the rented tuxedo and the dress shirt and bow tie. Selma arrived with her parents in her father's car. Her sister Dorothy and her husband, Abe, arrived in their own car a few minutes later. Selma was dressed in a beautiful white wedding gown and looked just like a beautiful princess. Heads turned when she walked in. My father in-law also wore a tuxedo. My mother-in-law wore a floor-length pink dress which she had purchased specially for our wedding.

Selma and I were called in before the rabbi, who read us the Hebrew marriage contract, the ketubah. The rabbi spoke about the importance of this day in our lives, and about how a Jewish couple should follow the principles and laws of the Jewish religion.

The guests began to arrive. They wished us mazal tov and helped themselves to the goodies that were being served. Uncle Irving was also garbed in a tuxedo, and my aunt wore a beautiful cocktail dress. My boss Harry

Stelzer was there, as well, with his girlfriend. Morris Siegelstein, Selma's old boyfriend, was also there, but neither one of us looked at him or spoke to him at all.

The wedding ceremony began shortly after noon. Selma and I were accompanied down to the wedding canopy by our respective parents. A choir boy preceded us singing a beautiful song in Hebrew. The maids of honor and the two best men, my brother-in-law and Selma's brother-in-law, followed the bridesmaids. They were followed by the ushers, the flower girl, and the ring boy. The rabbi performed beautifully, and it was a wonderful ceremony. I placed the wedding band on Selma's finger and made the required declaration, "Behold, with this ring I thee wed in accordance with the law of Moses and of Israel." Selma did likewise, placing a ring on my finger and repeating the same statement. A glass was placed under my shoe, and I smashed it. The custom of smashing a glass at a Jewish wedding is intended to remind the newlyweds that even at this moment of joy, they must not forget the destruction of the two holy Temples in Jerusalem.

As I stood beneath the wedding canopy, many things went through my mind. The human brain has unusual qualities, and at this profoundly happy moment, all kinds of scenes appeared to me. I saw myself having a wonderful life with Selma and raising a family. Then I saw myself in the gulag on the outskirts of Siberia. All of a sudden the gulag changed to the mud room near Afghanistan where we had lived for 3½ years next to a cow. I felt as if my head were spinning around and around, yet I was able to steady myself and hear the loud, reverberating voices in the wedding hall, "Kiss the bride! Kiss the bride!" And I did just that, for several minutes.

Selma and I were ushered out from under the wedding canopy and into the large dining room. We stood at the entrance and greeted all the guests as they came in. The food was delicious, and almost every one of the guests came to our table at some point to wish Selma and me mazal tov. Harry Stelzer, my boss, was just ecstatic when he greeted us. We received some very nice monetary gifts at the wedding.

After the wedding, Selma and I were ushered into the dressing room to change our clothing. I turned over the tuxedo and the dress shirt to my parents to return to the rental company. We said goodbye to my parents, because Selma and I were going to her parents' home, and from there, in the evening, to La Guardia airport for our flight to Miami Beach.

Selma and I rested for a couple of hours in her parents' apartment, then her father drove us in his Chrysler to the airport. We boarded a TWA airliner. Neither of us had ever flown before.

We arrived in Miami late in the evening and took a taxi to the Nautilus Hotel, on Collins Avenue in Miami Beach. I am a very romantic and passionate man, and my first night with the woman I love above all others was something that we will remember always.

The following morning at breakfast, we met quite a number of honeymoon couples. The same day, the concierge at the hotel suggested a company that would give us a bus tour of Miami Beach. There were lots of other honeymooners on the tour bus. The guide pointed out some of the famous hotels, in particular the Fontainebleau, which was then being built.

The guide also showed us the Kenilworth Hotel, which he said was owned by the famous entertainer Arthur Godfrey. A Jewish honeymoon couple sitting nearby whispered that Jews were not permitted at the Kenilworth. They said that Arthur Godfrey was a virulent anti-Semite. I couldn't believe it. In America, the land of freedom and equality, the land with the Statue of Liberty at its entrance, a Jew couldn't rent a room at the Kenilworth Hotel.

I felt very downcast, but I didn't let this unfortunate news spoil my wonderful honeymoon with Selma, and we enjoyed the tour of the Indian Village, where we saw an American Indian wrestle with an alligator.

The following day, Selma told me that she had an aunt who lived on Lincoln Road in Miami Beach and would very much like to visit her. I replied, "Selma, dear, I will do anything you want me to do!" We boarded a bus on Collins Avenue, paid our fare, and took our seats. Lots of other people got on, and I began to notice something strange. Whenever a black passenger boarded the bus, the white driver would say in a loud voice, "Get to the rear." Several black passengers sat down in the rear, although there were plenty of empty seats at the front of the bus.

I asked Selma what all this meant. She whispered in my ear, "Don't you know that Florida is a Southern state, where black people are discriminated against and must sit in the back of the bus?" I said, "Selma, dear, as a Jew and a Holocaust survivor, I can't accept that. It simply goes against every principle I believe in. To me a black human being is no different from a white human being. We may have paid our fare, but even so I refuse to ride on a segregated bus. Let's get off." Selma agreed with me, and we got off.

It was a long walk, but we finally got to Selma's aunt's apartment. Aunt Yetta, who had recently married for the second time, introduced us to her new husband. She served us a very good lunch and coffee. We complained a bit about the hot, humid Florida weather, but Aunt Yetta assured us that one would get accustomed to it after a while. She had lived in Florida now for several years and didn't mind the weather at all.

Our beautiful honeymoon ended the following Sunday, when we flew back to New York. We were met at La Guardia airport by Selma's parents, who drove us to my parents' apartment in the Bronx. My parents were away for the summer at their hotel, and we were going to stay in their apartment until our own apartment was ready for us to move in on September 1st.

Chapter 9

MARRIED LIFE, LL.B., INSURANCE BROKERAGE

That summer we lived rent-free in my parents' apartment and shopped around for furniture. We visited a number of furniture stores in the Bronx and purchased everything we needed for the bedroom, living room, and kitchen, with the understanding that it would be delivered to our new apartment on the first of September.

For the July Fourth weekend, we took the bus to the Oliver Country Club in order to be with my parents. They gave us a nice room in the hotel, and of course our stay was free. The Fourth of July weekend was usually a busy time for Catskills hotels, but this year the Oliver Country Club was far from fully occupied, and one could tell that it was going downhill. One reason was the volatile mix of guests. The very religious guests and the secular guests simply did not get along. It was an irremediable social mismatch, and my father and his partners still hadn't found a way to deal with the problem.

In addition, it was around this time that many hotels in the Catskills began to lose business because air travel was becoming popular and people were now taking their vacations in such places as the Rocky Mountains, California, and even Europe. My fears for the hotel proved to be correct. The Oliver Country Club went out of business two years later, and my parents lost all the hard work and money they had invested in it. Several years later just about all the Catskill hotels went out of business. There was no longer a Borsht Belt in the Catskills.

After the Fourth of July weekend, I went back to my job as a belt salesman and my five evenings a week at Brooklyn Law School. My poor Selma was home alone from morning until late at night, because I did not get back from school until ten or later.

Moving day came toward the end of August. The landlord, thanks to the intercession of Mr. Abramson, my uncle's real estate agent, gave us permission to move in our furniture during the last days of August. On September 1st we moved into our own apartment at 2608 Creston Avenue in the Bronx. We had been able to purchase our furniture because of the generous monetary gifts we got at our wedding: Selma's parents gave us $5,000, and Uncle Irving, Harry Stelzer, and the Feldman brothers also gave us generous monetary gifts, so our apartment was very nicely furnished.

Selma hadn't been able to find a teaching job in the Bronx, so she took a job as a social worker in the New York Department of Welfare for one year. She received a decent salary, which permitted us to live comfortably. In 1956 Selma was able to find a full-time teaching job in a Bronx elementary school that paid her more than she had earned as social worker.

On June 12, 1956, I graduated from Brooklyn Law School with Selma, my parents, and my in-laws in attendance. My graduation was a big event in my life. I had practically broken my back working all day and attending school every night with only the help of a Polish dictionary. I had proved to my relatives and my landsmen from Dynów that all of them were wrong when they tried to dissuade me from attending school and from hoping to become an attorney. It just goes to prove that if you are determined to achieve a goal in life, you can do it if you persevere and remain determined. And this is especially true in our America. When I was handed my diploma, I felt as if I had grown a few feet taller. It is difficult to describe what went through my mind at that moment.

Now that I had finished law school and passed the bar examination, I had to sit down and think calmly about my future. I was still selling ladies' belts in the garment industry, but I hadn't become a lawyer to sell ladies' belts. The change in my circumstances required a new plan. As I contemplated my future, something happened that required a more cautious approach to my planning. Toward the end of 1956, Selma became pregnant, and we were looking forward to having our first child. However, tragedy struck us when Selma had a miscarriage after several months. We were both heartbroken, and Selma couldn't stop crying. Our obstetrician told us that the baby had been a boy. I tried to comfort Selma and assured her that she would be able to have more children.

Selma soon became pregnant again. This time we retained an obstetrician in Manhattan. The new doctor gave Selma special pills to prevent another miscarriage. Around this time we purchased our first car, a second-hand

Plymouth. On January 2, 1958, Selma gave birth to a beautiful daughter, and we named her Phyllis. She wasn't just beautiful, she was a very good baby. My parents were overjoyed, and my in-laws couldn't stop bragging about their first grandchild. They came over several days a week to spend time with her.

My in-laws wanted us to move to Queens to be nearer to them. Selma wanted to continue teaching, but she couldn't leave Phyllis all alone. My in-laws said that if we moved near their apartment in Queens, they would baby-sit for Phyllis, and Selma could take a job as a teacher. We thought that might be a very good idea.

My in-laws found us an apartment on 52nd Street in a newly-built apartment complex in Woodside. It was only eleven blocks from where they lived. The new apartment was much larger than our apartment in the Bronx, and it was practically new. It had two bedrooms and two bathrooms, and the building was across the street from a very nice park with a playground for children.

I began to inquire about jobs with law firms and was disappointed to learn what small salaries they offered recent graduates of Brooklyn Law School. Graduates of the Harvard, Yale, and Columbia law schools had no problem getting good jobs with prestigious law firms. They were offered very good salaries. The best I could do was a job at a small firm with a weekly salary of $50. I learned that some Brooklyn Law graduates were willing to work without pay in order to get experience. Others started out by developing an insurance or real estate brokerage practice.

I certainly couldn't support my family on only $50 a week, especially since Selma was home taking care of Phyllis for the time being and couldn't work. I asked around and discovered that the Prudential Life Insurance Company had a debit insurance practice. A debit insurance practice involved selling small life insurance policies called burial insurance policies. The debit agent was assigned a certain territory that handled at least a couple of hundred insured clients. The debit agent would walk his territory almost every day of the week and collect the monthly premiums for the policies. He could sometimes sell larger life insurance policies in his debit district and could develop new clients recommended by existing clients. Some debit agents also developed a general brokerage practice that allowed them to sell fire or auto insurance policies to their debit clients, and some of the agents who did this earned $200 a week or more.

I mulled over the idea of becoming a debit insurance agent. When I discussed it with Selma, she agreed that it might be a good idea. After all, $200 a week was double the salary I earned at Stelzer. I knew by now that I was a good salesman, having learned the art of salesmanship in the tough New York garment industry. And I considered the fact that if I could develop a good relationship with my debit policyholders, I might later be able to count on them as law clients.

I searched for a good debit office and found one on the Grand Concourse in the Bronx. It was a Prudential Life Insurance office, and its manager at the time was Max Tunick. He assigned me a very good territory in the Mosholu Parkway area, which included some very nice apartment buildings. It was a good area for developing an insurance business.

After I made the decision to acquire a debit territory for my insurance enterprise, I had to tell Harry Stelzer that I was leaving. I asked if I could see him to discuss something important. When I entered his office, Harry waved me to a comfortable chair and asked, "What's on your mind, Larry?" I explained the situation, telling him that I would be leaving his employ to go into the insurance business, and once I had developed a decent brokerage, I would commence the practice of law. Harry Stelzer fully approved of my plan and wished me luck in my new undertaking. We parted warmly, and he asked me to keep in touch.

I developed a very good relationship with my debit clients. Some weeks I earned much more than $200. I became one of the best life insurance agents in the office. After several months, I took a general insurance brokerage examination and got my license as a general insurance broker. The name of the firm I formed was "Larry Wenig Insurance Brokerage Company," and my office was in our apartment in Woodside. I did very well, both as a life insurance agent and as a general insurance broker, selling fire and auto insurance policies to both individuals and businesses. The only problem was that I had to drive into the Bronx several days a week.

When my little princess Phyllis was two years old, Selma was hired as a substitute teacher in an elementary school in the Bronx. My in-laws were more than happy to stay with Phyllis while Selma was at work. She drove in to work in the Bronx on the days I didn't need the car to cover my debit territory.

Toward the end of 1959, Selma became pregnant again but, despite the special pills the doctor prescribed, tragedy struck us again, and after several months she miscarried. Selma and I and our parents grieved about the loss. Selma could not stop crying and asking, "Why? Why am I so cursed?" I tried very hard to comfort her and to convince her that we would have another baby. Early in 1961, Selma became pregnant again, and on October 21, 1961, she gave birth to a boy, whom we named Alan Irving Wenig. We named him Alan after my natural father, Aaron. His middle name honored my dear Uncle Irving, who had brought us to America after World War II and was always exceptionally good to us.

When Alan was eight days old, he was circumcised in our apartment in Woodside. This was a big family celebration that included not only our parents but all of our relatives and some of our close friends. Now we were truly happy because we had two children, a girl and a boy. Because of Selma's history of miscarriages, we decided not to have any other children.

Alan was a very handsome and active baby. He ran before he learned to walk. Phyllis enjoyed Alan very much, and loved to play with him. Things were turning out very well, for I was earning more and more money from my insurance business. We disposed of our second-hand Plymouth and purchased our first new car, a Chevrolet Bel Air.

Summers in New York City were hot, and air-conditioning was not yet widely available. In the summer of 1962 we rented a bungalow for the months of July and August on Lake Mohegan in upstate New York. Selma and the children spent the entire summer in the bungalow colony, and I came up on the weekends. At the bungalow colony Selma met Phyllis Lefkowitz, a friend of hers from Hunter College. Her husband, Alvin Lefkowitz, who was a dress manufacturer in New York, also came to the bungalow colony on weekends. The Wenigs and the Lefkowitzes became very good friends, and our friendship continues to the present day.

My insurance brokerage business was going very well, and in addition, after having obtained the appropriate license, I was selling mutual funds to my clients. It was time to start practicing law. I wanted to be a trial lawyer, and that required experience in litigation, which would only be possible in a law office that specialized in litigation. Glancing through the New York Law Journal one day, I came across an ad for a trial lawyer placed by the law firm of Max J. Gwertzman. The firm, one of the largest in New York City, was engaged in the practice of subrogation. Its office was located at 116 John Street, in Manhattan, within walking distance of several important courts.

It might be useful at this point to explain subrogation law. An individual or a business carries all kinds of insurance policies, such as auto, fire, and liability insurance. When an insured person is involved, say, in a automobile accident, and his vehicle sustains damages as a result, his insurance company will reimburse him. If the accident was caused by the other driver, the insurance company will commence a negligence action against the other driver for the amount it paid out in reimbursement. If the negligent driver also has insurance, his insurance company will defend him. In reality, one insurance company is suing another insurance company. The same principle is involved in fire or water damage situations caused not by the insured but by another party such as a negligent plumber.

Mr. Gwertzman interviewed me and offered me a job as a trial lawyer. To my shock, I learned that it only paid $50 a week. There was no alternative, however. I had to get trial experience. Fortunately I had no financial problems at the time, thanks to the income from the insurance brokerage I conducted from my apartment, which, of course, I had not mentioned during the interview.

Mr. Gwertzman introduced me to the firm's other, older trial lawyers: Mr. Nagelberg, Irvin Asofsky, Milton Pfefer, Sol Goldstein, Stanley Reiter, and Ronald Podolsky. The office manager was an elderly lawyer named Zig Sessler. The Gwertzman firm had its trial lawyers in the courts of Manhattan, Brooklyn, Queens, and the Bronx practically every day. It had cases pending in New York City and in Nassau, Suffolk, and Westchester counties. Mr. Gwertzman assigned Ronald Podolsky, a younger but very capable trial lawyer, to show me around the Manhattan courts. I was also to observe him in action during a trial in the State Supreme Court in New York County.

The case involved an action against a plumber who had caused a fire in a Manhattan apartment building while using an acetylene torch to repair a leaking water pipe. The fire damages were quite substantial. The insurance company that insured the owner of the building had been reimbursed for the damages. The Gwertzman firm had instituted an action against the plumber on behalf of the insurance company that had reimbursed the building owner. The plumber's insurance company was defending him. The jury had been selected two days before.

The trial took place on my second day with the firm. I was in court sitting next to Mr. Podolsky, but I didn't participate in the trial. I was there only to observe and learn. The trial lasted four days, and in the middle of it the plumber's insurance company settled the case. They did so because Ronald Podolsky, with the help of a city fire marshal, had proved that the plumber was negligent when he used the acetylene torch. This four-day trial gave me quite a bit of experience.

In the next few days I learned how to prepare a summons and a complaint as well as a bill of particulars. I sat in to observe the taking of a deposition.

A few days later, Ronald Podolsky was assigned a case in the Civil Court of New York County that involved a car accident. Our insured's vehicle had sustained substantial damages that we claimed were the fault of the driver of the other vehicle. The trial was set to be tried before a jury, and I sat next to Ronald Podolsky during the voir-dire, the process of selecting jurors. I liked what I saw and heard during the jury selection process. Feeling quite confident, I told Mr. Gwertzman that I was ready to start trying cases. Mr. Gwertzman told me to be patient and observe a few more trials, and to sit in on some more depositions.

Two weeks later, I was assigned my first trial in civil court. It involved an auto accident in which our vehicle sustained substantial damages. It wasn't a jury trial, but it went on for two days, with both sides producing witnesses and damage experts. I won the case, and the presiding judge awarded the insurance company I represented the full amount it had paid to our insured. Mr. Gwertzman and the other lawyers in our office congratulated me on my first victory. From then on, I tried numerous cases in all the courts of New York City, as well as in Nassau and Suffolk counties.

My relationship with Ronald Podolsky grew stronger and stronger. One day, when Ronald and I were having lunch in a restaurant near our law office, he confided that in addition to his job for Gwertzman, he had his own law practice, which he operated from his apartment in Manhattan. Of course, Ronald told me, neither Mr. Gwertzman nor the other lawyers knew about it. His clients were New York City police officers who were challenging their grades on promotional examinations. In several cases he had won promotions for his clients.

I then told Ronald about my insurance brokerage business. Of course, I told him to keep this to himself. I suggested that perhaps he and I could someday rent an office together near the Gwertzman office and start our own law practice, once we had developed our own clients. Ronald said that might be a good idea, especially since we had become such good friends.

However, our plan went on hold for a while. My father-in-law was diagnosed with prostate cancer in 1963 and underwent chemotherapy. In June 1964, his condition deteriorated, his cancer having spread to other parts of his body, and he was taken to Mount Sinai Hospital in Manhattan. We all hoped that the doctors would be able to stop the spread of his cancer. We prayed for a miracle, but unfortunately, the cancer was very advanced and he couldn't be saved. He passed away in Mount Sinai Hospital on July 2, 1964. We had all loved him very much. I personally had a very good relationship with my father in-law. There was a period of mourning, so for several months I couldn't talk with Selma about renting a law office with my friend Ronald Podolsky.

We had moved from the Bronx to Woodside several years earlier because Selma's parents wanted to babysit Phyllis and Alan while Selma was teaching as a substitute teacher in a Bronx elementary school. My father-in-law would drive my mother-in-law to our Woodside apartment, because she couldn't drive. Now that he was gone, my mother-in-law could no longer baby-sit for us, so Selma had to stop teaching.

We began thinking about buying our own house. We contacted some real estate brokers, and one of them found a nice brick ranch house in Bayside at 64-34 229th Street. The house stood on a 40- by 100-foot lot; had three bedrooms, a very large basement, and a very nice backyard; and was located less than two blocks from the Long Island Expressway, and only a half-block from the bus to the subway station. All of the other houses on the block were owned by young families our age with children. Within walking distance was a Conservative temple, the Oakland Jewish Center.

Selma and I decided to purchase the house, for which we paid $27,000. We moved in about two months after the date of purchase. As soon as we moved in, our neighbors came by to introduce themselves and their children, who were all around the same ages as Phyllis and Alan. Our new neighbors were very friendly and offered to help us get settled. We made some repairs to the house, put in new kitchen cabinets, and installed a central air-conditioning system. We also very quickly became members of the Oakland Jewish Center.

After the period of mourning for Selma's father and the purchase of our house in Bayside, I gave serious thought to opening my own law office in Manhattan, from which I would also continue my insurance brokerage business. I told Ronald Podolsky that I was ready to rent an office, provided he would join me and share the rent. I suggested that we could hire a part-time legal secretary. We would still work for Gwertzman, and at our own office we could prepare wills and do real estate closings or stockholder agreements. Since none of this would require court appearances, Mr. Gwertzman wouldn't find out about our outside practice.

Ronald went along with my idea. He suggested that we rent an office at 15 Park Row, about four blocks from Gwertzman. The building wasn't very distinguished, but it was good enough for us starting out, especially since the rent wasn't high. We rented a suite consisting of two offices, one for me and one for Ronald, a room for the secretary, a library, and a waiting room.

I developed several clients from my insurance practice, and I did some wills, real estate closings, and stockholder agreements for clients I had developed in the garment industry when I was a salesman for Stelzer. Podolsky mostly did police work as well as wills. Neither of us as yet had many law clients, so we continued to work for Gwertzman.

I was in court for Gwertzman clients almost every day, and as time passed I developed a very good relationship with many of the lawyers who represented the various insurance companies. I became acquainted with some of the company executives too, because I had to sit down with them to negotiate settlements.

One day Mr. Gwertzman assigned me a substantial water damage case that was scheduled for a pre-trial conference in the Supreme Court of Westchester County in White Plains. My opponent at the conference was Michael Saunders, the managing attorney of the Glens Falls Insurance Company. After we made our arguments, the judge advised Saunders to settle with me. We settled the case for 80 percent of our claim, which was a good settlement.

Mr. Saunders had noticed my heavy accent and, after we left the judge's chambers, he inquired about my background. I gave him a brief account of my family's history and our war experiences. In turn he told me how his middle-class parents had fled from Russia and the Bolsheviks during the October Revolution and had come to the United States. He was quite interested in my description of life in the Soviet Union and my views on communism.

Before we departed, Mr. Saunders told me that he liked the way I had presented my case before the judge, and added that he admired my perseverance in getting an education and becoming a lawyer. He said, "Larry, if you ever open a law office, I will give you as many cases as you can handle from the Glens Falls Insurance Company, whom I represent as its attorney of record." Furthermore, he said, he had a very good relationship with many insurance companies, and would see to it that I got some subrogation work from them.

When I told Mr. Saunders that I already had a law office, at 15 Park Row, he promised to send me some subrogation cases as soon as he returned to his office. Two days later I received a large number of subrogation cases from the Glens Falls Insurance Company.

I told Ronald Podolsky that I would be leaving Gwertzman at the end of the week and from then on would conduct my own practice full-time in our office. Ronald wished me good luck, but said that at this juncture he couldn't quit Gwertzman because he didn't have enough clients for a full-time practice. He said that he would stay on in our office, though.

Chapter 10

LARRY WENIG, ATTORNEY AT LAW

I gave Mr. Gwertzman notice that I would be leaving, but didn't say anything about setting up my own practice as a subrogation attorney. He wished me good luck and said he was sorry to be losing me.

My law practice began to boom--almost every day the mail brought in new cases from the Glens Falls Insurance Company, and also from the Maryland Casualty Insurance Company and the Reliance Insurance Company, whose managers I had met through Mr. Saunders. I had so many subrogation cases that I had to sell my insurance business. Cases bearing the name Larry Wenig, Attorney at Law, now appeared on the calendars of all five civil courts of New York City, as well as in State Supreme Court. My cases also occasionally ended up in the courts of Nassau and Suffolk counties.

My earnings increased from week to week. Very often I had to hire lawyers on a per-diem basis to help out when I had cases in different courts on the same day. I purchased my first Cadillac. Selma stopped working as a substitute teacher in the Bronx because the commute was too long and we no longer needed her earnings. Occasionally, Selma went to the civil court in Queens County for pre-trial conferences on my cases in Queens. One didn't have to be a lawyer to participate in a pre-trial conference.

Phyllis and Alan entered the elementary school located about three blocks from our house, and then went on to Cardozo High School, which was also within walking distance. I acquired some very substantial new clients--the Continental Insurance Company, Chubb Insurance Company, and the American International Adjustment Company--and had to hire a full-time lawyer to help handle the work.

What with all these developments, I felt that my office should be in a more prestigious building. One day, while walking back from the courthouse, I happened to meet Lou Turen, the senior partner of Turen & Turen, a firm that specialized in personal injury cases. Their office was located at 250 Broadway, a very fine building. I told Lou that I was thinking of moving out of 15 Park Row, and he offered to rent me space in his large suite of offices.

When I moved to the Turen & Turen suite, my friend Ronald Podolsky remained at 15 Park Row, but we continued to have a very warm and cordial relationship. My new law office was much larger and had a beautiful view. I hired a new legal secretary, Sylvia Ramos. She was an excellent legal secretary, very professional and very friendly. Thanks to Sylvia, Selma and I could sometimes go away for a few days of vacation. She almost became a part of my family.

Even though I had developed a very successful law practice which brought me rich financial returns, I never forgot that I was a Holocaust survivor. I always told the judges and other lawyers of my wartime experiences. I won respect from my client insurance companies, as well as from judges and lawyers. This was the period of the Cold War, and I made a point of warning the judges, lawyers, and insurance executives I met about the danger posed to our nation by the Soviet Union. I was also preoccupied with concern about the security of the beleaguered State of Israel.

During the Six-Day War in 1967 I was barely able to sleep, but Israel's stunning victory over its Arab neighbors lifted my spirits. I was very much involved in work on behalf of the State of Israel. I became an active member of the Zionist Organization of America and within a short time was the president of the North Shore Zionist District, one of the largest branches on Long Island. The North Shore Zionist District at that time had more than 400 members. Occasionally, the executive board held its meetings in the finished basement of our Bayside house.

In 1968 I decided to take my entire family, as well as my widowed mother-in-law, on a trip to Israel. We left for Israel in June via KLM. While in Israel we met my mother's three sisters and their families, who had survived the Holocaust and gone to Israel after the war. We also met Uncle Max Sarna and his two married sons, Eliezer and David, who were both officers in the Israeli Army and had fought in the Six-Day War.

Max told me at length about my natural father's family. In addition to the many Sarna relatives in Canada, I learned that I was related to two renowned Judaic scholars, my cousin Nahum Sarna and his son Jonathan. Nahum Sarna was a professor at the Jewish Theological Seminary in New York, and Jonathan Sarna was on the faculty of Brandeis University. Nahum Sarna's other son, David, was a scientist.

Max Sarna was a very learned man, and he made a great impression on me. He again tried to persuade me to change my last name, but once again I refused, explaining that my stepfather had not only brought me up, but had saved my life during our five-year ordeal in the Soviet Union.

Our first trip to Israel was a wonderful experience for all of us. We visited most of the historic places: Jerusalem, Hebron, Haifa, Masada, Jericho, Nazareth, and Bethlehem. We also went to the Wailing Wall and the Golan Heights, and took a walk in the Dead Sea. At the Wall, as is customary, I placed a slip of paper in a crevice with a prayer asking God to grant us good health. The trip to Israel was inspiring and moving. I felt that I had finally fulfilled the silent oath I had taken in August 1945 after the pogrom in Kraków, and I resolved to visit Israel regularly as long as my health permitted.

The day we got back from Israel I was tired because of the six-hour time difference, but I had to return to work because I had been away for almost two weeks. The other attorney in my office and my able secretary, Sylvia Ramos, had not neglected business but had competently handled whatever came up during my absence. Of course, the courts aren't as active during the summer, which is vacation time. In a couple of days I was able to adjust to the time change.

Around this time I began to experience some health problems. I sneezed constantly, I had a runny nose, and my eyes were red and teary. Friends introduced me to Dr. Herman Pelz, an allergy specialist in Queens. His office was packed with sneezing patients complaining about their allergies. Dr. Pelz told me right off that I had hay fever and possibly some other allergies. He gave me a series of tests which revealed that in addition to hay fever I was also allergic to dust, feathers, shrimp, mustard, peanut butter, and vinegar. He warned that on cold days I was not to go outside right after taking a morning shower. He suggested that I install a steam room in my house and use it several times a week. In addition I would have to come to his office every week for an injection. I did as Dr. Pelz said, installing a steam room in the shower room in our basement, and reporting faithfully every Friday for my injections. After several years, I was totally cured of all my allergies.

It was at this time that I experienced the devastating loss of my dear, good Uncle Irving, who died suddenly of a heart attack. My parents and I were grief-stricken by his death. He was such a wonderful and charitable person and so good to all of us. He brought us to America. He gave us a beautiful apartment in his building rent-free. He gave my father a job in his factory. He also gave father money to enter the hotel business, and from time to time he gave my parents extra money whenever they needed it. My parents, my sister, and I mourned for a long time the passing of dear Uncle Irving.

The goodness of Uncle Irving remained alive in his wife, Aunt Ruthie, and her children. They continued to let my parents have their apartment rent-free. Cousin Jerry took over the metal factory and continued to employ my father, just as my uncle had.

My law practice, meanwhile, continued to grow, for I was getting more and more cases from my insurance companies. I had acquired an important new client, Crum & Foster Insurance Company. Because of my strong relationship with the insurance companies and the respect I had among their managers, I was often able to settle cases before they reached the trial stage.

Despite the success of my law practice, and despite my happy marriage and the joy I derived from my wonderful children, Phyllis and Alan, there were still many, many matters that troubled me.

The security and survival of Israel were always on my mind. I was very concerned about the hostility of the Arab Muslim countries toward Israel. The Khartoum Resolution of 1968, generated at a meeting of the eight foremost Arab countries, produced the declaration "No negotiation, No recognition, and No peace with Israel."

My other concern was the welfare of the Jewish people in the Soviet Union. Anti-Semitism had been rampant in Russia under the tsars and even more under the Communists. In the early stages of the October Revolution in 1917, some Jews had joined Lenin, and some, such as Leon Trotsky, Grigori Zinoviev, and Yakov Sverdlov, became leaders of the Communist Party. Nonetheless, the Jews in the Soviet Union were butchered in staggering numbers.

Stalin was responsible for the murder of more than 600,000 Jews. He killed practically every Jewish leader of the Communist Party. He murdered practically all of the Jewish writers, poets, and artists. Among those whom Stalin executed were the well-known writer Isaac Babel, the famous theater director Vsevolod Meyerhold, the famous actor Salomon Mikhoels, the famous poet Itzik Feffer, and Dr. Miron Vovsi, the chief physician of the Red Army. In 1953, during the Doctors' Plot trial, the deaths of two important Politburo members, A. S. Scherbakov and Andrei Zhdanov, were attributed to Jewish doctors in the Kremlin. The announcement of the "plot" unleashed a wave of anti-Semitic reprisals in Russia. Stalin forced many leading Jews to sign a letter asking him to deport the entire Jewish population to the gulags of Siberia, "for safety." Novelist Vasily Grossman, the famous violinist David

Oistrakh, historian Isaac Mints, and Nobel physicist Lev Landau were forced to sign the letter. Trains were assembled in all the large cities to transfer the entire Jewish population to the gulags.

Fortunately, Stalin died on March 5, 1953, and his evil plan never came to fruition. Nonetheless, vicious anti-Semitism continued after Stalin's death. When Leonid Brezhnev became the leader of the Soviet Union, the anti-Semitism intensified. Official memoranda to Communist cells read as follows: "Vse Kromie Yevreyev: Everyone but the Jews." Jews were discriminated against in jobs, colleges, and academies.

As a result, an upsurge of Zionism developed among the Jews of the Soviet Union. They openly declared that they wanted to leave the Soviet Union and settle in their ancient homeland, Israel. These Jews who openly defied the Soviet state were incarcerated in gulags. They were called refuseniks.

One of the famous refuseniks was Nathan Sharansky, and when world Jewry took up his cry, the Soviet Jewish Movement was born. One of the organizers of the movement in America was Yacov Birenbaum. I immediately joined the movement and became a very active member on Long Island. I participated in demonstrations, and I delivered lectures on the plight of Soviet Jewry. I wrote letters to our congressmen and senators in Washington, pleading with them to take up the cause of Russian Jewry. Numerous letters on behalf of Russian Jewry went out from my law office to our officials in Washington. By this time, my very able legal secretary, Sylvia Ramos, probably knew more about Israel and the plight of Russian Jewry than the average American Jew.

At this point in history, which came at the height of the Cold War, I was concerned not only about the fate of Soviet Jewry and Israel, but also about the serious problems our nation faced from the bellicose leaders of the Soviet Union. They were beginning to make encroachments in the Middle East and were wooing the Arab Muslim countries by selling them their most modern offensive weapons.

As President of the North Shore Zionist District in Queens, I introduced the "Zionist Congressional Breakfast." The breakfast, to which we invited members of Congress from Queens and Nassau counties, took place once a year, usually in the spring, and was held at the Hillcrest Jewish Center on Union Turnpike. Our rabbi at the time was Israel Mowshowitz, a highly respected Jewish leader in New York City. Among those who attended were Representatives Benjamin Rosenthal and Geraldine Ferraro, and Senator Alfonse D'Amato. The breakfasts were always sold out. They were an important opportunity to tell our elected officials about our concerns regarding Israel, the Soviet Union, and the Arab countries.

I had an unusual experience, which I still think about even now, when Jimmy Carter, the former governor of Georgia, first contemplated running for the presidency. Presumably to get a sense of how the American people felt about his proposed candidacy, Governor Carter came to New York City to test the waters, and while there was the guest speaker at a Sunday forum sponsored by several Jewish organizations at the Garden Jewish Center of Flushing. I was present as the president of the North Shore Zionist District.

I was assigned to sit on the dais next to Carter because of my knowledge of the Soviet Union. I told him about my experiences as a political prisoner and found him to be very friendly and very polite. However, I soon discovered that he knew very little about the Soviet Union and its plan to engulf the democratic nations. He didn't even know the names of the important Soviet leaders, nor did he have much knowledge of Russian history or of the Arab people and the Islamic religion.

We parted in a very friendly manner, but I couldn't help asking myself, "This man wants to run for the office of President of the United States?"

When I think back on my appraisal of President Carter, I believe that my opinion was correct. His policies in Iran and North Korea, and his lack of knowledge of the Arab Muslim world, demonstrated that my assessment of Jimmy Carter was all too true.

Meanwhile, time moved on. My daughter Phyllis graduated from Cardozo High School and entered the State University of New York at Binghamton. Three years later my son Alan also graduated from Cardozo, and he too entered SUNY Binghamton.

So far everything had gone smoothly in my life as far as my health was concerned. Suddenly, things changed. I began to experience severe pain in my stomach. I underwent numerous tests, which revealed that my gallbladder was full of gallstones. My doctors decided on gallbladder surgery.

Selma drove me to Wyckoff Hospital in Brooklyn, which had a specialist in gallbladder surgery on its staff. After my gallbladder was removed, I was in severe pain during my ten-day stay in the hospital. My good Selma came to visit me almost every day. Ultimately, however, I recovered completely.

They say that when it rains, it pours. In the early hours of October 17, 1971, I received an urgent telephone call from my sister Hella asking me to come immediately to my parents' apartment in the Bronx because my father had fallen and was not feeling well. I rushed over, but by the time I arrived, my father was dead of a heart attack. I found my mother and sister sitting in the kitchen, crying. I tried very hard to console my mother, but she couldn't stop crying. Meanwhile, two undertakers came into the apartment.

Hella told me that immediately after my father expired, she had called the funeral home with which our Dynower society had a contract. I closed the kitchen door, so that my mother wouldn't see my father's body being taken out. It seemed as though the angel of death was starting to visit my family.

Early the next morning, I phoned all our relatives and friends, as well as Jacob Ores, the president of the Dynower society, informing them that my father had passed away. I told them that the funeral would take place the following day, and my father's body would be lying in the funeral home.

The next day the funeral home was packed with relatives and friends, including some employees, both Jewish and Christian, from Uncle's Irving's factory. A rabbi and the president of the Dynower society delivered eulogies. We left the funeral home and drove to the cemetery in Woodbridge, New Jersey. It is customary to say Kaddish, the prayer for the dead, when the casket is placed in the grave. The Kaddish prayer is always said by the son of the deceased. I wasn't his son, only his stepson, but since my stepfather's two sons from had perished during the Holocaust, I felt that I had a moral obligation to say Kaddish for him.

There is a Jewish religious custom for the family of the deceased to observe Shiva, a seven-day mourning period, usually in the deceased's house. During the Shiva period, members of the immediate family sit on small stools for the seven days of mourning, and it is customary for relatives and friends to visit the mourning family.

My mother was worried about whether she would be permitted to stay in the rent-free apartment that Uncle Irving had given to my father. As it turned out, my good and wonderful Aunt Ruthie, and her good children, Jerry and Norman, let her stay in that apartment rent-free until the day she passed away. My dear and good cousin Jerry, who took over my uncle's factory, mailed my mother a check every week in the amount of my father's weekly salary. I will always remember this noble gesture of my wonderful Aunt Ruthie and her son Jerry.

After my stepfather's death, I made it my business to call my mother every day, sometimes more than once a day. Selma also called my mother several times a week. And I made a point of visiting my mother at least once a week, usually on Sunday.

The winter of 1972 was very harsh and cold in New York. I can't recall whether it was in January or February of 1972 that we had a couple of days of heavy snowfall. The schools were closed for the day and the bus that took me to the subway station on Hillside Avenue wasn't operating. The snow drifts were so high that I didn't dare drive to the station, so I decided to stay home. Looking out the window of our living room, I saw the local children building snowmen in the middle of the street. Everything was white. I suddenly had the urge to write a poem. This was the first time in my life that I dared to write a poem.

WINTER

Snow is falling in the north,
Snowflakes glisten in the wintry sun,
The ground is a blanket of white,
Interspersed with footprints of all shapes and sizes.

Icicles are dangling from gutters and trees,
Silence is broken when they fall to the ground;
Daring bundled-up figures are making their way through,
Slipping, sliding, and falling on ice.

From a distance one can hear happy children's voices,
Navigating their sleds downhill in a great roar.
Nearby red-cheeked youngsters with dripping noses
Are rolling balls of snow, building snowmen.

Soon the spring sun will melt the ice and snow,
Swelling the rivers to their banks;
The snow birds will return from their winter abodes,
And all will be the same as before.

The next day the snow let up. The sanitation department was able to clear the streets during the night. My bus was in service again, and I took it as usual to the subway and was back in my law office. On returning to the office, I learned that my staff had been in the office the day I was absent, because they didn't have to travel by bus and the subway system had been operating.

The Zionist Organization of America often held its conventions in Israel. In August 1973, Selma and I went to the ZOA convention in Jerusalem. We had attended several earlier conventions, but this time we took along Phyllis, who was then 15 years old. Alan was already in Israel at a Zionist youth camp that summer. The convention delegates elected Selma and me to the national executive committee of the ZOA, a great honor. It was a very exciting and very productive convention. We met Israeli government officials and members of the Knesset, Israel's parliament. All told, we spent about two weeks in Israel, touring the country and visiting relatives.

From Israel we flew to Stockholm to visit my stepsister Susi. This was my first meeting with her. When we arrived at our hotel in Stockholm, Susi and her husband were waiting for us in the lobby. It was an unusual encounter. My sister and I were already on in years but we had never met.

Susi invited us to her apartment to get better acquainted. Naturally I wanted to know about my natural father, whom I had never even seen. My half-sister Susi, who was much younger than I, had no idea whether our father had ever tried to contact me. It occurred to me that perhaps he had tried, but my mother had interfered. This is one of the many mysteries of a life that can never be explained. I was very happy to have met my half-sister; we still keep in contact by mail.

After two days in Stockholm, Selma and I returned to New York. We arrived home late at night, and of course were very tired from the long trip. Early the following morning I called my mother, but there was no answer. That was rather strange, because it was very early and my mother should have been home. I called my stepsister Hella, who lived in the same building as my mother, and was shocked to learn that my mother was in Montefiore Hospital. She had polycythemia vera, a serious blood disease.

I rushed to the hospital. My mother didn't recognize me and couldn't even talk. I kissed her on the forehead, but there was no response. Her eyes were practically closed. I asked her doctor about her prospects, and he told me that she would expire soon.

It is difficult to describe the shock. When I left New York two weeks before to go to Israel, my poor mother had been in fairly good health. Now, two weeks later, she was on her death bed. My dear mother expired on August 23, 1973. She was buried in the Woodbridge cemetery in New Jersey.

It seemed as if the angel of death was crashing through the gates of the Wenig family to decimate us one after the other. My dear Aunt Ruthie was next on the list. She died in Florida. A little while later my dear cousin Norman, the son of Uncle Irving and Aunt Ruthie, collapsed at his front door and died of a heart attack.

In 1993, my stepsister Hella was diagnosed with cancer. She suffered for two years, during which time she was in and out of the hospital. We visited Hella during those two years whenever we were in New York. In April 1995, when Selma and I returned from Florida, we visited Hella in the hospital and she could hardly talk. She died on April 19, 1995.

Selma and I maintained a close relationship with our dear cousin Jerry and his wife Dolores. We visited each other both in Florida and in New York. Unfortunately, Jerry was diagnosed with prostate cancer, and he suffered greatly. Even so, Jerry and Dolores attended my grandson Matthew's Bar Mitzvah in New York a few weeks before he died. On November 4, 1998, Dolores called to say that Jerry had died. At that time I had a very severe cold. Nonetheless, Selma and I flew back to New York that same day in order to attend Jerry's funeral. Selma and I maintain a close relationship with Dolores, and we regularly get together in Florida.

A few weeks after my mother's death, I finally accepted the fact that she was no longer alive. I was ready to settle down again and enjoy my life with Selma and my children.

My hope of resuming a normal life was interrupted on October 6, 1973. I was in the synagogue with Selma on Yom Kippur, the holiest day of the year for the Jewish people, when a young man ran in screaming that Egypt and Syria had made a coordinated surprise attack against Israel. Everyone in the synagogue was shocked and stunned. I asked myself, and I am sure the other congregants asked themselves: What kind of people attack and invade other people on their most sacred holiday? I asked myself how a Christian country would feel if it were attacked and invaded by another country during the Christmas holiday. But on second thought I wasn't that surprised, bearing in mind everything I knew about Muslims and their hatred of infidels from my years in Soviet Uzbekistan.

Along with most of the other congregants I left the synagogue in order to get more information about the Arab attack on Israel. I ran home as quickly I could. On Yom Kippur, one isn't supposed to turn on or listen to the radio. I told myself that God would forgive me, given the grave news. When I heard all the details on the radio and, later, on television, I believe that my heart stopped beating. The news was simply devastating. More than 1,000 Syrian tanks had attacked the Golan Heights, where Israel had fewer than 200 tanks. Along the Suez Canal, fewer than 500 Israeli soldiers were attacked by close to 100,000 Egyptians.

I couldn't sleep that night, and for the next two days I didn't go to my law office. I was simply glued to the radio and the TV. When I heard Moshe Dayan, Israel's Defense Minister, speaking on TV, I could sense disaster and the disappearance of the State of Israel. I couldn't eat or sleep.

Over the next two days Israel mobilized its reserves and eventually repulsed the invaders, carrying the war deep into Syria and Egypt. The Arab states were swiftly resupplied by sea and air from the Soviet Union, which rejected U.S efforts to arrange a ceasefire. As a result, the United States belatedly began its own airlift to Israel. All of Israel's friends and supporters were grateful to President Richard Nixon for providing Israel with the weapons it needed.

Two weeks later, Egypt was saved from a disastrous defeat by the UN Security Council, which had failed to act while the tide was in the Arabs' favor. The evil Soviet Union had not been interested in peacemaking efforts when it looked like the Arabs might win. The same was true for Secretary-General Kurt Waldheim, who, we later learned, was a former Nazi. At least nine Arab states actively aided the Egyptian-Syrian war effort.

Israel's victory certainly lifted my spirits, and I became myself again. I went back to my office, and thanked my staff for keeping my law practice functioning efficiently and normally.

During those few days of despair, Selma had tried to cheer me up. I constantly kept in touch with the office of the ZOA, for I was a member of its national executive board, as well as a national vice-president.

At our first meeting after the end of the Yom Kippur war, there was a consensus among the members of ZOA executive board that despite Israel's victories on the battlefield, the war should be considered a diplomatic and military failure. A total of 2,688 Israeli soldiers had been killed.

My law practice had been growing steadily, for I was continually getting more work from insurance companies. I was in one court or another in New York City almost every day of the week. I won the respect of many of the judges, and at pre-trial conferences I always engaged the judges and lawyers in discussion about the international political situation. Some of them suggested that I should write a book about my experiences as a five-year political prisoner in the Soviet Union. I assured them that I would after I retired.

During summer vacations, Selma and I took overseas trips to various places. We went for two weeks each to Spain and Hawaii. In the summer of 1979, we took a very exciting trip to western Canada, where we visited the magnificent parks and mountains. On our Canadian tour we met quite a number of New Yorkers, some of whom told us that they were buying homes in Florida. House prices there, they said, were very reasonable, and it made sense to buy a house in Florida even if one only spent a few weeks in the winter escaping from the cold New York weather. Some of them told us that a new condo community called Strathmore Gate East was being built in Royal Palm Beach.

Selma and I decided to fly to Florida over the Labor Day weekend in 1979. We liked the model home that we were shown at Strathmore Gate East. We bought a very nice three-bedroom house there for $29,000. At this time in my life, I felt that I had a good legal staff in my law office. My son Alan had joined my firm after graduating from law school and passing the bar. I could depend on him, because he had become a very good litigator. I felt that it would be a very good idea to spend a couple of weeks in Florida during the cold New York winters.

In June 1982, the ZOA executive board appointed me to a delegation that was going to meet with members of the Israeli government in Jerusalem. We wanted to get a better understanding and first-hand knowledge of the previous year's war in Lebanon, when the PLO terrorists, including the chief terrorist Yasser Arafat, were driven out and went to Tunis. We also had a conference with Prime Minister Menachem Begin. I asked him whether he remembered the occasion when my father, my brother Shmulek, and I had met him in 1942 in Fergana, in the Soviet Republic of Uzbekistan, at the house of one of his friends from Wilno. Back then he was just another Polish soldier. Now, shaking hands and briefly talking to him, I felt his greatness and destiny. Begin apologized for not remembering me, explaining that his life had been so eventful that there were many incidents and people he could no longer recall.

Begin gave our delegation a rundown of the military and political situation in Israel and its problems with its Arab neighbors. He told us that the Israeli army was now at the gates of Beirut, and arranged for the Israeli army to take us on a tour of the area. An army officer drove me to the gates of Beirut and gave me a detailed account of the conflict.

On May 4, 1986, Selma and I received the Louis Brandeis Award, the highest honor given by the Zionist Organization of America. It was presented to us at a big banquet at Temple Shalom in Roslyn, Long Island. The presentation was made by Milton Shapiro, the national president of the ZOA. Also at the banquet was Dr. Joseph Sternstein, the immediate past president.

Meanwhile, my children were becoming adults. Phyllis graduated from SUNY Binghamton. She was interested in occupational therapy, for which she needed a master's degree, and enrolled at New York University. To make life easy for her and eliminate the long commute from our house, we rented a very nice apartment for her close to the university.

After receiving a master's degree in occupational therapy from NYU, Phyllis obtained a job as an occupational therapist at Mount Sinai Hospital in New York City. She continued to maintain her apartment near the university. She was dating Albert Russo, a Sephardic Jew whose parents were Holocaust survivors. Born in Greece, they had been sent to Nazi concentration camps but fortunately had survived. Albert, an accountant by profession, worked in his father's textile business.

In due course Phyllis informed us that she really liked Albert and wanted us to meet him. Selma and I were very impressed with Albert when she brought him to our house one Saturday. He seemed to be a very nice boy. When Albert brought Phyllis to his parents' home in Long Beach, New York, she made a very good impression on them, and they on her.

Albert eventually proposed, and Phyllis accepted. We invited his family to our house to get acquainted. Albert, his parents, and his two younger brothers, Cliffy and Larry, arrived at our house on a Sunday in the spring of 1982. Selma prepared a delicious meal of vegetable soup, salad, minute steak, and dessert and coffee. One of my clients at the time was a famous French baker, and his bakery, LaMarjolaine, made a large, delicious coffee cake for the party. It was a beautiful get-together of the Wenig and Russo families. We were very impressed with Albert's family, and they took a liking to us.

Albert's parents told us that they wanted to make the engagement party in about two weeks at their house. We even discussed a wedding date. Phyllis and Albert indicated that they would like to have their wedding at the beginning of the following year. Two weeks later Albert's parents made a very nice engagement party at their house. In addition to Selma and me, they also invited some of their relatives and friends.

Phyllis and Albert were married on January 15, 1983. At first they lived in an apartment in New York City because Albert wanted to be close to his father's business, which was located in lower Manhattan, and Phyllis wanted to be close to her job at Mount Sinai Hospital.

Albert's father had just acquired a substantial interest in 401 Broadway, a high-rise office building very close to the State Supreme Court and the New York County Civil Court. Because of its location, the building was home to a great many law firms. Albert said that his father could offer me a large suite at a reasonable rent. By then, my firm was too big for the premises I was subletting from Turen & Turen at 250 Broadway, and I needed more space. I accepted the offer and moved to 401 Broadway. My new office was very large, with several rooms and space for a large library and a conference room.

When Alan began his course of study at SUNY Binghamton, he intended to become a veterinarian. As a child he had been interested in animals. He occasionally brought home cats, and sometimes a neighbor's dog, and he had an aquarium with exotic fish. Talking over his plans with his college friends, he eventually decided to go to law school.

On graduating from SUNY Binghamton with very good grades, Alan went on to George Washington Law School. There he met and fell in love with a fellow student, Debra Kalmore. He asked us to come to Washington to meet her. Debra made a fine impression on us, and we approved. Debra's father was an accountant with a large firm in New York City. We later met the Kalmores at their home in Livingston, New Jersey.

Alan and Debra graduated from law school in 1986 and passed the bar exam the same year. They were married on November 16, 1986, and moved into a high-rise apartment overlooking the George Washington Bridge. Alan joined my law firm as a lawyer. I wanted to know whether he would like litigation practice, especially the practice of subrogation, in which my office specialized. Debra took a job with a large real estate law firm in New Jersey.

Alan found subrogation litigation quite interesting and decided to stay in that practice. I introduced him to the officers and managers of my client insurance companies and he made a good impression on them. I took Alan to the courts and introduced him to some of the lawyers and judges, and he was soon participating in pre-trial proceedings in the courts and also sitting in on some trials. Within a couple of months, he was trying cases on his own.

Selma and I soon became grandparents. Phyllis gave birth to three children, Matthew, Michelle, and Elena. Debra gave birth to Alex and Arielle. That made Selma and me very happy, as all our five grandchildren turned out to be very good children, and also very good students. They have made us very happy, and we have derived great joy from them over the years. We tried to see them and play with them as often as we could.

By now I had given up commuting to work by bus and subway, which took at least an hour and a half, and instead I was driving in every day. That was no fun, however, because I just couldn't handle the heavy traffic on the Long Island Expressway. I began leaving at 4:30 a.m., because that early it took only a half-hour get to the parking lot near my office building. The only vehicles I encountered on the way were milk and newspaper trucks.

As soon as I got into the office I would began dictating on my tape-recorder, and at about nine I went to the courthouses. I usually left for home at four, when there still wasn't much traffic on the LIE.

This schedule took a great toll on my health. I developed a heart condition and also had some prostate problems. I visited a cardiologist and a urologist in Queens, and was prescribed quite a number of pills for both conditions. I began to realize that I was getting older. My doctors suggested that I should slow down and take some time off for vacations. Selma and I went to Bermuda that summer, and we took some vacation time during the Christmas holidays at our house in Royal Palm Beach. While there, we furnished the house, but the furniture shopping took quite a bit of time and was quite stressful for both of us.

In June 1991 Selma and I were in Jerusalem attending the ZOA convention. We had been there barely two days when we received a telephone call from Seymour, Selma's brother in New York, saying that their mother had died on June 6th. The ZOA arranged for an immediate flight back to New York on El-AL. Needless to say, the sudden death of Selma's mother came as a shock; she had been in decent health when we left for the convention. Our entire family, along with relatives and friends, attended my mother-in-law's funeral.

Selma was heartbroken, for she had been very close to her mother. Since Selma's older sister Dorothy lived in Syracuse, Selma had always spent a great deal of time with her mother, taking her shopping and to doctors' appointments. My mother-in-law frequently stayed overnight at our house. We also took her to our Florida house to spend time with us there. It was some while before Selma accepted the fact that her mother was no longer alive, just as it had taken me some time to adjust when my mother passed away.

CHAPTER 11

RETIREMENT

MY HEALTH CONTINUED to deteriorate. My heart condition became more severe. Sometimes when I walked a few blocks I had difficulty breathing, and I had to stop and rest for a few minutes before I could go on. I had a very thorough examination by my cardiologist, Dr. Jose Meller, in Manhattan and he told me that my blood vessels were clogged. Dr. Meller arranged for me to have an angiogram at St. Francis Hospital in Roslyn, New York.

The angiogram was a dangerous procedure and quite painful, and it revealed that I did indeed have some blockage of my heart arteries. I was kept at the hospital over night, so that I could be monitored by the hospital staff. The doctor told me that for the time being open-heart surgery was not indicated and I could be treated with medication. He warned that cold weather was definitely not good for me and I would be much better off living in a warmer climate, especially during the winter.

This incident was very frightening. After I came home from the hospital, Selma and I had a serious talk about whether it was perhaps time for me to retire. I was almost 67 years old, and I was financially sound and could afford to retire.

We decided to move permanently to Florida. We would sell our house in Royal Palm Beach and move to one in Wellington, a much nicer place. Wellington was the home of the famous Polo Club. The area was horse country, and Selma liked horses.

We contacted a builder in Florida and told him that we would like to have a house on the water--something Selma had always dreamed of. The builder was currently building houses in a development called Lake Point, on the edge of Lake Wellington. He took us there and showed us a lot just across the lake from the Wellington Country Club. There were boats of all kinds on the lake. Selma was very excited by the sight, especially by the thought that she could go rowing. The builder also showed us a model house that he could build for us on the lot.

We decided right then and there to have the builder build us a house on the lot. The house would have three large bedrooms, a large kitchen, a large den, a large dining room, three bathrooms, a Jacuzzi, a steam room, and a two-car garage. The total price would be $250,000. We went back to the builder's office and signed a contract for the lot and the house, which, the builder told us, would take at least three to four months to build.

We phoned Phyllis and Alan and told them the news. They were both happy for us, but pleaded with us to spend part of the year in New York. We told them that we would discuss that upon our return to New York.

On our return to New York, Phyllis and Alan came to visit us. I told them that because of my age and my serious heart problems I had decided to retire and reside permanently in Florida.

Once again they both and pleaded with us to reside for some part of the year in New York. They told us that they loved us very much and wanted to be with us. I said that I fully understood their feelings, and we very much appreciated the fact that they wanted us to reside within easy visiting distance in New York. I told them to give us some time to think about it. I also told Alan that I would turn over my law practice to him, but I expected the firm to reimburse me for any consulting work I did. The name of the law firm would now be Wenig & Wenig Attorneys at Law. Before they departed, Phyllis and Alan asked us once again not to disappoint them by leaving New York.

Selma and I discussed the situation. We decided that we would become permanent residents of Florida and live there most of the year, but to make our children, our grandchildren, and ourselves happy, we would come to New York for the summers. Since we would be in New York only during the summer, we no longer needed our house in Bayside, so we decided to sell it and rent or purchase an apartment in Queens.

We looked for an apartment in Great Neck, but didn't like what the real estate agents showed us. Some friends suggested that we look at the North Shore Towers in Queens. We had always seen the high-rise buildings of the North Shore Towers when we traveled on the Grand Central Parkway, but we had never paid much attention.

I made an appointment with the rental agent of the North Shore Towers, a very nice woman named Judy Goodman. Mrs. Goodman explained that the North Shore Towers complex was a co-op. Most of the residents owned their apartments, but there were some apartments that could be rented. The complex, a gated community situated on about 110 acres, included a golf course, tennis courts, and large outdoor and indoor swimming pools. The three apartment buildings each had 34 floors and 618 apartments, and the complex had its own electrical plant. It also had excellent indoor facilities.

Mrs. Goodman took us down to the arcade, where the indoor facilities were located. As we walked along the arcade, which was roughly a quarter of a mile long and connected the three buildings, she pointed out the restaurant, bank, movie house, supermarket, fruit and vegetable store, art store, dry cleaning establishment, beauty parlor, card-playing facilities, and a large entertainment hall where lectures were given.

Then she took us into the gym, which had every type of exercise equipment. We went on to the large indoor pool area, which had a large whirlpool, steam and sauna rooms, and shower facilities for both men and women.

Selma and I were very impressed. Surely there was no other facility like the North Shore Towers in all of New York City. I told Mrs. Goodman that we would like to rent an apartment on a high floor. Not a single apartment was available for rent at that time, but she promised to contact us as soon as the situation changed. I told her that we would be staying at our Bayside house until September, and then would be going to our Florida house. I asked her to call whenever an apartment became available. If it was after September, she was to call Phyllis in New York.

About two weeks later, I contacted a real estate broker in Queens to say that we wanted to sell our house in Bayside but couldn't vacate before September. Within a few days the agent brought a family to look at then house, and they decided to purchase it right then and there. We had purchased our house for $27,000, and we sold it for $275,000. At the time of this writing, the value of the same house is about $600,000. When we closed on the house, we put our furniture in storage and went back to Florida some time in mid-September of 1989, and we inspected the house in Wellington which the builder had just completed. The closing followed upon our approval, and we moved in shortly thereafter. We became permanent residents of Florida. We voted in Florida, registered our car in Florida, and obtained Florida driver's licenses. Of course we also paid Florida taxes.

Our house in Wellington was just magnificent. It had a breathtaking view of Lake Wellington. The enclosed pool was very large and the patio was enclosed with the pool area.

We moved our furniture from our Royal Palm Beach house into our new Wellington house, and we put the Royal Palm Beach house up for sale. We sold it through a real estate broker, and we lost money on the deal. Then we went on a shopping spree to purchase some additional furniture, paintings, and large pots with artificial flowers and large green leaves.

The house was now beautifully decorated. Our next purchase was a large boat with an electric motor. Selma and I really liked rowing our new boat on the lake, but we occasionally used the motor when we became tired. Of course we also greatly enjoyed swimming in our large beautiful pool.

One day, while relaxing in my Jacuzzi, I had a flashback of an entirely different period of my life. The human mind is so wonderful the way it can do this. I saw myself as a vrag naroda ("enemy of the people") in the gulag on the outskirts of Siberia. We were packed together there, fifty-five people on three layers of wooden bunks, with only a one-seat outhouse. The next flashback I had in my Jacuzzi was of the small mud room where my family of five had lived next to a cow in the Soviet Muslim Republic of Uzbekistan, close to the border of Afghanistan. How life had changed for me! I told myself how fortunate I was to have this complete turn of events in my life.

Since my mind was always focused on Israel and its problems with the Arabs, I decided to devote some of my time to a serious study of Islam, the religious culture that had shaped the Arab mentality with its hostility to Jews and Judaism. I purchased a copy of the Koran, and borrowed some books on Arab history from the Wellington library.

Toward the end of March, Judy Goodman called to say that three apartments had come up for rent at the North Shore Towers. I told her that I would have my daughter, Phyllis, make an appointment to look at the apartments.

I called Phyllis, and she went to North Shore Towers the next day. Phyllis called us from the sales office and said that she had only liked one of the three apartments. It was a corner apartment with a decent-sized kitchen, a dining room, a large living room, two bathrooms, a balcony, and two terraces. The former occupant, a doctor, had just passed away. Phyllis said that the apartment needed some work but would be very nice.

I told Phyllis that I wanted to speak to Judy Goodman. Without seeing the apartment, but based what Phyllis told me, especially the fact that it was on the 27th floor, I told Judy that I would take it. I asked what the monthly rent was, and she replied $2,000, with a two-year lease.

I felt that the rent was a little too high, but Judy said that I had to make a decision immediately, because corner apartments went like hotcakes. She also told me that the management had to do some work on the apartment, as well as put in a new refrigerator, gas stove, washing machine, and drier, so it would not be ready for us to move into until the end of April. I decided to rent the apartment, and Judy said she would mail me the two-year lease. I was to return it to her with two checks, each in the amount of $2,000. One check was to cover the first month's rent, and the second was a security deposit.

Phyllis was delighted by our decision. I told her that we would return at the end of April, and would move directly into our North Shore Towers apartment. I asked her to arrange for the storage company to deliver our furniture there.

We arrived at the North Shore Towers before noon one day at the end of April, and Phyllis was waiting for us in our apartment. When we entered and inspected it, Selma and I were thrilled. It was a beautiful apartment, and the view from our 27th floor balcony was just breathtaking. When I looked to the left, I could see Little Neck Bay. When I looked to the right, I saw Jones Beach. When I looked straight ahead, I saw a forest of trees. I grabbed Selma and Phyllis, hugging and kissing them because I was so happy with our decision to live there for the summer months. Our furniture arrived in the afternoon, as scheduled, and our good daughter Phyllis had filled our refrigerator with all kinds of food.

After arranging our furniture and unpacking the clothing we had brought with us from Florida, we went down to the restaurant in the arcade of our building for supper. Not having eaten lunch that day, I was very hungry, and I ordered a big meal for supper: minestrone soup, salad, my favorite eggplant parmesan, and chocolate cake and coffee. Selma and Phyllis had smaller meals.

After supper, the three of us took a walk in the large arcade. I came across an old client of mine, Henry Willner, and his wife Frieda, who had been living in the North Shore Towers for several years. Henry said, "Larry, you've moved into the greatest place. There isn't another place like it." Henry and Frieda introduced us to some of their friends.

The next morning, I went down to try out the gym. The first piece of equipment I went on was the treadmill. There was a TV on the treadmill, and I was able to watch the news and listen to the various TV commentators. I paid no attention to how long I spent on the treadmill, going at a speed of four miles per hour. When I stopped, I noticed that I had been on the treadmill for an hour and a half. After that I got on the stationary bicycle for about 10 minutes. After the bicycle, I did some weight lifting. I relaxed for a few minutes, and then went swimming in the large indoor pool, and spent a few minutes in the whirlpool, which was in the same area as the swimming pool. After swimming, I took a shower and got dressed in the locker room. I didn't go to either the steam room or the sauna that day.

Over the next few weeks I spent four or five days a week in the gym and the pool, and I did the same exercise routine each time. All of a sudden I began to experience severe back pains, but I didn't pay much attention to them. Now that I was retired, the gym and the swimming pool gave me something to do. When the back pain became too bothersome, Selma would massage my back with aspercreme before I went to bed.

I kept up the same regimen, but at last my back pain became so excruciating that I could no longer exercise and even had difficulty walking. A friend recommended a doctor in Great Neck. Dr. Bloom gave me a thorough examination, in fact a quite painful examination, because he twisted my body this way and that. He asked whether I was doing any exercises, and when I said yes, he had me describe my regimen in detail. When I did so, Dr. Bloom said in a loud voice, "Are you crazy? Are you out of your mind? You're close to 70 years old, and you go on the treadmill for an hour and a half!"

Dr. Bloom sent me to see an orthopedic surgeon. The surgeon diagnosed my back pain as a herniated disk, probably caused by my strenuous exercise in the gym. He said that he would try to help me with medication in order to avoid surgery, but I was no longer to go to the gym. The only exercise I was permitted was walking--not swimming--in the pool. By now I was in such severe pain that I had difficulty walking, and I spent quite a bit of time in bed, taking the prescribed medication.

Meanwhile, Dr. Bloom's office called and told me that my blood test had revealed that my body was not absorbing vitamin B-12. I was to come in once a month for a vitamin B-12 injection. This news, coming upon my back problem, left me depressed and despondent. I had retired to take it easy after all my trials and tribulations, and now I was almost an invalid, in terrible pain, and barely able to walk. In a way it was my own fault; I should have asked the gym personnel to plan a routine for me suited to my age and condition.

When I went to see Dr. Bloom for my monthly B-12 injection, I complained about my severe back pain. Dr. Bloom gave me an epidural, which in time lessened my pain.

Much of my time was now spent visiting doctors. In addition to my herniated disk problem, my heart condition had deteriorated. When I took a long walk, I would often feel that I was going to faint. I made another appointment with my cardiologist, Dr. Meller. He examined me thoroughly and arranged for a thallium stress test.

The test revealed that I had severe valve blockage and needed an angioplasty. Dr. Meller made arrangements for me to undergo the procedure at St. Francis Hospital in Port Washington. The angioplasty was performed by Dr. Ari Ezrati, a friend of my son-in-law, Albert, and it was successful. Within a few days I felt much better and no longer experienced any faintness while walking.

On the other hand, I still had severe back pain from my herniated disc. I went back to Dr. Bloom, and he sent me to Dr. Richard Blanck, a neurologist. Dr. Blanck prescribed a new medication and suggested physical therapy. When I told him that I would soon be returning to Florida, he told me to consult Dr. Richard S. Baylin, a neurologist in Boca Raton.

On our return to Florida in mid-September, I made an appointment with our family doctor in Wellington, Dr. Robert Rubin, for my B-12 injection and a general examination. I also made an appointment with Dr. Baylin, the neurologist in Boca Raton. Dr. Baylin agreed with the New York doctors. At this point in my life I shouldn't undergo surgery for my slipped disc. As an alternative he recommended a physical therapy clinic in Lake Worth and gave me a prescription for the therapy.

I began visiting the clinic several days a week. It was quite large, with a great many patients, both young and old, and all kinds of exercise equipment. The young woman who was my physical therapist did many exercises with me, both by manipulating my body and by having me use the equipment. At first the exercises were painful, but after several weeks at my back pain disappeared. I was eventually discharged from the center, but the therapist told me that I would have to do the same exercises at home for the rest of my life. She also told me that swimming and spending time in the Jacuzzi were also good therapy. I have certainly followed her advice. I swim in my pool in Florida practically every day, and I really enjoy being massaged by the warm water in the Jacuzzi.

Since I was now no longer in pain, I decided to go ahead with a project I had long had in mind: a book about my experiences as a political prisoner in the Soviet Union. I purchased a computer and a printer and began writing. I had no documents or diaries, nothing to consult except my memory, but it so happens that I am blessed with an excellent memory and I remember many of the events in my life. The book I wrote, *From Nazi Inferno to Soviet Hell,* was published by the Ktav Publishing House in 1999.

Several newspapers published reviews of my book. The longest and best review was the one in the New York Law Journal, the most prestigious legal newspaper in America. In addition, I was interviewed on cable TV stations in Nassau, Suffolk, Queens, and New York. I was also interviewed on NBC-TV in Florida, on the Mosaic Hour, and on the Bloomberg Radio Network Station in New York City.

I sent copies of my book to our newly elected President George W. Bush, and to Vice-President Cheney and Secretary of State Colin Powell. I also sent copies to our senators and congressmen. I delivered lectures about my book in temples in New York and Florida. I also gave a lecture at the Barnes and Noble bookstore in Bay Terrace, Queens.

It was a wonderful feeling when my book was published because I wanted the world to know about the brutalities perpetrated against the Jews not only by Hitler but also by Stalin. After my book was published, I developed confidence in myself as a writer, and I began to write Op-Ed pieces on important political and international issues. Some of these were published both in New York and in Florida. I also continued my activities in the Zionist Organization of America.

As I have already mentioned, I have been active in the ZOA for many years, and was both a national vice president and a member of the national executive board. When Morton Klein was national president, he asked me several times to attend meetings of the Conference of Presidents of Major Jewish Organizations in his place. This was a very great honor.

I still remember the meeting in May 1997. Our guest speaker was John M. Shalikashvili, the Chairman of the Joint Chiefs of Staff. In the question-and-answer period after his address on the military situation in the Middle East, I asked, "General Shalikashvili, if the government of Israel were to ask you whether Israel should give up to the Arabs the Judean Heights, in Judea and Samaria, as well as the Golan Heights, what would you advise, as a military expert?"

General Shalikashvili hesitated, then replied that he would do it only if the Arabs signed a real peace treaty with Israel!

I happened to be sitting next to Colonel T. Collins, a member of General Shalikashvili's staff. When I told him that I had been born in Poland, he said, "Then you speak Polish?"

"Of course," I replied. Colonel Collins said that General Shalikashvili had also been born in Poland and was fluent in Polish.

After the meeting, Colonel Collins introduced me to the general, and we spoke for a while in Polish. I promised to send him a complete account of my experiences in the Soviet Union. We said goodbye with the warm Polish phrase "Do widzenia."

When I returned home, I sat down at my computer and drafted a letter to General Shalikashvili. The last sentence was "Sto lat niech zyje lat," which means "May you live a hundred years." This is a verse from the song we sang in Poland on our birthdays. Several weeks later, I received a very warm letter from the general and a signed photograph. I felt quite honored, and reproduced both the letter and the photo in *From Nazi Inferno to Soviet Hell.*

At another meeting of the Conference of Presidents, the guest speaker was Haydar Aliyev, the President of Azerbaijan, who was in the United States for a meeting with President Clinton. I knew that Aliyev had been a lieutenant general in the KGB, so I didn't have much respect for him. We spoke in Russian, and when I told him about my wartime experiences, he offered his apologies for the treatment my family had received in the Soviet Union. "Now, however," he added, "we are all democrats." Knowing his background, I said to myself, "Some democrat!" Aliyev suggested that we take a picture together. I also included this picture in *From Nazi Inferno to Soviet Hell.*

Chapter 12

HEALTH PROBLEMS

My heart condition worsened, and so did my prostate problem. I returned to New York in April 2001, and from time to time had fainting spells when I got up suddenly from a bed or chair. I kept exercising in the gym at the North Shore Towers, but now I went on the treadmill for only half an hour and at a speed less than four miles per hour. I also did less weight lifting in the gym.

One night toward the end June, while getting out of bed, I fainted and collapsed on the floor. Selma dialed 911, and an ambulance took me to the North Shore Hospital in Manhasset. I was examined by Dr. Singer and Dr. Ram Jadonath, and they concluded that my heart condition had deteriorated to such an extent that I needed a defibrillator implant.

This really scared me. I was afraid that my life was coming to an end. The defibrillator was implanted in my chest around the Fourth of July weekend, and I spent several days in the hospital. Since I am not a good patient and I can't tolerate any pain, Selma hired a private nurse to stay with me at night. Upon my discharge, Dr. Jadonath informed me that my defibrillator must be checked in a hospital every three months.

Once I was home, I looked at the lump on the left side of my chest and I didn't like what I saw. I was embarrassed to go swimming at the gym, because the people at the pool would look at my chest lump and ask about it, and I had to keep explaining what that ugly lump was all about.

Meanwhile, we had become the owners of our North Shore Towers apartment. The lease we had signed two years earlier had expired in April. It was not renewable, but rather than move out we had decided to purchase the apartment. The price was $170,000.

Knowing that I was not in good health, and loving Selma very much, I made her the owner of our North Shore Towers apartment, just as I had made her the sole owner of our house in Wellington, Florida. The apartment needed some work in order to make it really nice. We carpeted the living room and our bedroom, and set up one room as an office. We also tiled the kitchen floor, and totally rebuilt both bathrooms. The entire cost of renovation was about $30,000.

I now had a beautiful house in Wellington, Florida, and a very nice apartment at the North Shore Towers, which had recently been renamed the North Shore Towers Country Club. However, my health was not at all good. My heart condition had continued to deteriorate. When I got up suddenly, my blood pressure dropped precipitously, and I felt faint and sometimes fell to the floor. I had a very good cardiologist in New York City, Dr. Jose Meller, but I was now looking for a cardiologist who was also a family doctor. I found him in Dr. Theodore Tyberg. His office was in Manhattan, but it was easily reached by bus from the North Shore Towers Country Club. Dr. Tyberg changed some of my heart medication, but continued my monthly injection of vitamin B-12.

My prostate condition had also deteriorated. Dr. Tessler, my urologist in Manhattan, had passed away, so I asked Dr. Tyberg to recommend a replacement. He told me he would recommend one of the best urologists in Manhattan, Dr. John Williams, whose office is located at 820 Park Avenue.

On my first appointment, Dr. Williams gave me the PSA blood test and a bladder test. I had to strain to pass my urine. Dr. Williams changed my medication, and directed me to visit him twice yearly, before leaving for Florida and as soon as I returned.

The North Shore Towers Country Club is a great place, with wonderful cultural facilities in addition to its wonderful physical facilities. Among other amenities, it has two monthly newspapers, the *North Shore Towers Courier* and the *Tower Times*. From time to time the clubhouse hires excellent outside entertainers. In addition, several times a month there are lectures on such topics as health problems, investments, the history of opera, and current political events. I have given lectures there on current events, and in particular the Israeli-Arab conflict. Senators, representatives, and other elected officials often come to report on their work.

As for our beautiful home in Wellington, we had encountered some problems. The house was in a community known as Lake Point. It wasn't a condo community, and the 130 homeowners had to take full care of their houses on their own. This often entailed a great deal of work and expense for the homeowner. Among other things, one had to hire a gardener, painter, pool service company, and exterminator.

For those who lived at Lake Point all year, it was not a problem to be there when an outside service company came to do the necessary repair or maintenance work on the house. In addition, we often had a problem finding someone to watch the house during our summers in New York.

Selma and I began to ask ourselves why two people really needed such a big house. Moreover, we were spoiled by convenience of living at the North Shore Towers Country Club, where all the work and maintenance on our apartment were done by the co-op management. We decided to look for a high-rise condo building in the Palm Beach area with facilities similar to those at the North Shore Towers Country Club.

Milton Gold, a dear Zionist friend of ours, lived in a condo community in West Palm Beach known as The Lands of the Presidents, and also as the President Country Club, because three of its high-rise buildings are named Washington, Jefferson, and Lincoln. The other three are named Parliament, Consulate, and Envoy.

The Lands of the Presidents was exactly the sort of place we were looking for. The condo complex consisted of six high-rise buildings and a number of one-story houses. A gated community occupying about 230 acres of land, the complex had two magnificent golf courses, quite a number of tennis courts, and an excellent clubhouse with a gourmet restaurant. Milton's apartment was in the Envoy building, the finest building at the President Country Club.

Milton invited us to visit him. We were enthralled by his magnificent apartment with its breathtaking view of Palm Beach. I am by nature a person who makes snap decisions, and I told Selma right then and there that we should sell our Wellington house and purchase an apartment at the Envoy. Selma, who usually takes her time making decisions, agreed right away. I asked Milton whether he could arrange for us to purchase an apartment on a high floor in the Envoy building. That same day he introduced us to Charlotte Sharkey, the real estate broker for the condo, and we told her what we wanted.

There was nothing available on a high floor of the Envoy, but Charlotte showed us some apartments in the other buildings. We didn't like them, and we told Charlotte that we were only interested in the Envoy building. She promised to call if anything became available.

Around the end of March 1999, Charlotte called to say that a two-bedroom apartment had just come up for sale on the 16th floor of the Envoy. It was owned by a Mexican citizen who had just passed away and his children, who resided in Mexico City, were willing to sell it. Charlotte told us to come right away, because the apartment was a hot commodity and some other brokers might try to sell it.

Selma and I drove over to the Lands of the Presidents to see the apartment. We were stunned by its size and beauty. It was 2,000 square feet, and consisted of a very large living room, two very large bedrooms, a nice-sized kitchen, and a huge terrace overlooking Lake Mangonia, and with a view of the Atlantic Ocean. The terrace was large enough to accommodate three lounges, a table, and several chairs. The apartment was completely furnished, and the children of the former resident were willing to sell it with all its furnishings, bedding, towels, dishes, and kitchen utensils. They were asking $225,000 for the apartment, including the furnishings.

Real estate prices in Florida at that time were very low, and I had a feeling that the children wanted a quick sale, so I made an offer of $185,000 cash, no mortgage. Charlotte agreed to submit my offer but said that they would never accept. I felt sure that I was going to get the apartment

The following morning, Charlotte reported that the sellers were willing to sell for $185,000 and wanted a quick closing. I told her that we were ready to proceed to the closing as soon as details could be worked out.

I gave Charlotte a deposit to show that I was as anxious to purchase the apartment as she was to sell it. I explained that I wanted to have a title search and an inspection of the apartment by the Northstar Inspection Services, which would look over the plumbing system and do the environmental testing of the apartment. Although it was now the middle of April, and I had to return to New York for the summer, I told Charlotte that there was no reason why we couldn't close on the title by mail.

We went back to New York as scheduled, and the contract was executed by mail between Mexico, West Palm Beach, and New York City. The closing took place on June 15, 1999. Once again I thought that it was a good idea for Selma to be the owner of the apartment.

While still in Florida in April, I gave our Wellington house to a local real estate broker with instructions that we were willing to sell for $230,000. The real estate broker said that the house was really beautiful, but no one was going to pay that much, because Florida real estate prices were very low.

In August, the broker called to say that she had a solid purchaser who was offering $175,000. As much as I didn't like the offer, I accepted because of the weak real estate market.

We returned to Florida in September, and the taxi drove us straight to our new apartment in the Envoy. The new apartment was magnificent, but Selma and I decided to make it even more beautiful. We hired Dale Weidman, the excellent decorator who had done our Wellington house, to decorate our new apartment at the Envoy. Dale suggested that we get rid of the old carpeting and install new carpeting in both bedrooms. He picked out the new carpeting as well as a beautiful chandelier for the dinning room area. He changed the lighting fixtures in other parts of the apartment, had the whole apartment repainted, and rearranged the furniture, incorporating some pieces we had brought from our Wellington house.

When we moved into the Lands of the Presidents, our lifestyle changed dramatically. In Wellington we had very little social life, just attendance at Friday evening services at Temple Beth Torah, and occasional lectures during the week by Rabbi Stephen Pinsky. In contrast, the President Country Club has a magnificent clubhouse, an excellent restaurant, and frequent lectures. The Envoy building has its own party room, called North One, on the ground floor, and we have parties there four nights a week. Our Envoy neighbors are very fine people and very friendly. The building also has a very large pool with a waterfall.

Charlotte Sharkey recommended Dr. Robert A. Wacks, whose office is in the St. Mary's Hospital complex, a short drive from the Envoy. Dr. Wacks, whom I visit at least once a month, is a very fine doctor, and he is dedicated to his patients. I have always found him to be friendly and patient. He spends a great deal of time with me, making sure that I am properly diagnosed and properly treated.

In October 1999, we closed on the sale of our Wellington house, losing about $70,000 on it. We gifted our furniture from the house to the Jewish Community Center Thrift Store of West Palm Beach. The furniture we gifted was appraised at more than $10,000.

Through the autumn of 1999, I was preoccupied by political developments. The first of these was the failure of the so-called Oslo Peace Agreement after Yasser Arafat refused to accept the generous proposal made by President Clinton and Prime Minister Ehud Barak. Knowing the history of the Arab people, I was neither surprised nor disappointed, for I had always felt that the Oslo Agreement would be a great tragedy for the State of Israel. Soon after this the second Intifada broke out.

I submitted Op-Ed pieces on various aspects of the Arab-Israeli conflict to a number of newspapers. Most of them were published by the *Sun-Sentinel* and the *Jewish Journal,* both Florida papers. The South Florida *Sun-Sentinel* is an excellent paper and a good friend of the State of Israel. Victoria Preuss, the editorial page editor, is a very intelligent and decent human being, and she accepted almost all of the Op-Ed pieces I submitted to her.

The New York Times, to which I have subscribed for over 30 years, refused to publish any of my Op-Ed pieces or any of my letters on the Arab-Israeli conflict. *The Times* is no friend of Israel. Some of my friends have canceled their subscriptions to the *Times* because of its anti-Israeli policy.

In April 2000 we again returned to New York for the summer. My heart condition was still deteriorating, and my prostate was becoming larger. I constantly saw my doctors, and regularly checked my defibrillator at the North Shore Hospital. Despite these problems, I still managed to attend meetings of the ZOA executive board at the national office in Manhattan, and I gave lectures on the Arab-Israeli conflict at the North Shore Towers. I also kept in touch with my son, Alan, advising him on legal matters.

On the morning of September 11, 2001, I was at home reading the *New York Times* as usual when the telephone rang. I answered it to hear one of my friends screaming, "Larry, are you aware that Arabs just crashed two airplanes into the Twin Towers of the World Trade Center?" I hung up and turned on the TV. I couldn't believe what I saw. My law office was about a block and half from the World Trade Center. My first thought was whether Alan and the other lawyers and staff were all right. And naturally I was very concerned about all my fellow Americans who were working in the World Trade Center. I knew that there were thousands and thousands of them. I used to go to the World Trade Center whenever I visited my law office during the summer months in New York and I frequented the many stores located there.

I immediately called the office and got Alan on the phone. He told me that they were all right, but the office was full of soot and my faithful secretary Sylvia was hiding under her desk and screaming. Alan told me that they were vacating the office and would try to get out of Manhattan.

I was glued to the TV, and when I saw the towers fall and the World Trade Center disappear I felt that my heart was dropping into my stomach. Selma and I were unable to eat on that tragic day. Who could eat, when our country had been so cruelly attacked? We couldn't take our eyes off the TV.

About 8 p.m. our doorbell rang. We opened the door, and there was Alan. He was pale and covered with soot. His shoes were practically black with soot from the Trade Center collapse. Alan told us a horrendous story. He had wanted to go home to New Jersey, but that was impossible because the transit system in Manhattan had stopped operating. His entire staff of lawyers and secretaries had walked over the Brooklyn Bridge, hoping to find some transportation there. Not finding any buses, he walked all the way to the Long Island Railroad station at Atlantic Avenue, hoping to get to our apartment. After waiting for several hours, he was finally able to board a train, which took him to Great Neck, and from there he took a taxi to the North Shore Towers.

When he got there, our security personnel stopped the taxi to find out who Alan was and what he was up to. They were suspicious because his clothing and face were covered with soot. The security at the North Shore Towers entrance gate was severely tightened on that horrible September 11th. Alan told us that our security guards had searched the taxi, and had made the driver open the trunk. It was only after the search that they allowed Alan to enter the premises of the North Shore Towers.

When he reached our apartment, Alan was so tired he could hardly walk. He phoned Debra to tell her where he was and that he was okay. Then he took a hot bath. Afterwards, Alan described the horrendous scene at the World Trade Center, had a cup of hot tea, which was all he wanted, and went to sleep.

The next morning, after breakfast, Alan asked me to drive him to the Long Island Railroad station in Great Neck, because he wanted to go home and be with his family. Selma brushed Alan's suit, which was filthy with soot, and I cleaned his shoes. He had difficulty walking that morning, because he was so exhausted from walking for several hours the day before. I drove Alan to the Great Neck station and stayed with him until a train arrived. I kissed Alan goodbye and asked him to call us as soon as he arrived home.

Selma and I were relieved to learn that our son-in-law, Albert, had not gone to his office at 401 Broadway that fateful morning. Albert usually drove to his office after the heavy traffic on the Long Island Expressway subsided. When he heard about the attack on the World Trade Center, he knew that he couldn't get to Manhattan and so had remained home.

The events of 9/11 stunned the entire nation. We had always assumed that we were safe from attack, protected by two oceans. We knew now that this was not so. People were fearful and anxious. Many were afraid to travel by air. My daughter-in-law, Debra, even refused to drive across the George Washington Bridge for several months.

Nevertheless, Selma and I flew down to Florida just a few days after the tragic events of 9/11. I will never forget our experience at Kennedy Airport. It took a very long time to board the plane because of the very thorough searches we had to undergo.

An upsurge of patriotism was our response to those evil Muslim hate-mongers. We all wore flag pins in our lapels and attached large American flags to our cars. We simply wanted to show the Muslims that they would never defeat us. There was a sad mood in the Lands of the Presidents, and it was palpable wherever I went, on the street, in stores, and in the restaurants. I resumed my program of reading books on the history of Islam in order to have a better idea of what we in the non-Muslim world are facing.

Back in New York for the summer of 2002, the first thing I did was make an appointment with Dr. John Williams, my urologist. I was experiencing great difficulty in urinating and had to strain severely. Dr. Williams took a number of tests, including an echogram, and they revealed that my bladder did not empty fully. Dr. Williams told me that this was a serious problem, but he would wait one more year to determine whether I should undergo prostate surgery.

My heart condition didn't get any better either, and my fainting spells continued whenever when I got up suddenly from a bed or chair. One day in June 2002, after I came back to our apartment from the gym at the North Shore Towers, I blacked out and fell down, smashing my head against the closet door. Blood flowed from my head as I lay on the floor.

Selma immediately drove me to the North Shore Hospital, where the emergency room doctors put eight staples in my head. I was kept in the hospital for four days, in order to determine the cause of my fainting spells. The doctors in the hospital kept in touch with Dr. Theodore Tyberg, my New York cardiologist. One of the doctors asked whether there was anything that caused me aggravation. I told him that I was upset about the deaths of our 3,000 Americans on September 11th and about the Intifada in Israel, where people were being blown up on buses and on the streets.

We returned to Florida in September. All that year I attended the monthly meetings of the ZOA in Delray Beach. I also did a great deal of swimming in our very beautiful pool at the Envoy building. I am exaggerating when I use the word "swimming.' Mostly I just walked in the pool, because my doctors had told me that walking in water was good exercise.

In March 2003, I attended an Israeli Bond Dinner at the President Country Club and purchased $5,000 worth of Israeli bonds--a $1,000 bond for each of my five wonderful grandchildren. Support of the State of Israel has always been one of my paramount activities.

In April 2003, we returned to the North Shore Towers. Although my heart condition had always been my main concern, and I always made my first medical appointment with Dr. Theodore Tyberg, my cardiologist, this time I made my first appointment with Dr. John Williams, my urologist.

I saw Dr. John Williams in May and again had a series of tests, including an echogram. The echogram revealed that my prostate had become so enlarged that it was preventing my bladder from releasing the bulk of my urine. Dr. Williams said that this was very dangerous and we needed to address it right away. Some day, and it could be in the near future, I might be in a place where there was no hospital nearby, and I might die because I would not be able to pass my urine. The only solution was surgery, as soon as possible.

I am by nature a coward when it comes to pain. I simply can't tolerate it, and I knew that surgery involves pain. However, I realized that there was no alternative. Selma, as always, was with me in Dr. Williams's office. I looked at her, and then told Dr. Williams that since there was no other solution, I was reluctantly willing to undergo the surgery. He told me to go home and he would make all the arrangements.

Dr. Williams called several days later to say that he had made reservations for me at the New York Presbyterian Hospital for the second week in June. I asked Dr. Williams to inform Dr. Theodore Tyberg, my cardiologist, that I would be undergoing prostate surgery. Dr. Tyberg is also affiliated with the New York Presbyterian Hospital.

My good and dear daughter Phyllis arrived at our apartment around five in the morning on the day of my scheduled hospital appointment, and she drove Selma and me to the hospital. My good and dear son Alan arrived at the hospital a bit later that morning. At the hospital, I underwent pre-surgery procedures and all kind of tests.

The surgery had been scheduled for the next morning. The surgery, I was told, would not involve any incision on my body, as it would be done through my penis. When I heard that, I developed goose bumps. I was assured that I would not feel any pain because I would be anesthetized.

Selma and my children were with me the next morning when I was taken in a wheelchair to the operating room, and they all kissed me on the forehead. I saw Dr. Williams and another doctor in the operating room. Each of them was dressed in a green gown, and had an instrument of some kind on his head. I was administered some medication and fell asleep.

I woke up a few hours later and was told that the operation was over and had been a success. At that point, I didn't feel any pain. However, some time later when I was given a urinal bottle, I felt such great pain that I kept screaming as I passed urine into the container. The nurse explained to me that the pain was the result of the surgical procedure. She asked me to control myself and not scream so loudly. Selma and Phyllis were with me practically the entire day.

Dr. Williams came to visit me late that afternoon. He walked in just as I was given the urinal to pass urine again. I felt such severe pain and screamed so loudly that people outside the hospital building must have heard me. When Dr. Williams heard me scream, he said that he had performed numerous similar surgeries and had never heard any of his patients screaming so loudly. He told me and Selma that I must have some mishegas, which means "craziness" in English, a Yiddish expression which he probably learned from some of his Jewish doctor friends. After hearing me screaming again on the second day, Dr. Williams decided to keep me in the hospital two days longer, hoping that I would stop screaming. Dr. Williams told Selma and Phyllis that he had never had a patient who was so susceptible to pain.

I was scheduled for discharge after four days, but because I still couldn't tolerate the pain, I wasn't released for six days. I was driven home again by my dear Phyllis. Selma hired a private nurse to stay with me for the first week at home.

After two weeks, I was fully recovered and my urinary problem had improved dramatically. I now passed my urine normally, without having to strain myself, and I felt like a young boy again. I was glad that I had agreed with Dr. John Williams and undergone the surgery. I was only upset because I had not been able to attend the Congressional Mission in Washington on behalf of Israel, which took place while I was in the hospital.

After my prostate surgery I felt that my health was finally improving, and that I would soon be well again even though I still had the nagging problem of fainting spells when I got up suddenly. Alas, my good mental disposition after the surgery didn't last very long.

In the spring of 2004, while in Florida, I began to feel severe pain in my esophagus whenever I swallowed food. For several months I tried to ignore the pain, thinking that it might be no more than a sore throat. I didn't even mention it to Dr. Wacks when he administered my monthly vitamin B-12 injection, even though the pain was becoming progressively more intense.

When we returned to the North Shore Towers that April, I began to realize that the pain in my esophagus was not going to go away. Late in May, I went to see Dr. Martin Edelstein, my doctor in New York, for my general checkup and my vitamin B-12 injection. I told him about the severe pain in my esophagus whenever I ate. Dr. Edelstein asked me how long this had been going on. When I told him, he said, "You mean to say that you never told your Florida doctor?" Dr. Edelstein was quite concerned, and told me to made an immediate appointment for an upper endoscopy with Dr. Alan Sloyer at the North Shore Gastroenterology Associates.

I was able to get an appointment with Dr. Alan Sloyer, whose office is in Great Neck, in the early part of June, two days before we were to leave for Florida to attend the Bas Mitzvah of a granddaughter of Selma's cousins, Morris and Agnes Stern. After the Bas Mitzvah we were scheduled to drive to Washington to participate in the ZOA's Organization's Congressional Mission on behalf of Israel. In Washington we had already made appointments to meet with several senators and representatives, as well as some State Department officials. I had made reservations at a motel in Washington for the duration of the Congressional Mission. We were going to be driven to Washington by Dave Solomon and his wife, Muriel. Dave is the president of the ZOA chapter in South Palm Beach County. After the Congressional Mission, we had reservations in a motel in Pennsylvania for the Bas Mitzvah of the daughter of Selma's niece, Lisa Kletter.

June 13, 2004, was our fiftieth wedding anniversary, but it was also the day when we had to leave for Florida, so Phyllis and Albert celebrated our anniversary earlier. They took us out on the Sunday before our anniversary to a very nice Italian restaurant in the theater district in Manhattan, and they gave us matinee tickets for the same day to see *Fiddler on the Roof.* Phyllis and Albert and our grandchildren Matthew, Michelle, and Elena had lunch with us. After the lunch, picture-taking, kissing and hugging, and wedding anniversary greetings, they left, and Selma and I went to see *Fiddler on the Roof.* We really enjoyed the new production of this wonderful show.

The following day I went to Dr. Sloyer's office for the upper endoscopy. When I awakened from the anesthesia, he told me that in addition to the upper endoscopy, he had taken a biopsy of my esophagus. Dr. Sloyer told me that he would know the results in a few days. I told him that I would be leaving for Florida in two days, and from there would be going to Washington and Pennsylvania. I said would call him from Florida to get the results of the tests. I still really thought that the severe pain in my esophagus must be a simple sore throat.

A few days later I called Dr. Sloyer's office from Florida. His secretary said that he was busy with a patient and couldn't come to the phone. I told her that my name was Larry Wenig and I was calling from Florida about a very important matter. The secretary asked me to wait a second while she buzzed Dr. Sloyer. He immediately got on and told me that he had some very bad news. "The biopsy shows that you have a cancerous esophagus," he said. I practically fell to the floor, and momentarily lost the ability to speak. After I recovered from the shock, I asked Dr. Sloyer, "What should I do?"

"Come right back to New York and see me as soon as you get here," he replied.

At that moment, Selma was in the gym at our President Country Club. I fell onto my bed, and my mind entered into another realm. Suddenly, in this mental realm, I saw my own funeral at the Gutterman Memorial Chapel in Woodbury, New York. I saw my dear Selma there with my children, my grandchildren, my friends from the North Shore Towers, and my Zionist friends. A cold sweat spread over me and dripped from my face. My heart was beating so fiercely that I could hear its loud pounding.

Selma returned from the gym, and when she saw me in bed, she asked me why I was so pale and sweaty. I answered, "Selma, dear, I have esophageal cancer."

She screamed, "Oh no!" But then Selma, the eternal optimist, kissed me on the forehead and said, "Larry, try to be optimistic." She reminded me that Jonathan Sarna, my cousin who is a professor at Brandeis University, also had been diagnosed with cancer of the esophagus and had been totally cured. However, I wasn't the least bit optimistic. I always like things to be in order, and I always plan for any eventuality.

I asked Selma to sit down on the bed, because we had to have a serious talk. "Selma dear, we have to be realistic. I am close to the age of 80, and I guess my time is up." I reminded her that several years before we had purchased a funeral plan with the Gutterman Memorial Chapel, which would take care of our funerals. Pursuant to that plan they would ship our bodies to their chapel in New York and would bury us in the cemetery in New York. I also reminded her that we had even selected and purchased caskets.

I told Selma that I wanted Rabbi Joseph P. Sternstein, a past national president of the Zionist Organization, to officiate at my funeral. If he was not available, then I would like Rabbi Arnold Marans of the Sephardic Temple in Cedarhurst, Long Island. Finally, I reminded Selma that our son-in-law, Albert, had promised to give us two burial plots in the large Russo family plot at the Beth David Cemetery on Long Island. Selma started to cry. "Please, Larry dear," she said, "you mustn't talk like that; you're going to survive this cancer, and you'll be all right."

We called Phyllis and Alan, and told them the sad news. They were as shocked as we were. They asked when we would be returning to New York, and I told them that I hadn't yet decided. Then I cancelled our various motel reservations and informed the people whom we would have been seeing in the next few weeks that we had been forced to change our plans.

I was unable to eat any lunch or supper that day, and went to bed early, but I couldn't sleep. I tossed and turned all night. The next morning, after breakfast, I told Selma that I wanted to return to New York that very day. Selma doubted that we would be able to get airline reservations on such short notice, but it turned out that JetBlue Airways had two seats available on a flight at 10:15 that morning. The price was exorbitant, but I had no choice. I had to get back to New York.

We quickly packed a carry-on suitcase, called a taxi, and set out for West Palm Beach airport. The taxi arrived a bit late. When we got to the airport, we asked the security people to search us quickly because I had to get to New York for health reasons. The JetBlue agent at the entrance desk said that the plane was about to take off, and I began running to the departure gate. Selma was running behind me, and she fell and hurt herself. Some bystanders helped her up, and I asked the agent at the gate to ask the captain to hold the plane for a moment so that we could board. They shoved us into the plane.

Selma and I sat down in our assigned seats. I took the window seat, and Selma sat down next to me. The plane took off, and I closed my eyes. All of a sudden, I recalled that November 11th would be my eightieth birthday, and I didn't know whether I would be alive to celebrate it. I slept through the flight, but Selma woke me up when we landed at Kennedy Airport. We took a taxi to our North Shore Towers apartment.

We called Phyllis and Alan, and told them we were back. I asked them to get the names of the best doctors in New York who specialized in cancer of the esophagus. I also called our dear friends Alvin and Phyllis Lefkowitz, whose niece was a radiologist at the Sloan-Kettering Cancer Center. A few hours later Phyllis called back. Her niece had recommended Dr. David H. Ilson at Sloan-Kettering, one of the top oncologists in the field of esophageal cancer.

In the next few hours I called all my relatives and friends in Florida and New York to tell them about my cancer. I also called my relatives in Israel, and my stepsister Susi in Stockholm. Everyone I spoke to assured me that they would pray for me. They asked my Hebrew name, and the Hebrew names of my father and mother, so that the prayers for my recovery could be recited in the proper traditional format.

Before long, in synagogues in Florida and New York and some other states and countries, people would be praying for my recovery. My relatives in Israel would be praying for me at the Wailing Wall in Jerusalem. When I learned that so many people were praying for my recovery, I decided to have a positive attitude. I would not be depressed, and I would conquer my cancer, as I had conquered my other illnesses.

My daughter-in-law Debra called that night and told me that she learned that the Sloan-Kettering Cancer Center had a very good female surgeon named Dr. Rush, who specialized in esophageal surgery.

The next morning I called Dr. Theodore Tyberg, my cardiologist, and Dr. John Williams, my urologist, informing them that I had been diagnosed with esophageal cancer. The same morning, I telephoned the office of Dr. David Ilson, the oncologist at Sloan-Kettering, to make an appointment. His secretary said that she could give me an appointment in eight days, provided Dr. Ilson could get the endoscopy and biopsy reports from Dr. Sloyer. She suggested that I see an esophageal surgeon beforehand, so I called Dr. Rush's office and set up an appointment for three days later.

Phyllis drove us to the Sloan-Kettering Cancer Center to see Dr. Rush. When we arrived, my good son Alan was already there waiting. Dr. Rush was a fairly young woman and a very pleasant person. She explained that oftentimes it is necessary to remove the esophagus and raise the stomach. I got goose bumps. Sometimes, she said, the surgery is preceded by chemotherapy and radiation treatments, and in some cases these come afterward. Dr. Rush said that she would contact my cardiologist to see if I was a candidate for surgery, and added that Dr. Ilson, the oncologist, would determine whether my cancer was operable.

Several days later, Phyllis drove us in for my appointment with Dr. David Ilson, and once again Alan joined us at the hospital. Dr. Ilson had already read the endoscopy and biopsy reports from Dr. Sloyer, as well as the report from Dr. Rush. After a thorough examination, he told me that he still didn't know whether I was a candidate for surgery. He was going to have me check in to Sloan-Kettering for two weeks of round-the-clock chemotherapy treatments and daily radiation treatments..

On a fateful Monday in July 2004, Phyllis drove me once again to Sloan-Kettering, where I was checked in and assigned a room and a special nurse. After a series of tests, a catheter was inserted into my arm, and chemotherapy fluid began to flow into my body. That afternoon I was wheeled into the radiation room for my first radiation treatment.

On Wednesday morning, my third day in the hospital, I experienced a sharp pain in my left chest. It became so severe that I blacked out. It was soon determined that I had suffered a heart attack. In consultation with Dr. Tyberg, the Sloan-Kettering doctors replaced the drugs I had been taking for the past several years with some new medication. They thought that the drugs I had been taking might have interfered with the chemotherapy treatment, possibly causing a negative reaction in my heart. The radiation treatments continued, and in about two days, when my heart condition stabilized, the chemotherapy treatments were resumed.

After two weeks I was told that I would be released from the hospital because I had received the maximum dosage of chemotherapy, but I would still need four more weeks of radiation. I was hardly able to walk. The doctors insisted that I begin walking in the hospital corridors, and I tried very hard to do so, but I needed Selma's assistance to keep from falling. My dear Selma came to the hospital to be with me each and every day.

My weakened condition would have made it impossible for me to come in from Long Island every day for the next four weeks to get radiation treatments. Instead it was arranged for me to stay at the Helmsley Medical Tower, a hotel about three blocks from the hospital, and basically used by outpatients of the hospital, and also by some doctors. I was prescribed 13 injections at the hospital pharmacy that Selma would administer to me over the next two weeks while I was staying at the Helmsley Medical Tower.

On my first night at the Helmsley Tower Hotel, I decided to take my first shower in two weeks. When I got out of the shower and commenced drying myself with a towel, my Guidant defibrillator went off with such a loud knock that I almost hit the ceiling. I gave a loud scream, and I thought that my body was exploding.

My defibrillator had never before activated. Selma got me into bed, then called Sloan-Kettering and asked to speak to a cardiologist. When a cardiologist got on the phone, Selma told her what had just happened and asked whether she should bring me back to the hospital. The cardiologist assured

Selma that it wasn't necessary, but told her to call my treating cardiologist in the morning.

The next day Dr. Tyberg arranged for me to be examined at the cardiology department of New York Presbyterian Hospital, which is a couple of blocks from the Helmsley Medical Tower. A young doctor checked out my defibrillator and found that it was in good working order. He faxed the report to Dr. Tyberg, and Dr. Tyberg called to tell me not to worry, everything was fine as far as my heart was concerned. (In June 2005, I learned that my Guidant model defibrillator was defective and that one young person implanted with this defective defibrillator had died. Sadly, the Guidant company never informed hospitals and doctors of the danger. I became very depressed when I learned that I had a ticking bomb in my chest. I had difficulty sleeping, and I suffered a great deal, knowing that I was walking around with this ticking bomb. I lived in trepidation for a few months, but my doctors eventually replaced my defective defibrillator with a Medtronic defibrillator.)

For the next four weeks I walked from the Helmsley Medical Tower to the hospital seven days a week to get my radiation treatments. I got weaker and weaker by the day. When I looked at myself in the mirror, I was so pale I looked like a ghost. Selma occasionally did some cooking in the kitchen of our hotel suite, and sometimes we went to a little nearby diner for lunch or dinner.

When the four-week radiation treatment ended, I was examined by Dr. David Ilson, my oncologist, and Dr. Bruce Minsky, the radiation specialist. Dr. Ilson said that it would be quite a few weeks before we knew whether the cancer cells had been destroyed. Dr. Minsky said the same thing, and warned that during the next weeks I would have a very, very difficult time. I would be very weak and tired, and would have difficulty walking.

Phyllis drove us home. My eyes lit up when I caught sight of the high-rise buildings of the North Shore Towers. I was so happy to be home again. Exhausted from the long car ride, I just fell into my bed. Lying there, I made up my mind to have a positive attitude and fight my cancer just as I had fought all my previous battles; once again, I told myself, I would succeed in achieving my goal.

When I got out of bed the next day, I had difficulty taking even two steps, yet I told myself that I must go on fighting. I asked Selma to walk with me in our corridor on the 27th floor of the building. For the first few weeks I was so weak that all I could do was walk with Selma holding by hand, and I could barely make it along the full length of the corridor. I was unable to go down to the arcade for a longer walk. I certainly couldn't go to the gym to exercise on the treadmill or swim in the pool. This was the beginning of August 2004, and throughout that month I was confined to my apartment, except for some walking with Selma's support in the corridor.

But I was determined and I pushed myself, and in September I forced myself to take the elevator down to the arcade and walk with Selma there. The arcade at the North Shore Towers is about a quarter of a mile from end to end. At first, I was only able to make one round trip, only half a mile. It is difficult to describe how weak and tired I was, and I even had difficulty talking. Yet I was determined, and I continued to force myself to do things that were beyond my physical strength. In these difficult moments, I reminded myself of what Dr. Bruce Minsky had told me--that the next few months would be very, very difficult.

In September 2004, I began to eat a little bit better, but my weakness was still there, and I still had to hold on to Selma to keep from falling. The High Holidays came, but I was not able to go to the synagogue. This was the first time since my arrival in the United States that I had failed to go to the synagogue on the High Holidays. I did a little praying in our apartment.

Despite my infirmity, I closely followed the pre-election news in 2004 on radio and TV. Selma and I always voted in Florida. This year, because of my illness, we requested absentee ballots. We filled them in and returned them to the election board in Florida.

The hurricanes that hit Florida in October did considerable damage at the Lands of the Presidents complex. More than 700 trees on its two golf courses were lost. Our Envoy building was so severely damaged that all the interior walls would have to be replaced. Judy Mestman, one of our neighbors, informed us that the parquet floors in the living room and kitchen of our apartment had buckled and would have to be replaced. Our kitchen cabinets were badly damaged and would also have to be replaced. We also sustained severe damage to both bathroom floors, as well as to the wallpaper in the kitchen and the bathrooms.

Hearing this bad news, I called the Mike Myers Insurance Agency. Mike Myers is an agent for the State Farm Insurance Company, from which we had purchased all our insurance policies since moving to Florida. I told Kimberly Perez at the agency that I had retained Harold M. Lightman, Public Insurance Adjusters, Inc, to handle our hurricane damage claim. Harold M. Lightman is a highly respected public insurance adjuster in Florida. I also asked our dear and good neighbor Judy Mestman to let Mr. Lightman into our apartment so that he could assess the damages we had sustained. He contacted the adjuster from State Farm and they set up a date to meet in our apartment and assess the damages together. I must say that State Farm is a very decent and respectable insurance company, and it acted in a very responsible manner, compensating us for all the damages we sustained to our apartment

Meanwhile, as the month of October proceeded, I began to feel much better. The food that I ate went down smoothly, and I no longer felt any pain in my esophagus. Dr. David Ilson had me come in for an examination and a CAT scan, and sent me to see Dr. Alan Sloyer for an upper endoscopy and a biopsy of my esophagus.

Three days later Dr. Sloyer's office called and asked me to come in. When Selma and I arrived, Dr. Sloyer gave us the unbelievable news that my esophageal cancer was in total remission. (I later received the same news from Dr. Ilson.) I almost jumped off my chair, and I was ready to grab Dr. Sloyer and hug and kiss him. I asked Dr. Sloyer and Dr. Ilson whether I could return to Florida. They both said that I could, but to stay out of the sun as much as possible. Of course I grabbed my dear Selma, and I couldn't stop kissing her in Dr. Sloyer's office. Phyllis was there, and I hugged and kissed her too.

At this moment of great joy, I told myself that it was my good disposition and positive attitude that had given me the strength to endure the pain and to fight on and lick my esophageal cancer. And I reflected that the many people in America and Israel who were praying for me had also helped me to defeat it.

We returned to our apartment, and I immediately called my son to tell him the good news. Next I called JetBlue Airways and got a flight to Florida for November 2. Then I called all my relatives and friends to tell of my recovery and to thank them for their prayers.

When we entered the Envoy building in Florida, I couldn't believe what my eyes saw that day. It is almost impossible to describe the damage to our building and our apartment caused by the October hurricanes. I contacted Marvin Domb, the president of Gold Coast Flooring & Interiors Inc., and asked him to make all the necessary repairs, including replacing the floors and the kitchen cabinets.

It was at this period of life that I decided to write this, my second book. In it I have described my life in America from the time of my arrival on these blessed shores. I have told of my accomplishments in my new country, the greatest of which was marrying the most wonderful and beautiful girl that I ever had the great good fortune to meet--my wife, Selma. Although the bulk of this book deals with the ups and downs of my personal life and my concerns about my deteriorating health, I want to emphasize that the Holocaust, the events of 9/11, the Arab Intifada in the ancient kingdom of Judea, and the anti-Semitism that is again raising its ugly head throughout the world have always been foremost in my mind, even during my serious illnesses.

Chapter 13

My Political Views and Assessment of Current Events

In studying history, I have learned that there is something evil in the human species, namely discrimination, persecution, and anti-Semitism. The strong always have contempt for the weak. The good-looking have contempt for the ugly or the less good-looking, the rich have contempt for the poor, and the majority always have contempt for, and persecute, the minority.

From the moment they were forced to leave their ancient kingdom of Judea some 2,000 years ago, the Jews have always been a tiny minority in the various countries in which they settled. They were always the "Wandering Jew." They settled everywhere, but mostly in the countries of North Africa, the Middle East, and Europe.

Some Christians of Europe persecuted and murdered the Jews not only because they were a minority but because they were considered to be "Christ-killers." The stigma of this accusation is based on viciousness, malice, and false facts. Blaming Jews for the crucifixion of Jesus is outrageously absurd.

In the time of Jesus, Judea was no longer governed by Jewish law, but by Roman law. Just as the countries of occupied Europe in World War II were governed by German law, and not by their own, because they had been conquered by Nazi Germany, so too Judea had been conquered by the Roman Empire and therefore was governed by Rome. The applicable law in Judea in the time of Jesus was Roman law, not Judean law. Similarly, the judges of the Sanhedrin, or high court, were appointed by the Romans. The Roman government also appointed Caiaphas, the High Priest.

According to ancient Judean law, no trial by the Sanhedrin could be held at night, but the New Testament tells us that the trial of Jesus took place at night. This proves that the trial was conducted under Roman law, not Judean law. Furthermore, under Jewish law, a trial that could bring a death penalty had to be conducted over two days, but according to the New Testament, the trial of Jesus took place on one night, and not over a two-day period.

Jesus was accused of claiming that he was the King of the Jews. The ruler of Judea at that time was the Emperor in Rome. Claiming to be king was a crime against the Emperor, and for this crime Jesus was convicted and sentenced to death. Jesus was convicted because the Romans regarded him as a rebel. They executed him by crucifixion, a method common under Roman law but strictly forbidden under Judean law.

In Mel Gibson's movie *The Passion of the Christ*, Jews are portrayed as jeering when Jesus is led to his crucifixion. Of course, I wasn't there when Jesus was led away to be crucified, but I have had some relevant experiences. In 1939 and 1940, when my family lived in Soviet-occupied Lwów, we were ordered to participate in public demonstrations and parades on May Day and October Revolution Day. We had to enthusiastically shout such slogans as "Glory to the Great Stalin," "Long live the Communist Party," and "Glory to the Great October Revolution," and officials stood by to report us if we did not perform as expected. Based on this personal experience, I believe that the Roman authorities in Judea ordered some Jews to go out and jeer at Jesus on his way to his crucifixion.

The belief that Jews were responsible for the crucifixion of Jesus has, over the centuries, brought terrible tragedies and disasters to the Jewish people in predominantly Christian countries. In the eleventh century, Jews were burned alive in York Castle, and were expelled from England. During the crusades, Jewish blood flowed like water in the Rhineland. Jews were burned alive during the Spanish inquisition. Jews were raped and slaughtered during the pogroms in tsarist Russia. The greatest tragedy befell the Jewish people during the Holocaust. Six million Jews were killed, the greatest such disaster in Jewish history.

Many of my American-born Jewish friends ask why I talk so much about the Holocaust, and about anti-Semitism, and about the security and survival of the State of Israel. They advise me, "Larry, you have done so well for yourself in America, you have a wonderful wife and children, yet all you have on your mind is the Holocaust, anti-Semitism, and Israel."

I explain over and over that the Holocaust simply petrified me and changed my life forever. I know that some Holocaust survivors in America don't carry this heavy burden and they lead normal lives without worrying about such issues. I am not one of them. I tell my American-born Jewish friends that the persecution and sufferings of my fellow Jews during the past 2,000 years have profoundly affected my life, and never leave my mind. I explain to them that certain events in my life are always with me, in my mind and in my heart. I cannot forget my visit to Auschwitz in July 1945, right after our escape from the Soviet Union.

A Polish Christian guide showed us around and described how the Germans had operated the camp. An endless stream of trains poured out frightened, helpless Jews, young, old, babies. They were brutalized, confused, terrified. Packed like sardines in the gas chamber, they were suffocated by Zyklon-B gas. The screams of the choking victims could be heard far and wide. After the screaming stopped, the doors to the gas chambers were opened and the dead bodies fell out. The gold and silver crowns were pulled from the mouths of the dead. Their hair was cut off. Their bodies were cut open and the fat was removed. We saw the mountains of soap made from the fat, the stacks of coiled rope made from the hair. When everything useful had been extracted from the bodies, they were burned to dust in the crematories.

I trembled in terror as the guide explained all this on that fateful day in July 1945. What I saw that day was something no mind could comprehend. I asked myself whether human beings could really perpetrate such evil. For some time thereafter I was unable to sleep or eat.

Another thing I constantly recall is the pogrom against Jews in Kraków on August 11, 1945. I saved myself from the mob by running as fast as I could. The pogrom took place less than three months after the end of World War II, when, as it is often claimed, anti-Semitism had subsided because the Holocaust had sensitized the world to its evil.

I tell my American Jewish friends how deeply they disappointed me when so few acted to save European Jewry during the Holocaust. Their response: "Larry, shh, shh, you're making too much noise." I tell them in return that no one is going to shush me, for I am determined to remind the world of the great injustices it has done to the Jewish people for the past 2,000 years.

I castigate American Jewry for its indifference and passivity. During the Holocaust they sat at their desks, or even hid under their desks, but did nothing. I tell my American Jewish friends that I will never hide under my desk, I will stand on top of my desk, pointing my finger. I will shout about the crimes perpetrated against the Jewish people in the past and continuing today.

I want to remind my Jewish American friends about the many pogroms throughout history that decimated the Jews of Europe. To give one example, the Bogdan Chmielnicki pogrom in Ukraine began in 1648 and continued through 1649. The first wave of violence destroyed the Jewish communities east of the Dnieper River. Thousands of Jews fled across the river. The Cossacks and the peasants followed and murdered them. It is estimated that 100,000 to 200,000 Jews died.

More recently was the Kishinev pogrom on April 6-7, 1903, in Russia. Government agents stirred up the pogrom with a poisonous anti-Jewish campaign in the newspapers that incited the populace. When the body of a murdered Christian child was found, and a young Christian woman patient committed suicide in the Jewish hospital, the mob became violent.

According to the official statistics, 49 Jews lost their lives and more than 500 were injured, some of them seriously; 700 houses were looted and destroyed and 600 businesses and shops were looted. The material loss amounted to 250,000 gold rubles, and 2,000 families were left homeless. Public opinion throughout the world was aroused, and protest meetings were organized in London, Paris, and New York. President Theodore Roosevelt sent a letter of protest to the tsar, who refused to accept it.

The great writer Leo Tolstoy expressed his sympathy for the victims, condemning the tsarist authorities for their complicity in the pogrom. The Russian writer Vladimir Korenko described the pogrom in his story "House No. 13." Chaim Nachman Bialik, the greatest Hebrew poet of the twentieth century, also described it in one of his most moving poems, "The City of Slaughter." In another powerful poem, "If Thou Wouldst Know," actually written some years before the Kishinev pogrom, Bialik extolled Jewish martyrdom down through the ages. I always cry when I read these beautiful poetic works.

There are so many incidents and tragedies that could be recounted. Remember the Crown Heights pogrom in New York City in 1991--a pogrom in the liberal, democratic United States! Or consider the shameful behavior of the Canadian government in 1939, when implored by a delegation of Jews to admit Jewish refugees fleeing Hitler and the Nazis. They asked Fred Blair, the top immigration official, how many Jews Canada could take in. He replied, "None is too many."

And as anyone who reads the newspapers or watches TV knows, hatred against Israel and Jews is spreading throughout the world. A case in point: Michel Rocard, the former Prime Minister of France, publicly condemned the Balfour Declaration as a "historic mistake" because it paved the way for the creation of the State of Israel. Moreover, on December 20, 2001 the French ambassador to England, Daniel Bernard, dismissed Israel as "that shitty little state." And who can forget Britain's Prince Harry attending a costume party callously dressed as a Nazi storm trooper?

I was also shocked at the recently published book by former President Jimmy Carter, *Palestine: Peace Not Apartheid*. The book shows Jimmy Carter's lack of understanding of history and terrorism.

Here is a quote from the book: "It is imperative that the general Arab community and all significant Palestinian groups make it clear that they will end the suicide bombings and other acts of terror when international laws and the ultimate goals of the Road Map for Peace are accepted by Israel."

To me, Jimmy Carter has implicitly justified the murder of Israeli lives at the hands of Palestinian Arab terrorists. I asked myself, why did Jimmy Carter write this seemingly anti-Semitic book? I was discouraged by a report written by the distinguished Harvard professor, Alan M. Dershowitz. According to this report, Jimmy Carter receives millions of dollars from the rich oil-producing Arab countries, especially from Wahabbi Saudi Arabia.

Also according to Dershowitz's report, in 1970 Jimmy Carter received large sums of money from a bank controlled by the Saudi Royal family, in order to bail out of the Carter family peanut business. Also, in 1993 the Saudi Royal family contributed $7.6 million to the Carter Center.

I want to emphasize to my American Jewish friends that hatred of Jews is not limited to Christians. It is a pernicious vice shared by many Muslims. A few shocking and distressing examples drawn from recent press:

Dr. Umayma Ahmad Al-Jalahma, of King Faisal University in Saudi Arabia, accuses Jews of using the blood of non-Jewish teenagers in making Purim hamantashen (pastries) and Passover matzo.

Sheik Abdul Rahman al-Sudayyis, the senior imam of the Grand Mosque in Mecca, recently made the following statement in London: "Jews are the scum of the human race, the rats of the world, the violators of pacts and agreements, the murderers of prophets, and the offspring of apes and pigs."

Standing beside this apostle of "diversity and equality" was a junior minister in the Blair government. To Britain's shame, he uttered not a single word in response to this despicable statement.

But I have something to say. I say to this imam, "You are a creature from the Stone Age, and you represent desert Islam." I would remind the imam that in 2004, five of the ten Nobel Prizes were awarded to the sons of pigs and apes: How many such awards have ever been given to Muslim Arabs? Instead they will be remembered for inventing the shahid (suicide bomber) if they do not reform their religion.

I would also tell the Stone Age imam from the Grand Mosque in Mecca what some of the greatest minds in human history have said about Jews and Judaism:

"The Jew is that sacred being who has brought down from heaven the everlasting fire, and has illumined with it the entire world. He is the religious source, spring, and fountain out of which all the rest of the peoples have drawn their beliefs and their religions."

--Leo Tolstoy, quoted by Chief Rabbi J. H. Hertz, *A Book of Jewish Thoughts* (Oxford University Press, 1966).

"Some people like the Jews, and some do not. But no thoughtful man can deny the fact that they are, beyond any question, the most formidable and the most remarkable race which has appeared in the world."

--Winston Churchill, quoted by Geoffrey Wheatcroft, *The Controversy of Zion* (London: Sinclair Stevenson).

"The Jew gave us the Outside and the Inside--our outlook and our inner life. We can hardly get up in the morning or cross the street without being Jewish. We dream Jewish dreams and hope Jewish hopes. Most of our best words, in fact--new, adventure, surprise, unique, individual, person, vocation, time, history, future, freedom, progress, spirit, faith hope, justice--are the gifts of the Jews."

--Thomas Cahill, *The Gifts of the Jews* (New York: Doubleday, 1998).

"One of the gifts of the Jewish culture to Christianity is that it has taught Christians to think like Jews, and any modern man who has not learned to think as though he were a Jew can hardly be said to have learned to think at all."

--William Rees-Mogg, quoted by Chief Rabbi Jonathan Sacks, *Radical Then, Radical Now* (London: Harper Collins, 2000).

"It is certain that in certain parts of the world we can see a peculiar people, separated from the other peoples of the world and called Jewish people. . . . This people is not only of remarkable antiquity but has also lasted for a singular long time. . . . For whereas the people of Greece and Italy, of Sparta, Athens and Rome and others who came so much later have perished so long ago, these still exist, despite the efforts of so many powerful kings who have tried a hundred times to wipe them out, as their historians testify, and as can easily be judged by the natural order of things over such a long spell of years. They have always been preserved, however, and their preservation was foretold. . . . My encounter with this people amazes me."

--Blaise Pascal, *Pensées*, translated by A. J. Krailsheimer (Harmondsworth: Penguin, 1968).

"The Jewish vision became the prototype for many similar grand designs for humanity, both divine and man made. The Jews, therefore, stand at the center of the perennial attempt to give human life the dignity of a purpose."

--Paul Johnson, *A History of the Jews* (London: Weidenfeld & Nicholson, 1987).

"As long as the world lasts, all who want to make progress in righteousness will come to Israel for inspiration as to the people who had the sense for righteousness most glowing and strongest."

--Matthew Arnold, *Literature and Dogma* (London: Smith, Elder, 1876).

"The Jews embarrass the world as they have done things which are beyond the imaginable. They have become moral strangers since the day their forefather Abraham introduced the world to high ethical standards and to fear of Heaven. They brought the world the Ten Commandments which many nations prefer to defy. They violated the rules of history by staying alive, totally at odds with common sense and historical evidence.

"They outlived all their former enemies, including vast empires such as the Romans and the Greeks. They angered the world with their return to their homeland after 2000 years of exile and after the murder of six million of their brothers and sisters. They aggravated mankind by building, in the wink of an eye, a democratic State which others were not able to create in even hundreds of years. They built living monuments such as the duty to be holy and the privilege to serve one's fellow men. They had their hands in every human progressive endeavor, whether in science, medicine, psychology or any other discipline, while totally out of proportion to their actual numbers. They gave the world the Bible and even their 'savior.'

"Jews taught the world not to accept the world as it is but to transform it, yet only a few nations wanted to listen. Moreover, the Jews introduced the world to one God, yet only a minority wanted to draw the moral consequences."

--Olive Schreiner, quoted by Chief Rabbi J. H. Hertz, *A Book of Jewish Thoughts* (Oxford University Press, 1966).

"If there is any honour in all the world that I should like, it would be to be an honorary Jewish citizen."

--A. L. Rowse, *Historians I Have Known* (London: Duckworth, 1995).

As the foregoing quotations make clear, many great scholars, statesmen, and authors think very highly of Jews and are quite respectful of them, yet our media, newspapers, and TV networks have shown a gross bias and naked hatred for the Jewish state of Israel. Articles and news clips in the *New York Times*, the *Boston Globe*, the *Los Angeles Times*, the *Atlanta Journal-Constitution*, the *Times of London*, *CNN*, the *BBC*, and thousands of newspapers and TV networks around the world have sought to demonize the State of Israel, the only democracy in the Middle East and the only Jewish state in the world.

I accuse the world media of gross incompetence. I accuse the world media of abrogation of journalistic integrity. I accuse the world media of sheer and transparent prejudice against Israel and the Jews. I accuse the world media of pandering to the Islamic nations' hatred of anything Jewish.

As a student of history, I have often asked myself why the Jews, persecuted, humiliated, and murdered, especially in Europe, did nothing to escape the brutality perpetrated against them during their 2,000 years of exile. I ask myself why the Jews in the Diaspora did not organize and return to their ancient homeland of Judea.

Searching for an answer, I have learned that for centuries the rabbis told the beleaguered Jews to wait for the coming of the Messiah, for only the Messiah could bring them back to their ancient homeland. Finally, some people became exasperated with this approach, and the Zionists grew up among them in the nineteenth century.

At first, many of the brave young people who became Zionists were prevented from returning to Palestine by their Orthodox parents and their religious leaders. Some of these young people disregarded their parents' admonitions, fled from their parents' homes, and went to Palestine to build up the ancient homeland. In many cases the parents mourned for them as if they were dead because of their refusal to heed rabbinic admonitions.

I will never forget that the teacher in my Hebrew school in Poland told us that when the Messiah comes, the dead will rise from their graves and roll underground all the way to Jerusalem, the ancient capital of Judea, and there they will meet the Messiah. Until then we need not do anything. I believed such nonsense then, but not now.

It is very disheartening to know that there are still fanatical sects like the Netorei Karta and the Satmar Chasidim that oppose the existence of the State of Israel because it was not founded by the Messiah. So much Jewish suffering over the millennia can ultimately be blamed on fanatical rabbis of this stripe and their preachment that Jews must await the Messiah to have their own state. These fanatics have contributed to the deaths of millions and millions of Jews.

Think too of the passivity of the American Jewish community during the Holocaust. American Jews were and are very charitable, but they did nothing to save their fellow Jews from the gas chambers and crematoria of Auschwitz.

They laud Franklin Delano Roosevelt as a great President and a friend of the Jews, yet he refused to admit the Jewish refugees on the *St. Louis*. Think too of his indifference to the report on the Warsaw Ghetto brought to him by Dr. Jan Karski, a very decent human being and a Polish Catholic, who heroically risked his life to sneak into the ghetto of Warsaw and bring information about the concentration camps to America. And think about how Roosevelt ignored the pleas of Treasury Secretary Henry Morgenthau, Congressman Emanuel Celler, and other Jewish leaders when they asked him to bomb the railroad tracks that led to the Auschwitz death factory and the gas chambers and the crematoria.

Think too about Harry Bingham, a very decent Christian and human being who was the U.S. vice consul in Marseilles after the fall of France. Ignoring his instructions, he issued visas to more than 2,500 Jewish refugees fleeing the Nazis, among them the famous artist Marc Chagall. Did Bingham get a medal? No, for his pains the Roosevelt State Department fired him.

The catastrophe that befell our nation on September 11, 2001 was a wake-up call. Until then we felt that we were secure because of our two natural borders, the Atlantic and Pacific Oceans. We failed to understand the hatred Arab Muslim fundamentalists, jihadists, and Islamofascists have for us infidels. We failed to understand that there are evil people in the world who are willing to blow themselves up in order to kill people of other religions.

Much of our ignorance of this problem I blame on our liberal media. When innocent people are blown up in the streets of Israel, our media blame Israel because of its occupation of supposedly Palestinian lands. Throughout history Jews have always been blamed for catastrophes, even the bubonic plague in Europe.

Since the media do not bother to report objectively and honestly on the Arab-Israeli conflict, I will now present some important information about the actual facts.

History of the Arab-Israeli Conflict

The ancient kingdom of Judea embraced all of what is now the State of Israel, including Gaza and the West Bank territories of Judea and Samaria, as well as the area that is now the Kingdom of Jordan. Judea was invaded and conquered by the Roman Empire. The Jews revolted twice against the Romans. Both revolts were brutally crushed and, as punishment, the Romans changed the name of Judea to Palestine. Many Jews were expelled from the country and resettled in Europe and North Africa.

The Jews in Europe were persecuted, and many were killed. Jews were not permitted to own land, nor were they allowed to become members of the guilds. They were persecuted, robbed, and mistreated in every imaginable way. Toward the end of the nineteenth century, some European Jews decided to return to their ancient homeland. Thus began the Zionist movement. Jews cannot be considered occupiers of Palestine, because as history shows, they were simply returning to their ancient homeland.

In 1917 the British government enacted the Balfour Declaration, which called for the establishment of a Jewish state in the entire territory of the ancient kingdom of Judea, which also includes the present territory of the kingdom of Jordan.

After World War I, the newly created League of Nations awarded Great Britain a mandate to create a Jewish state in all the land that comprised the ancient kingdom of Judea, as set forth in the Balfour Declaration.

In 1922 Great Britain violated the provisions of the mandate by ripping out 78 percent of the territory of ancient Judea and creating a new state which they named Trans-Jordan.

Britain imported Abdullah, a member of the Hashemite clan from Saudi Arabia, and appointed him Emir of Trans-Jordan. Britain betrayed the Jews in this way to suit its colonial interests. The League of Nations did absolutely nothing to stop Great Britain from violating the mandate.

After World War II and the Holocaust, the United Nations enacted a resolution to divide the 22 percent of what remained of the land of the ancient kingdom of Judea, creating two states, one Jewish and the other Arab. Despite the tiny size of the piece of territory the United Nations assigned to the Jewish state, the Jews agreed to this partitioning of their ancient land.

On April 15, 1948 the Jews of the Yishuv declared their territory an independent state, which they named Israel. The neighboring Arab countries, in violation of the United Nations partition resolution, invaded the newly created Jewish state in an attempt to throw the Jews out and into the sea. The Israeli Jews defeated the invading Arab armies and signed a truce agreement with some of the invading Arab countries.

In June 1967, the neighboring Arab states began violating the truce agreement, again with the intention of destroying the Jewish state. A war broke out, and again Israel managed to defeat the Arabs. Israel captured the Sinai desert and its ancient territories in Judea, Samaria, and Gaza, as well its ancient capital, Jerusalem.

There is a cardinal rule in history that if an aggressor nation invades another nation and is defeated, it pays a heavy territorial price for its aggression. A good example would be World War II. Germany invaded many countries, was defeated, and paid a heavy territorial price. Large parts of Germany were transferred to Poland and Czechoslovakia, and some to Russia. No one has ever said that they should return these territories to Germany.

But of course Israel is different, and Jews throughout history have always been treated differently. According to the European countries, Israeli Jews must compromise with their Arab enemies who still seek the destruction of Israel by giving up the West Bank territories.

History of Islam and the Koran

American political officials, commentators, and journalists are unbelievably ignorant about the history of Islam and about the Koran. To counteract this to some extent, I present below a short account of Arab Muslim history, and I quote certain Suras (chapters) of the Koran that describe how Muslims are instructed by their sacred text to deal with "infidels," as they call people of other religions. Many of the facts outlined below come from the book *Understanding Islam*, by Thomas W. Lippman.

At the time of the birth of Muhammad, the prophet and founder of Islam, the Arabian Peninsula was populated by numerous tribes and clans and families. Arab society was violent and barbarous. The practice of infanticide was widespread and accepted. Unwanted girls were buried alive the day they were born. While there were many Jews and Christians living in Arabia, most of the Arab people were pagans.

The city of Mecca was the religious and commercial center of the Arabian Peninsula. The powerful Quirash tribe dominated the city of Mecca. Every Arab tribe and clan had its own pagan idol, and these were stored in the shrine of the Kaaba, in Mecca. It is believed that the Kaaba contained about 300 idol gods.

Like Zeus in Greek mythology, in the Kaaba the most powerful and feared god was Allah. The Arabic name "Allah" means "God."

Almost every day of the year, one or another tribe came on a pilgrimage to Mecca to worship its idol in the Kaaba. Arabia was a desert, and the city of Mecca needed food and other supplies for the pilgrims. In order to get food, spices, wine, fruit, and even textiles, large camel caravans traveled from Mecca all the way to Syria and back. The pilgrims purchased products of every kind when they came to Mecca to worship their idols, consequently boosting the economy of Mecca.

Muhammad is believed to have been born in 570 C.E. to the Hashemite family in Mecca. Descendants of this family have long been important leaders in the Arab Muslim world. In modern times, the Hashemite Faisal became the king of Iraq, and Abdullah became the king of Jordan.

Muhammad's father, Abdullah, died before he was born. His mother, Amina, died six years later. Upon her death, Muhammad was entrusted to the care of his grandfather, Abdel Muttalib. When he died two years later, Muhammad was turned over to his uncle Abu Talib, an important merchant who operated large camel caravans that regularly trade in Syria.

Muhammad apparently accompanied some of the caravans to Syria. While there he encountered Christians and Jews and absorbed the idea of monotheism from them. Muhammad was fascinated by the idea of one God.

We are told that Muhammad was a shrewd operator on those trips to Syria. Khadija, a wealthy widow who owned a business that sent numerous caravans to Syria, hired him to manage some of them. She was so impressed with Muhammad's ability that she asked him to marry her. Muhammad was 25 years old when he married Khadija, and she was 40 years old.

Khadija bore six children, five of whom died, which was a misfortune for the Muslim people, because it left Muhammad with no sons to survive him, only a girl, Fatima. After Khadija's death in 618 C.E., Muhammad had at least nine other wives and several concubines, but he had no other children. Muhammed was 53 years old when he married Ayesha, his last wife, who was a nine-year-old child.

Muhammad often sought solitude in a cave on Mount Hira, near Mecca. The Koran tells us in Sura 97 that in the month of Ramadan in the year 610 C.E. the angel Gabriel appeared to him one night when he was meditating in the cave.

The appearance of the angel Gabriel to Muhammed is designated in the Koran as the Night of Qadr ("night of glory" or "night of power"). Sura 97 of the Koran tells us that this is when Allah called Muhammad to be his messenger. Muslims believe that the angel Gabriel commanded Muhammad, "Recite." Muhammad asked, "What shall I recite?" As recorded in Sura 96 of the Koran, the angel replied, "Recite in the name of your Lord who created man from clots of blood! Recite! Your Lord is the most bountiful one, who by the pen taught man what he did not know."

The Koran does not give any details about how the angel made himself known. It says that "a gracious and a mighty messenger, held in honor by the Lord of the Throne," revealed himself to Muhammad (Sura 89:19). "He stood on the uppermost horizon; then drawing near, he came down within two bows' length or even closer, and revealed to his servant which he revealed" (Sura 53:7).

Muhammad was so shaken by the revelation that he ran home, chilled and trembling, and asked Khadija to cover him with a blanket. Each subsequent revelation is said to have caused Muhammad to fall down in groaning, sweating fits. This is why some Christian scholars think that he may have been an epileptic.

The great poet Dante, in "The Divine Comedy," consigned Muhammad to the ninth circle of the Inferno, with the "sowers of schism and of discord." Because of the tradition that Muhammad actually fell down, groaning and sweating, as revelations came upon him, Henry Treece, in his history of the Crusades, attributed Muhammad's revelations to the sun-crazed musings of a semiliterate trader lulled into a trance by the swaying of his camel. Tor Andrae, one of Muhammad's first modern Western biographers, observed, "It has long been thought that Muhammad was epileptic."

After the Night of Qadr, Muhammad began to share his revelations with the people of Mecca. He encountered great difficulties in converting them to the new religion. Some of the Meccans accused him of madness, fakery, and flights of poetic fancy. In three years, he was able to make only 30 converts to Islam, among them his wife Khadija, his cousin Ali, and Abu Bakr, a wealthy merchant.

After a time Muhammad was able to make more converts, which caused some apprehension among the leaders of the Quraish tribe in Mecca. When Muhammad began to preach more widely, the community of believers grew, and so did the hostility of the Quraish. They were hostile because Muhammad was denouncing the gods who represented tradition and order. He was espousing a faith that chose religious brotherhood instead of tribal identity for the foundation of society. Moreover, he threatened the commercial profitability of the pagan activities centered on the Kaaba, which the Quraish controlled.

The Quraish subjected the early Muslims to severe treatment. They tortured them by fire and with heated rods of iron. The Muslim victims were chained and exposed naked to the heat of the midday sun, or made to lie with heavy rocks placed on their chest. This was a difficult period in Muhammad's life.

In 620 C.E. Muhammad made his famous night journey from Mecca to see the heavenly throne. According to Sura 17 of the Koran, Muhammad went up to see the heavenly throne on Borak, a winged horse. However, he first shuttled to what the Koran calls the farthest temple; from there he went up to the heavenly throne and then returned to Mecca the next morning.

Muslims claim that the farthest temple he shuttled to was the Temple Mount in Jerusalem, where the ancient Jewish Temple stood. According to Muslim belief, this one-night journey to the heavenly throne was an exalting spiritual experience that consoled Muhammad in his darkest hours when the leaders of the Quraish were making life miserable for the Muslims.

Shortly after the night journey, Muhammad was at a pilgrims' fair outside Mecca where he met some men from Yathrib, a city about 280 miles north of Mecca. Yathrib was populated by three Jewish tribes and two pagan Arab tribes, the Aws and the Khazraj.

At that time there were approximately 30,000 Jews in Yathrib, and they had some influence on the two Arab pagan tribes. Yet there were problems in Yathrib that led to disputes and even wars between the two Arab tribes, and wars between the two Arab tribes and the Jewish tribes.

When Muhammad learned about the quarrels in Yathrib, he told the men from Yathrib about his problems with the leaders of the Qurash, who were torturing his converts to Islam. They returned home and told their people of their meeting with Muhammad. At the fair the following year, 621, a delegation of 12 men from Yathrib, probably both Jews and Arabs, returned to Mecca and entered into an agreement with Muhammad that he would be welcome to reside in Yathrib.

In 622, a delegation of 75 citizens of Yathrib formally invited the community of Muslims to move to Yathrib. Muhammad was initially hesitant to move, as he believed that Mecca, with the shrine of Kaaba, was the center of Arabia. However, common sense dictated that he and his Muslim followers move to Yathrib, where they could live in peace, and where, hopefully, he would be able to convert some Arabs from that area to Islam.

Muhammad finally decided to settle with his Muslim followers in the city of Yathrib, where he could establish a useful power base. They left Mecca in small groups so as not to arouse the suspicion of the Quraish. The migration was completed on September 24, 622. That event in Islamic history is known as the *hijra* (or hegira, in English). The number of Muslim followers that went with him to Yathrib was a little more than 200.

Yathrib now became the new home of Islam and was renamed al-Medinat al Rasul, "the City of the Messenger." Yathrib has since been known as Medina. Muhammad found himself now in different and more promising circumstances than in Mecca. He could preach openly, and he was welcomed by the people of Medina.

There was no strong ruling power in Medina, so Muhammad's temporal authority grew rapidly. His first act of governance as "Commander of the Faithful" was the issuance of a charter establishing the relationship between the three groups that made up the population of Medina: his followers from Mecca, the Medinese *ansar* ("helpers"), and the Jews. The charter guaranteed religious freedom to the Jews. It declared that Muhammad would be the arbiter of disputes.

Muhammad's primary goal now was to convert the 30,000 Jews in Medina to Islam. He obviously thought that they would be an easy target for conversion because they were already monotheists. To entice the Jews he designated Saturday as the day of congregational prayer. In other words, Saturday would be the Muslim weekly holy day. He also directed the *qibla* (the direction of prayer for Muslims) toward Jerusalem. Muhammad closely observed the customs of the Jews and the details of their religious practice. He noticed that Jewish boys were circumcised on the eighth day after birth. We know that Muslims also undergo circumcision.

Muhammad probably heard Jews greeting each other with the words *Shalom Aleichem* ("Peace to You"). Muslims also greet each other with *Salem Aleikem.*

Muhammad probably noticed that Jews do not eat pork. Muslims also do not eat pork.

Muhammad probably noticed that the Torah, the Old Testament, is chanted, not read, at religious services. The Koran also is chanted, not read, by the Muslims.

Muhammad probably noticed that Jews fast on certain days during the year. Muslims too fast during the month of Ramadan.

Muhammad probably noticed that Jews gave a great deal to charity. Muslims too give to charity.

Muhammad observed that Jews prostrated themselves during the Yom Kippur services. Muslims also prostrate themselves when praying.

Muhammad noticed that when a Jewish person dies, his or her body is washed, wrapped in a white shroud, and buried on the day of death. Muslims follow the same procedure when a Muslim dies.

Thus it seems that Muhammad learned a great deal from the Jews in Medina and adopted their customs.

The working agreement with the Jews, however, did not last long. Muhammad naively expected the Jews to accept his religious message and his temporal authority and he became angry when they did not. The Jews mocked his revelations and scorned him for his imperfect understanding of the Jewish scripture.

Since the Jews in Medina refused to convert to Islam, Muhammad took revenge by changing the day of congregational prayer from Saturday to Friday. The Jews had their weekly holy day on Saturday, and the Christians had their weekly holy day on Sunday. Muhammad changed the *qibla* from Jerusalem to Mecca.

Knowing that the Jews did their shopping for Saturday on Fridays, Muhammad ordered the stores closed on Friday afternoon, in order to make it difficult for Jews to purchase their provisions.

Muhammad saw Jews as treacherous, claiming that they supported the Quraish in Mecca and violated their charter with the Muslims. The Jews did not simply rebuff Muhammad's religious message, they also ridiculed him. The Koran speaks of Jews in harsh terms.

In the Koran, Allah says, "Because of their iniquity, we forbade the Jews good things which were formerly allowed them, because time after time they have debarred others from the path of Allah; because they practice usury--though they were forbidden it--and cheat others of their possessions" (Sura 4:160).

Respect for Jews as "people of the book" gave way to excoriation and contempt; the Koran denounces the Jews as blasphemers and corrupters, and even associates them with pagans as the strongest enemies of Islam (Sura 5:85). "Those to whom the burden of the Torah was entrusted and yet refuse to bear it," says the Koran, "are like a donkey laden with books" (Sura 62:5).

Two of the three Jewish tribes of Medina were expelled from the city. The third Jewish tribe, the Qurayza, supported the Quraish during the Battle of the Trench, and when that engagement ended, the Muslims inflicted a terrible vengeance on the Jews. All the men, 608 in number, were beheaded; the women and children were sold into slavery.

At one time there were about 30,000 Jews in Medina, but Muhammad wiped them out even though they were the ones who saved Muhammad and Islam from extinction when they and the two Arab tribes opened the gates of Medina for him and made it possible for him to spread his message. If Muhammad had stayed in Mecca, the Quraish would have liquidated Muhammad and the few hundred Muslims there, and that would have been the end of Islam.

After the elimination of the Jews in Medina, and after the Quraish Army retreated from the Battle of the Trench, Muhammad felt that he could now challenge the Quraish of Mecca.

He gathered a band of at least 1,000 Muslims, and they marched on a pilgrimage to worship at the Kaaba in Mecca. When Muhammad and his Muslims approached the city, the Quraish leaders sent out a delegation to negotiate with him. Both sides entered a ten-year agreement known as the Treaty of Hudaibiya.

The treaty, signed in 628 C.E., allowed the Muslims from Medina to come to Mecca on a pilgrimage every year, commencing in 629 C.E. In 630 C.E., Muhammad broke his agreement with the Quraish and invaded Mecca with a large army and took possession of the city. The Muslims smashed the idols and threw them out of the Kaaba.

The principle of the Treaty of Hudaibiya is applied by Muslim countries when they enter agreements with infidel nations. In other words, any agreement a Muslim country enters with an infidel nation can be broken by the Muslim country, based on the principle of the Hudaibiya agreement.

Muhammad died on June 8, 632, leaving no will or any instructions as to who should succeed him upon his death. Muhammad left no son. His only child, Fatima, was married to Ali, Muhammad's cousin.

No one could claim succession to Muhammad's position as spiritual leader, as Muslims considered Muhammad to be the last prophet. He was the one to whom God told everything there is to know, and therefore there could be no other prophets. But someone had to have temporal authority to govern the Muslim community. Someone had to negotiate with non-Muslim tribes, levy taxes, and raise armies.

Several of Muhammad's companions turned to Abu Bakr, who was one of the first converts to Islam as well as Muhammad's father in-law. Muhammad's last wife, Ayesha, was the daughter of Abu Bakr. Abu Bakr was designated as Khalifa, or Caliph, successor to the temporal authority of the Prophet. This was not an election, it was simply a designation of Abu Bakr by a group of insiders from Medina.

The decision to award the caliphate to Abu Bakr instead to Ali, Muhammad's cousin and son-in law, created a schism in Islam that endures to this day. Thanks to this split, about 80 percent of the world's Muslims are Sunnis and 20 percent are Shiites.

The Shiites, or Shia, believe that Ali should have been the Caliph after Muhammad's death, because he was Muhammad's cousin and the husband of Fatima, Muhammad's daughter. Sunnis are defined as followers of the *sunna,* the "path" or "way" of the prophet, whereas the name Shia derives from the words *shiat Ali,* or "partisans of Ali." The Shiites are predominantly in Iran and Iraq, and the Sunnis and Shiites carry hatred for each other.

Abu Bakr died two years after he was designated as Caliph, and he was succeeded by Umar (Omar), also a Sunni. Umar was assassinated ten years later, and Uthman (Othman), another Sunni, was designated as Caliph.

When Muhammad died, there was no Koran. The Jews had the Torah, the Christians had the New Testament, but the Muslims had no book. It was Caliph Uthman who ordered the official compilation of the Koran, and it was put together many years after Muhammad died.

Muslim scholars explain how the Koran was compiled. After receiving God's revelations through the angel Gabriel, Muhammad shared these revelations in sermons to his fellow Muslims. When he gave these sermons, scribes wrote down them. Sometimes, if the scribes were not actually present, the Muslims who had heard Muhammad's sermon reported and the scribes wrote down whatever they said Muhammad had said. Muslim scholars claim that the Koran is the verbatim account of God's revelations that the angel Gabriel gave to Muhammad.

According to Muslim author Salman Rushdie, in his book *The Satanic Verses*, some of the scribes who wrote the Koran, probably more than 20 years after Muhammad died, added their own beliefs and interpretations, and therefore the Koran is not the verbatim revelations of God.

In addition to the Koran, Muslims also follow the *hadith*. This consists of a vast collection of statements on various matters by Muhammad and descriptions by people who knew him about how he conducted himself in all aspects of daily life. The hadiths summarize the duties, practices and beliefs of the true Muslim, and they are expressed in The Five Pillars of Islam

The first pillar is the *shahada*, or profession of faith: "There is no god but God, and Muhammad is the messenger of God." As I understand it, this means that Allah is the only true God, and it is an error to worship any other god.

The second pillar of Islam is prayer. Muslims pray five times a day.

The third pillar of Islam is *zakat*, "alms-tax," a mandatory donation to charity.

The fourth pillar of Islam is fasting during the month of Ramadan. The fast of Ramadan celebrates two very important events in Muslim history: the Night of Qadr, when the angel Gabriel appeared to Muhammad in the cave and delivered God's first revelations to him, and the victory of 300 Muslims from Medina over 1,000 Quraish soldiers in the Battle of Badr in 624 C.E.

The fifth pillar of Islam is the *hajj*, or pilgrimage. Pursuant to this pillar of Islam, every Muslim, man or woman, is obligated to make a pilgrimage to

Mecca at least once to worship at the Kaaba. The reason for the pilgrimage to Mecca is to commemorate Abraham's obedience to God's command to sacrifice his son--according to Muslims, this was Ishmael and not Isaac, as Jews and Christians believe.

I have been studying this matter for a very long time, and after analyzing the Koran and the history of the Arabs, I have come to the following conclusion. Unless the Muslim religion reforms, just as the Christian and the Jewish religions have reformed over the centuries, and unless the Koran is reinterpreted by modern, civil, peace-minded Muslims, the non-Muslim world will never be able to live in peace.

I am now going to list certain Suras of the Koran to demonstrate the religious component of the hatred Muslim fundamentalists have for people of other religions.

"O Prophet! Make war against the unbelievers [all non-Muslims] and the hypocrites and be merciless against them. Their home is hell, an evil refuge indeed."

--Sura 9:73

"When you meet the unbelievers in jihad [holy war], chop off their heads. And when you have brought them low, bind your prisoners rigorously. Then set them free or take ransom from them until the war is ended."

--Sura 47:40

"The punishment of those who wage war against Allah and his messenger and strive after corruption in the land will be killed or crucified, or have their hands and feet and genitals cut off, or to be expelled out of the land. Such will be their humiliation in the world, and in the next world they will face an awful horror."

--Sura 5:33-34

"When we decide to destroy a population, we send a definite order to them who have the good things in life and yet sin. So that Allah's word is proven true against them, then we destroy them utterly."

--Sura 17:16-17

"Then when the sacred months have passed, kill the infidels [all non-Muslims] wherever you find them, and take them prisoner, and besiege them, and lie in wait for them in every place of ambush. But if they repent and establish prayer, and pay the due taxes, then let them free. For Allah is forgiving, merciful."

--Sura 9:5

"In order that Allah may separate the pure from the impure, put all the impure ones [all non-Muslims] one on top of another in a heap and cast them into hell. They will have been the ones to have lost."

--Sura 8:37

"How many were the populations we utterly destroyed because of their sins, setting up in their place other peoples."

--Sura 21:11

"Remember, Allah inspired the angels: I am with you. Give firmness to the believers. I will instill terror into the hearts of the unbelievers: you smite them above their necks and smite all their fingertips off them."

--Sura 8:12

"Verily, the tree of Zaqum will be the food of the sinful [all non-Muslims]. Like molten brass, it will boil in their insides. Like the boiling of scalding water, seize him and drag him into the midst of the blazing fire. Then pour over his head the penalty of boiling water."

--Sura 44:43-50

These selections from the Koran help to explain attacks like the one that took place on September 11 and reveal why Arab Muslim fundamentalists have such hatred for people of other religions. It is because of this hatred that I am so very concerned about the safety and security of our America, as well as the safety, security, and survival of Israel. It is this concern that keeps me up at night.

Unfortunately, most European governments and even our own government and media do not as yet understand this problem. Our government considers Saudi Arabia to be an ally. Yet consider what our Saudi so-called allies are still teaching their students in their madrassas:

"Everyone who does not embrace Islam is an unbeliever. . . . One who does not call the Jews and Christians unbelievers is himself an unbeliever."

To offer greetings to a Christian at Christmas--even to wish them "Happy holidays"--is "a practice more loathsome to God . . . than imbibing liquor, or murder, or fornication."

Jews "are worse than donkeys." They are the corrupting force "behind materialism, bestiality, the destruction of the family, and the dissolution of society."

Muslims who convert to another religion "should be killed because [they] have denied the Koran."

Democracy is "responsible for all the horrible wars" of the twentieth century, and for spreading "ignorance, moral decadence, and drugs."

When I was a boy in prewar Poland, most of my reading was in history. In those days I thought that kings, presidents, and prime ministers were vastly superior to the rest of us and had almost godlike qualities. I was in such awe of kings, presidents, and prime ministers in those days--and I am almost embarrassed to write this--that I used to ask myself, "Do they do the same thing in a bathroom that I do?"

It didn't take me long to conclude not only that the rulers of the world do the same thing the rest of us do in the bathroom, but they also make the same mistakes. The American government persists in treating the Arab states as friends, and they always turn against us, biting the hand that feeds and protects them, whether by an oil embargo, or raising prices, or threatening Israel, or in some other nefarious way.

Our European Allies

Our so-called European allies are behaving the same way they did when Hitler and the Nazis came to power in Germany. If the European countries had acted strongly and with determination against Hitler in the 1930s, World War II would never have taken place.

When President Bush decided to take a strong position against the Muslim terrorists and invade Iraq, many of our so-called European allies refused to give us any assistance in that struggle.

These same so-called allies blame Israel for all the problems the world faces from Muslim fundamentalists and Muslim terrorists. They are now urging President Bush to force Israel to make huge land concessions to the

Palestinian Arabs and to establish as quickly as possible a Palestinian state, with its capital in Jerusalem.

These so-called allies want President Bush to force Israelis to give up their homes in Judea, Samaria and Gaza, the provinces of the ancient kingdom of Judea. I want to tell these so-called friends of ours that first, to set an example, they should give up the lands they currently occupy to the previous owners.

Let Russia return to Germany the part of East Prussia it annexed at the end of World War II, and to Japan the southern part of Sakhalin.

Let England return the Falkland Islands to Argentina. What right do the Brits have to the Falkland Islands? The Falklands are part of Argentina.

I urge the Brits to return Gibraltar to Spain. Gibraltar is Spanish territory.

I have the same message for France. I want to remind my readers that several years ago the French Prime Minister, Lionel Jospin, while visiting Israel, called Jerusalem the "capital of the Palestinian Authority." A few years later, in 1966, President Jacques Chirac announced that "Syria has a moral right to demand the return of the Golan Heights."

I now state to those French anti-Semites that Germany has a moral right to demand the return of Alsace-Lorraine. I also ask France to permit the return of the millions of Germans they expelled from the German provinces of Alsace and Lorraine.

France annexed Corsica from Genoa. Italy, the successor state to Genoa, must get the island of Corsica back from the French.

I hope that the Arab attacks in Britain and riots in France will at least give these countries some understanding of the serious problems Israel is facing. The bombings in London and the fires in France, perpetrated by evil Muslim jihadists and Islamofascists, may finally convince Britain and France that the Palestinian Arabs are not interested in peace with Israel, but in its destruction.

I hope that England and France will finally realize that a Palestinian state is not only a very bad idea for Israel, it is a bad idea for Europe.

Dr. Condoleezza Rice, our Secretary of State, has urged Israel to seize the best chance for peace by helping to establish a Palestinian state. I would suggest that our Secretary of State should read some of the pronouncements made in the official Friday sermon broadcast by a senior Palestinian Muslim figure, Ibrahim Mudyris. According to this senior cleric, the diplomatic process will achieve a return to the borders Israel had before the 1967 war. Then, in the final stage, Ibrahim Mudyris said, will come the destruction of Israel, "the way Muhammad returned there as a conqueror."

Mudyris said further: "We tell you, Palestine, we shall return to you, by Allah's will, we shall return to every village, every town, and every grain of earth which was quenched by the blood of our grandparents and the sweat of our fathers and mothers. We shall return, we shall return. . . .

"No one on this earth recognizes the 1948 borders. Therefore, we shall return to the 1967 borders, but it does not mean that we have given up on Jerusalem, Haifa, Jaffa, Lod, Natanyah and Tel-Aviv, Never!"

It is important to bear in mind that treaties with Arab countries are often not worth the price of the paper and ink. Israel signed a peace agreement with Egypt and returned every inch of land it had captured in the 1967 war. Pursuant to the agreement, Egypt was to establish diplomatic relations with Israel and send an ambassador to Israel. The same peace agreement provided that Egypt must stop any and all hate propaganda against Israel. At the inception of the second Intifada by the terrorist Yasser Arafat, Egypt recalled its ambassador from Israel.

On April 18, 2001, the following appeared in the Egyptian government-sponsored newspaper *Al-Akhbar*: "Thanks be to Hitler, of blessed memory, who on behalf of the Palestinians revenged in advance against the most vile criminals on the face of the earth. Although we do have a complaint against him, for his revenge on them was not enough."

During lectures about my book *From Nazi Inferno to Soviet Hell*, as well as lectures on the history of Islam and the Koran, the audiences ask many questions. They ask about the anti-Semitism on our college campuses. They ask why some of our print media are so biased against Israel, and why the Presbyterian and Anglican churches are calling for divestment in Israel. And of course, I am asked why the Bush administration has changed its policy to the detriment of Israel. I will now try to answer all these questions, each under its separate topic.

The upsurge of anti-Semitism on our college campuses:

Our universities are filled with anti-Semitic professors. Some of our universities have imported Arab Muslim professors who spew hatred toward Israel, and brainwash our students to hate Israel. In addition, many of our professors are very ignorant about the Muslim religion.

Our print media:

Most of our newspapers have a leftist slant, and their writers and editors are ignorant about the reality of the Arab Muslim world. They are ignorant about the history of Islam and the Koran, and they have a hatred for Israel.

The *Los Angeles Times* has an almost psychopathic hatred for Israel. In my own mind I have renamed it the *Los Angeles Pravda*. Here is an example of its rabid hatred for Israel: After Israel expelled its own Jewish people from Gaza, an editorial in the *Los Angeles Pravda* read "Israel Leaves But Gaza Is Hardly Free!"

Here is another editorial from the *Los Angeles Pravda*: "The precipitator of this economic crisis has been 'closure,' a multifaceted system of restrictions on the movement of Palestinian people and goods, which the government of Israel argues is essential to protect Israelis in Israel and the settlements." In other words, Israel has no right to protect its citizens from the Arab suicide bombers.

Another example is the *New York Times* whose publishers have long been self-hating Jews. From 1896 to 1935 publisher Adolph S. Ochs was totally opposed to the creation of the State of Israel. The next publisher of the *New York Times* was Arthur Hays Sulzberger. He buried news about the Holocaust in the back pages of his paper. The slaughter of the Jews in Austria and Italy in 1943 appeared on pages 6 and 35 respectively. Arthur Hays Sulzberger was one of the founders of the American Council for Judaism in 1942, an organization of Jews whose sole purpose was to fight against the creation of a Jewish state in Palestine.

When Israel expelled the Jewish settlers from Gaza, which was a part of the ancient territory of the kingdom of Judea, the *New York Times* said that this was "only the beginning," and declared that Ariel Sharon "must be forewarned" that giving up the West Bank must be next.

Not only is the *New York Times* unsympathetic toward Israel, but its editors are ignorant about the Muslim Arab world. The *New York Times* is not only a danger to the security and the very survival of Israel as a Jewish state-- its ignorance is also a danger to our own American security

Disappointing Jewish leftists in the United States and in Israel:

Thomas L. Friedman is a columnist for the *New York Times*. Several years ago I attended a lecture by Friedman at Temple Emanu-El in Palm

Beach. He had been invited by the Brandeis Organization of Florida to speak on the Arab-Israeli conflict, and in particular the Oslo Peace Agreement.

Outside the temple were numerous demonstrators from various Jewish organizations. As a matter of fact, I was an organizer of the demonstration, and I listened to Friedman's talk. He spoke about the Oslo Peace Agreement that the leftist Israeli government had entered into with the Yasser Arafat. He praised the Oslo Agreement as a brave step by the Israeli government. He told the audience that the Arab Muslim world is now a different, more progressive world. As an example of the progressive new Arab Muslim world, he told us about meeting an Arab girl at a hotel in Beirut who told him that she had met her husband through the Internet.

We also learned about it on 9/11, and at the bombing of the Khobar Towers in Saudi Arabia, and at the bombing of the U.S.S. Cole.

In his column in the *New York Times* on May 13, 2004, Friedman wrote, "Why did the administration always-rightly bash Yasir Arafat, but never lift a finger or utter a word to stop Ariel Sharon's massive building of illegal settlements in the West Bank?"

On May 16, 2004, he wrote, "What do the Shiite extremist leader Moktada al-Sadr and his Mahdi Army have in common with the extremist Jewish settlers in Israel? Answer: More than you'd think. Both movements combine religious messianism, and a willingness to sacrifice their followers and others for absolutist visions, along with a certain disdain for man-made laws, as opposed to those from God."

I would say to Friedman, "Tom, if you believe what you have written in your columns, then why don't you turn over your house to the American Indians? If you refuse to do that, then you are a two-legged hypocrite."

In all fairness to Friedman, I must say that he is intelligent and very well educated. However, as far as Jewish history and the history of the Arabs are concerned, his brain is flat.

It is difficult for me to understand why any Jewish organization or synagogue would invite Tom Friedman to lecture on Israel.

Leon Wieseltier, the literary editor of the *New Republic*, is another disappointment as a leftist Jew. He happens to be the son of Holocaust survivors. Wieseltier is a good writer, but in his columns he bashes the Jews who live in the provinces of Judea, Samaria. and Gaza, which are all part of the ancient kingdom of Judea.

The same can be said of Rabbi Michael Lerner, the editor of *Tikun magazine*. In his magazine he, too, bashes the Jews who reside in their ancient homeland of the kingdom of Judea, namely the provinces of Judea, Samaria, and Gaza.

Rabbi Bruce Warshal, the publisher emeritus of the *Jewish Journal of Florida*, also bashes the legitimate Jewish residents of the provinces of Judea, Samaria, and Gaza.

These people don't realize that because of their hateful writings about the patriotic Jews who reside in Judea, Samaria, and Gaza, they are undermining the safety, the security, and the very survival of Israel as a Jewish state.

I also want to include among these disappointing leftist Jews Martin Indyk, our former ambassador to Israel. It is very difficult for me to understand how someone so ignorant of the Arab Muslim world could have been appointed our ambassador to Israel.

Also included on my list is Noam Chomsky, who is a linguistics professor but an ignoramus about history. Noam Chomsky has called the wonderful American Jewish professor Alan Dershowitz a "Stalinist-style thug." I also want to mention Norman G. Finkelstein, a college professor. Norman G. Finkelstein, who is a child of Holocaust survivors, calls Elie Wiesel the "resident clown of the Holocaust circus," and he hates Israel with venom.

I remind my fellow American Jews that when Lenin and his Bolsheviks finally defeated the commanders of the counter-revolutionary White armies, some of the Jewish Bolsheviks went into action. Leon Trotsky and Grigori Zinoviev became members of Lenin's Politburo. The duo of Trotsky and Zinoviev traveled to Russian cities and addressed Jewish crowds everywhere. They told the Russian Jews that their lot had finally changed for the better. They told the Russian Jews that there would be no more pogroms. There would be no more raping of Jewish woman by the Black Hundreds. They said that Jews would from now on treated the same as Russians.

Zinoviev, especially, told the Russian Jews that they no longer had to be Jews. In his loud, screeching voice, Zinoviev urged the Jews of Russia to stop being Jews.

During Stalin's purges in the 1930s, Zinoviev was sent to the death chamber of the Lubyanka Prison. His last words before his execution were "Hear, O Israel, our God is the one God," and not in Russian but in Hebrew: *Shema Israel Adonai Eloheinu, Adonai Echad*. His landsman Trotsky had his brain smashed with a hammer by a KGB agent in Mexico. Their fate should be an example to all Jews who try to forget that they are Jews.

In contrast to the many apparently anti-Jewish Jews, and to those Christians who are indifferent or hostile to Israel, I want to acknowledge my gratitude to our wonderful Christian friends, the good and decent people of the Evangelical churches of America. You have such wonderful and decent leaders: Reverend Pat Robertson, Reverend John Hagee, Jerry Falwell, Albert Stearns, Gary Bauer, Congressman Tom DeLay, and Frank Gaffney of the Center for Security Policy. I am convinced that you will continue to stand by the State of Israel, and you will not permit the Arabists and the anti-Semites of our State Department to endanger the very survival of the Jewish state. May God bless you for all the wonderful help you are rendering to Israel.

As for our State Department and some of our elected leaders, the State Department has a history of Arabists and anti-Semites leanings. It has long objected to the establishment of a Jewish state on the ancient territory of the kingdom of Judea.

When our good and decent President Harry Truman supported the idea of establishing a Jewish state, practically every top official of the State Department at that time was opposed to it. Our then Secretary of State, George Marshall, threatened to resign if President Truman proceeded with the idea of establishing a Jewish state in Palestine.

That hatred toward Israel still exists today among some of the officials in the State Department. Every new Secretary of State, upon first entering the State Department building, encounters this hateful attitude toward Israel.

Consider James Baker, Secretary of State during the administration of the first President Bush. James Baker isn't only an anti-Semite, he is an Arabist. He once reportedly said to President Bush, "F- - k the Jews, they don't vote for us anyway." James Baker's law firm represents the oil-producing Arab countries and is probably raking in billions from his Arab clients. The second President Bush called upon him to deal with the situation in Iraq, presumably because he is so close to so many Arabs.

I wonder how many of my fellow Americans know about Edward Abington, a former State Department official who is now a lobbyist for the PLO terrorist organization. The annual salary of the President of the United States is $400,000. Edward Abington's annual salary as a lobbyist for the terrorist PLO is $600,000, not bad for a former State Department official.

I was initially pleased when Dr. Condoleezza Rice was appointed Secretary of State. It didn't take me long, however, to realize that Dr. Rice had been affected by the Arabist and anti-Zionist atmosphere in the State Department.

On her second visit to Israel, Secretary Rice asked the Israeli government to supply the terrorist PLO with weapons and allow the evil Hamas terrorist organization to participate in the upcoming Palestinian Arab election. As my readers no doubt recall, our own government has put Hamas on the list of terrorist organizations.

Can you imagine Dr. Rice asking the government of Afghanistan to supply the Taliban and Al-Qaeda with weapons, or to allow the Taliban and Al-Qaeda to participate in elections in Afghanistan?

I became even more upset when Secretary Rice stayed up a whole night browbeating Israeli officials in order to force them to relinquish control of the border crossing between Gaza and Egypt, which is known as the Philadelphi Corridor, the very crossing that has long been a major source of weapons smuggling from Egypt to Gaza. Some of these weapons, including surface-to-air missiles, could be smuggled to Judea and Samaria, the so-called West Bank.

If you doubt that our State Department is dominated by a prevalent pro-Arabist atmosphere, read this:

During the second week of November, 2005, the Senate Judiciary Committee convened a hearing entitled "Saudi Arabia: Friend or Foe in the War on Terror?" The hearing was inspired in part by the Saudi Arabia Accountability Act, initiated by the Zionist Organization of America, and co-sponsored by Senator Arlen Specter and Congress Anthony Weiner. The pro-Arab State Department refused to send anyone to testify at the hearing. The Saudis also refused to participate.

Based on her actions and statements over the last few years, I have concluded that Secretary Rice is totally ignorant about the Muslim Arab world, and by her actions is endangering the very survival of Israel as well as our own security here in America.

At the same time I must acknowledge that we do have some excellent people in in the State Department. One of them is John Bolton, who briefly served as our representative to the United Nations under the second President Bush.

My message to my fellow Americans:

My dear fellow Americans, in this book I have poured out my heart about the tragedy that has befallen the Jewish people for the past 2,000 years, and especially the Holocaust, where so many members of my family were turned to dust in Auschwitz.

As a Holocaust survivor, I am deeply concerned about the security and survival of Israel as a Jewish state.

I arrived on these blessed shores in June 1946. I was weak, emaciated, practically a skeleton. My blessed new country nourished me, gave me hope, and inspired me to become a human being again. This blessed country of ours opened to me the gates of its schools and colleges, and I became a very successful attorney.

It didn't take me long to learn what a wonderful country I was living in. I found my fellow Americans to be wonderful, warm, and friendly people. That is something I never found on the European continent.

Let me share some of my concerns for our beloved America. We are confronting an evil enemy, fundamentalist Muslim Arabs, the Wahhabis, the jihadists, and the Islamofascists who seek to destroy our way of life.

I lived for three and a half years in in the Soviet Muslim Republic of Uzbekistan, where I attended a predominantly Muslim school. It was there that I learned about the hatred Muslims have for Christians and Jews. I will never forget what a Russian Christian once told me: "If these Muslims could, they would slaughter us like sheep!"

I give lectures on Islam and the Koran both in New York and in Florida, and I am surprised at how little my fellow Americans know about these subjects, and about the dangers we are facing from Muslim extremists.

The leftist media here and in Europe have misrepresented the danger to our country. They perpetually blame Israel for our problems with the Arabs. They think that by bashing Israel and making it a sacrificial lamb, they can please and satisfy the Muslim Arabs.

My main concern is the security of our America and of Israel. In my opinion Europe is a lost cause. Europe's leaders are Chamberlains, and I am afraid that in this twenty-first century, Europe will be a Muslim continent. By the end of this century, one will no longer hear church bells in Europe. At the end of the twenty-first century, Europeans will be hearing a man calling from the tower of a mosque five times a day, and the people will throw themselves on the ground chanting, "Allahu Akbar, God is Great."

I hope and pray that this isn't going to happen to our beloved America. My fellow Americans, we must be on guard and protect ourselves.

Our ignorant leftist media and college professors keep telling us that the Muslim suicide bombers must be blamed on Israel, that the Muslim religion is a religion of peace, that the Koran itself is a book of peace. The truth, however, is that the Muslim religion is not a religion of peace, in the hands of the extremists.

The Western world has been fortunate so far. In 732 we had Charles Martel of France, who defeated the Muslims at Tours, only 200 miles south of Paris, and prevented them from conquering Europe. In 1683, Pope Innocent XI and King Jan Sobieski III of Poland saved Europe by defeating the Turkish Muslims at the gates of Vienna.

Unfortunately, at this grave moment in history we don't have good leaders like Charles Martel, Pope Innocent XI, and Jan Sobieski III. My fellow Americans, don't listen to the gullible politicians who say that Saudi Arabia is our friend. Saudi Arabia is the fount of the fanatical Wahabi branch of Islam.

Osama bin Laden was educated in Saudi Arabia. We must never forget that 15 of the 19 hijackers of 9/11 were Saudis. We must not forget that the Saudi rulers are the powerbrokers who keep the price of oil so high. Our Saudi "friends" produce a barrel of oil for about $5 and charge us $60.

I have been a supporter of our current President Bush, but lately he has disappointed me. I liked President Bush back when he was brave and honest--when he said, for instance, that Texas driveways are longer than the width of Israel at its waist, where most of its population and industry is located.

But when Israel began to build a wall to protect its citizens from being blown up by Arab suicide bombers, President Bush changed his tune. He told the government of Israel that checkpoints and detours cause too much inconvenience for the Arabs. That is evidently more important to him than saving Jewish lives.

Another of my disappointments is that President Bush goes along with Israeli and American Jewish leftists in supporting the establishment of an Arab state in the provinces of Judea, Samaria, and Gaza. He claims that a Palestinian state will be peaceful and democratic.

And I ask you, my fellow Americans, based on what you see happening now in Iraq, do you believe that a Palestinian state would be peaceful and democratic?

I want to remind President Bush that within days of the murderous 9/11 attacks he declared, before a joint session of Congress, "Every nation in every land now has a decision to make. Either you are with us, or you are with the terrorists!"

So many people are ignorant of the history of the Arabs on the soil of the ancient kingdom of Judea that I feel I must clarify some things not only to our government but to the leftist Israelis and the self-hating leftist American Jews.

Mark Twain visited Palestine in 1867. In his book about his travels, *The Innocents Abroad,* he described it as "a desolate country whose soil is rich enough but is given over wholly to weeds--a silent mournful expanse. . . . A desolation is here that not even imagination can grace with pomp of life and action. . . . We never saw a human being on the whole route. . . . There was hardly a tree or shrub anywhere. Even the olive and the cactus, those fast friends of worthless soil, had almost deserted the country."

This description by Mark Twain should clarify once and for all to Israeli leftists, to our own self-hating leftist American Jews, and to our government what Palestine was like in 1867. It was a virtually unpopulated disaster area.

Palestine was not built up until the arrival of brave young Jews from Russia and Poland who settled there toward the end of the nineteenth century and early in the twentieth. They returned to their beloved ancient homeland, cultivated it, and built cities and industries. Until then the land had been almost empty, but now Arabs from neighboring countries began moving into Palestine to benefit from its new prosperity and get jobs that had become available for the first time in centuries because of the work of these Zionist Jewish pioneers.

It is the descendants of these Arab interlopers and immigrants who now call themselves Palestinians. There has never ever been a Palestinian state, or a Palestinian king or queen; there has never ever been a Palestinian language--their language was and is Arabic. Moreover, there has never ever been a Palestinian people. The Arabs in Palestine are and always have been Arabs.

And they have no desire for peace with Israel!

Just listen to the words of the PLO leaders that President Bush and our State Department describe as partners for peace.

Jibril Rajoub, Palestinian Authority National Security Advisor, said in an interview on Al-Arabiya TV: "The West Bank is still occupied and resistance [i.e., terrorist activities] is a legitimate right."

Muhammad Dahlan, Palestinian Authority Minister of Civil Affairs, as reported by the Palestinian News Agency on November 6, 2005, called for national unity "to complete what was achieved in the Gaza Strip. To liberate Jerusalem and the West Bank and for the refugees to take by force the right to return to their houses."

Muhammad Hijazi (Abu Khaled), senior Fatah operative in the northern Gaza Strip, stated, according to *Al-Bayan* on November 7, 2005: It is important to continue "the path of jihad and [active] resistance until all Palestinian land has been liberated"; Fatah weapons are legitimate, and Fatah and others have "the right to respond to the occupation's crimes."

Or consider these excerpts from an officially sanctioned sermon broadcast by Palestinian Authority TV on May 13, 2005. The preacher was Sheik Ibrahim Mudeiris, a paid employee of the Palestinian Authority:

"Allah has tormented us with the people most hostile to the believers--the Jews. Thou shalt find the people most hostile to the believers to be Jews. Allah warned his beloved Prophet Muhammad about the Jews, who had killed their prophets, forged their Torah and sowed corruption throughout their history. With the establishment of the state of Israel, the entire Islamic nation was lost, because Israel is a cancer spreading through the body of the Islamic nation, and because the Jews are a virus resembling AIDs from which the entire world suffers.

"We [Muslims] have ruled the world before, and by Allah, the day will come when we will rule the entire world again. The day will come when we will rule America. The day will come when we will rule Britain and the entire world--except for the Jews. The Jews will not enjoy a life of tranquility under our rule, because they are treacherous by nature, as they have been throughout history. The day will come when everything will be relieved of the Jews--even the stones and trees which were harmed by them. Listen to the Prophet Muhammad, who tells you about the evil that awaits Jews."

We Americans must never forget the danger we face from these Islamofascists, the danger our nation faces from these evil people.

Remember that it was an Arab Muslim extremist who, on our very shores, assassinated Rabbi Meyer Kahane.

Remember the Arab Muslim extremist bombing of PanAm Flight 103.

Remember the Arab Muslim extremist bombing of the World Trade Center in 1993.

Remember the Arab Muslim extremist bombing of the Marine barracks in Lebanon.

Remember the Arab Muslim extremist bombing of the U.S. military barracks in Saudi Arabia.

Remember the Arab Muslim extremist bombing the American embassies in Africa.

Remember the Arab Muslim extremist bombing of the *U.S.S. Cole.*

Remember the Arab Muslim extremist attack on the Twin Towers on September 11, 2001.

Remember the beheading of Daniel Pearl, the reporter for the *Wall Street Journal.*

Remember the beheading of the young American boy Nick Berg in Iraq.

Remember what Sheik Ibrahim Mudeiris, a paid employee of the Palestinian Authority, said in a TV sermon on May 13, 2005: "We Muslims have ruled the world before, and by Allah, the day will come when we will rule the entire world again. The day will come when we will rule AMERICA!"

I hope that these historical facts will finally convince our government that the establishment of another Muslim Arab state on the land of the ancient kingdom of Judea is a very bad idea.

My message to the decent Muslim people:

You will have noticed, in reading my book, that I do not limit my criticisms to Muslims. I also criticize Israeli leftists, American self-hating Jewish leftists, as well as my own American government.

I respect the decent, well-educated, secular Muslim people, and I respect the Muslim religion. However, you are doing absolutely nothing to bring to your own people your message of decency, civility, and respect for other religions. You are afraid to speak out and bring your message to the Muslim world. You are hiding under your desks, just as American Jews did during the Holocaust.

I urge you to follow my example: Stand atop your desk and point your fingers at the Muslim world. Start screaming at the Muslim world about their perversion of the Muslim religion.

Don't be afraid to criticize Muhammad himself for his actions and his behavior. Muhammad was a human being. According to the Koran, Muhammad was a prophet, but he was also illiterate, and by trade he was a camel driver.

The Koran claims, just as Jews claim, that King David was a prophet. You are probably aware that Jews have always criticized King David for sending Uriah the Hittite to be killed so that he could marry Uriah's wife, Bat Sheva. Why don't you decent and civilized Muslims criticize Muhammad for doing things that we today recognize as immoral?

I want you to be brave and unafraid to speak the truth to the Muslim people. I plead with you to explain to the Muslim people that they should not heed the radical clerics who call for a jihad against the people of the non-Muslim world.

I plead with you to work hard to make the Muslim religion reform itself, just as the Christian and Jewish religions have reformed themselves, and continue to reform themselves.

My message to the government and people of Israel:

I plead with you to remain strong and not succumb to the pressure of the anti-Semitic countries of Europe. Remember, it is still the aim of the Arab countries to wipe you off the map. The present generation of Arabs in Judea, Samaria, and Gaza, brainwashed for so many years, are by no means ready to make peace.

Do not give up a single settlement in Judea, Samaria, or in Gaza. This land is your land.

Remember that the Jews have no future in viciously anti-Semitic Europe, and they will eventually have to leave the European continent, for so long the cemetery of the Jewish people. Europe now has about twenty million Muslims, and that may make for even more anti-Semitism.

I hope that the Jews of France, England, Germany, Russia, and the other European countries will not make the same mistakes my parents made in the 1930s by not leaving that anti-Semitic continent. I urge all the Jews of Europe to leave now, before it is too late.

The only country the European Jews should go to, and the only country where they will be accepted, is Israel. Therefore, Israel must not give up a single inch of its ancient land, for it will be needed to resettle the European Jews.

I can assure you that the majority of Jewish Americans will stand by you, and they will not repeat the same mistake they made during World War II, when they did so little to save European Jewry during the Holocaust.

I also want you to know that America is the most decent and humane country on our planet. I am convinced that the good decent American Christians will stand by you and support you in those difficult times. My message to you is, in words taken from our sacred liturgy, is "chazak ve-amatz: be strong and determined."

Finally, I have some advice for Prime Minister Ehud Olmert. My country is in a big mess in Iraq. That is why my government would like to show the American people that we are making progress with the Arabs by helping to create a "democratic" Palestinian state in Judea, Samaria, and Gaza.

The next time Secretary of State Rice comes to visit you in Jerusalem and demands that Israel give more territory to the PLO terrorists, Mr. Prime Minister, your response should be to sing her a chorus of "From the Halls of Montezuma to the Shores of Tripoli."

If Dr. Rice asks why you are singing this song, you should respond: "Madam Secretary, many years ago your country was invaded by Mexico and your ships in the Mediterranean Sea were attacked by pirates from North Africa. At that time, you had some good and strong Presidents, and they dispatched your Marines. The North African pirates were liquidated, the Mexicans were beaten back. Many of your citizens were butchered in a place called the Alamo. After the Mexicans were defeated, they paid a heavy price for their aggression. Your country annexed a huge area of Mexican territory, which became four of your states, Arizona, New Mexico, Texas, and California."

Then say to Dr. Rice, "Madame Secretary, you have no intention of giving Arizona, New Mexico, Texas, and California back to Mexico."

Her response may be, "But you are different!" And then you say, Madam Secretary, after the Holocaust we took an oath, 'Never Again.' We will never permit people to do this to our people again. Madam Secretary, we will not give up a single inch of our land to the PLO terrorists. We are going to complete the wall and separate our country from the PLO terrorists."

I urge you, Mr. Prime Minister, not to agree to the establishment of a Palestinian state. I hope, Mr. Prime Minister, that you have learned something from the war Hezbollah unleashed on Israel in July 2006. I hope, Mr. Prime Minister, that you have learned from the stupidity of expelling your citizens from Gaza and turning Gaza over to the Arabs. Now the Arabs of Gaza are firing their missiles into Israel practically every day.

I urge you, Prime Minister, and you, the people of Israel, be strong and determined.

I have stood on top of my desk for quite a long time, pointing my fingers in numerous directions. I have screamed and yelled at Jews, Christians, and Muslims. But now I have finally lost my voice, and I have a sore throat. Therefore, I have stepped down from my desk, and I am sitting on a chair behind my desk. My elbows are resting on my desk, and my palms are covering my forehead and my eyes. Sitting at my desk in this position, I have just had a thought, and I want to share it. Our world has recently been struck by great natural disasters--the tsunami in South Asia, Hurricanes Katrina, Rita, and Wilma in the United States, the earthquake in Pakistan. I ask myself, Could Mother Nature be sending us a warning?

My hope and prayer:

So many sleepless nights, as I toss about in turmoil, I keep asking myself, Why there is so much hatred on our planet Earth? Why do we keep having so many wars, in which so many people are killed?

Why do we have religious wars? Why do people of one religion make war against another people of a different religion?

Why is there so much hatred and persecution of the people of one religion by the people of another? Why do those of one religious group discriminate against those belonging to other groups?

I believe, and I hope that everyone on our planet Earth believes, that God created this world of ours, and that He created life.

I believe, and I hope that we all believe, that there is only one God who created us and to whom we all pray.

Every religious group prays to the same God, and every religious group has its own name for this same God.

Every religious group says its own prayers to this same God. Jews have a name for this same God. Christians have a name for this same God, and Muslims have a name for this same God.

God loves all of us equally, whether we are Christian, Muslim, or Jewish. Therefore, as a Holocaust survivor, I ask myself, Why can't we have respect and love for each other? Why is there so much hatred in this world of ours that brings on killing and the destruction on our planet Earth?

As a Jew, I carry no hatred toward any Christian or Muslim. Judaism has taught me that he who saves one life saves the whole world.

I hope and pray that one day it will dawn on us how wrong we have been for so long, that hating and making war on each other makes no sense.

My fervent hope and prayer is that we will wake up some day and follow the preaching of Isaiah, transforming the tools of war into instruments that will help cure the diseases that plague our lives. And I hope and pray that our minds will be cured of the disease of hate, and there will no more wars on our planet Earth.

Printed in the United States
98349LV00004B/43-126/A

9 780978 942793